Mr Pepys

SAMUEL PEPYS

From the portrait by John Hayls painted in 1666

(*By permission of the National Portrait Gallery*)

Mr Pepys

An Introduction to the Diary together with a Sketch of his Later Life

By

J. R. Tanner

GREENWOOD PRESS, PUBLISHERS
WESTPORT, CONNECTICUT

Originally published in 1925
by G. Bell and Sons, Ltd., London

Reprinted from an original copy in the collections
of the University of Illinois Library

First Greenwood Reprinting 1971

Library of Congress Catalogue Card Number 71-110870

SBN 8371-4549-X

Printed in the United States of America

CONTENTS

CONTENTS

INTRODUCTION

LIKE the tomb of a Pharaoh, Pepys's *Diary* was reserved for discovery by a later age than his own. The six volumes of shorthand which contain it, lay undeciphered in the Pepysian Library at Cambridge for 100 years—from 1724, when the library passed to Magdalene College under Pepys's will at the death of John Jackson his heir, until 1825, when the work of deciphering it having been completed the first edition was published.

In 1728 the volumes had attracted the passing notice of Peter Leicester, a visitor to Cambridge who, on May 22,[1] wrote to John Byrom, the poet and stenographer, to report his discovery and to advise Byrom to visit Cambridge and inspect them; but the suggestion was never followed up. In 1818, however, Evelyn's *Diary* appeared, in which Samuel Pepys was many times referred to, and this led the reigning Master of Magdalene, George Neville, to think that the six volumes in

[1] H. B. Wheatley, *Pepysiana*, p. 73.

the Library lettered "Journal" might be worth examining. He shewed them to his uncle Lord Grenville, who as Secretary of State for Foreign Affairs was familiar with secret characters, and he translated a few pages which justified a further examination. The result was that in the spring of 1819 the manuscript, together with Lord Grenville's translation and an alphabet and a list of signs which he had drawn up, was handed over to John Smith, an undergraduate of St. John's College, to be deciphered. At the outset Smith was assured by an expert stenographer to whom he shewed the *Diary*, that neither he "nor any other man would ever be able to decipher it," but by working at it for nearly three years, "usually for twelve and fourteen hours a day, with frequent wakeful nights," he at length accomplished the task.[1] He found that the system of shorthand employed by Pepys was that described by Thomas Shelton in a book published in 1641 under the title of *Tachygraphy*.

The edition of 1825, bearing the title *Memoirs of Samuel Pepys, Esq., F.R.S. . . . comprising his Diary . . . and a Selection from his Private Correspondence*, was prepared under the superintendence of Richard Griffin Neville, third Baron Braybrooke, the Visitor of Magdalene, in whose gift as the

[1] John Smith's letter of March 23, 1858, quoted in *Pepysiana*, p. 75.

owner of Audley End the Mastership of Magdalene lay; and he issued a second edition in 1828. In these editions the original *Diary* was abridged [1] and heavily expurgated,[2] and the editor found himself charged in consequence with having "used the pruning-knife with too much freedom" and excluded "the most entertaining passages." The result of this criticism was that in the preface to the third edition, published in 1848-9 under a new title, *Diary and Correspondence of Samuel Pepys, F.R.S.* . . . , many of the omitted passages were inserted, "with the exception only of such entries as were devoid of the slightest interest, and many others of so indelicate a character that no one with a well-regulated mind will regret their loss; nor could they have been tolerated, even in the licentious days to which they relate." The editor had paid a tribute to the labours of the decipherer which, for a generation that was inclined to be effusive in its prefaces, appears singularly frigid: "In justice to the Reverend John Smith [3] (with whom I am not personally acquainted) it may be added that he appears to have

[1] In the original edition of 1825 scarcely half the MS. was printed.

[2] M. Lucas-Dubreton speaks of Lord Braybrooke as "auteur de notes estimable mais d'une pruderie exigeante" (*La petite vie de Samuel Pepys Londonien*, 1923, p. 17).

[3] John Smith had been ordained in 1824, and from 1832 was Rector of Baldock, Herts.

performed the task allotted to him of deciphering the shorthand Diary with diligence and fidelity, and to have spared neither time nor trouble in the undertaking." In 1854 a fourth edition appeared with a rearrangement of the notes and some additions to the correspondence; and in 1875-9 Mr. Mynors Bright added nearly a third to the matter already published, accounting for about four-fifths of the whole *Diary*. Finally, in 1902 Mr. Henry B. Wheatley printed all but some thirty pages.[1] "L'histoire de ce manuscrit" . . ., writes the French biographer of Pepys, "est une petite illustration sans malice à mettre en marge d'une étude sur les transformations psychologiques du peuple anglais."[2]

The key-problem of Pepys's *Diary* is whether he ever intended it to see the light. Robert Louis Stevenson, a man of letters writing for a public, found it difficult to believe that Pepys had no ultimate public in view, and he offers two reasons in support of his conclusion to the contrary—the first, "of capital importance," that the *Diary* was not destroyed, and the second, that the author "took unusual precautions to confound the cipher in 'rogueish' passages," shewing "that he was

[1] To this last edition it may perhaps be objected that it does not contain enough to satisfy the more exacting claims of literary scholarship, but includes too much for a work intended for popular use.

[2] Lucas-Dubreton, p. 17.

thinking of some other reader besides himself." [1] The first would be more convincing if there were not innumerable instances in which mortal illness and imminent death have been responsible for a failure to destroy documents. In this connexion it must also be remembered that while Pepys lay dying at Clapham the *Diary* may have been in York Buildings on the other side of the Thames. The second may only have been an additional defence against the casual explorer among his books, or perhaps, as Mr. Percy Lubbock suggests, "to disguise the nakedness of his confidences, even from himself." [2] In any case Stevenson's impressions, formed in 1881,[3] were derived from the Mynors Bright edition of 1875-9; the more intimate details of the diarist's frailties, and the minuter particulars of his symptoms, which make an intention to publish so improbable, had not yet been given to the world by Wheatley. We may say rather, as Stevenson himself does elsewhere in his article,[4] that the *Diary* was "a private pleasure,"—Pepys, the supreme egotist, "making reminiscences" for himself. Perhaps also the artist in Pepys was

[1] *Familiar Studies of Men and Books* (1886), p. 302.

[2] *Samuel Pepys*, p. 32.

[3] The paper afterwards published in *Familiar Studies* was preceded by an article in the *Cornhill* of 1881 (xliv. 31).

[4] *Familiar Studies*, pp. 299, 303.

striving after self-expression. "To give form to the life which he tasted so keenly, that was all he wanted, and from this point of view the *Diary* is a purely artistic creation."[1] And when it was finished, it had an indirect utility. When in 1669 Pepys was on his defence before the Commissioners of Public Accounts he wrote, "Among the many thousands under whose observation my employment must have placed me, I challenge any man to assign one day from my first admission to this service in July 1660 to the determination of the war, August 1667, . . . of which I am not this day able upon oath to give an account of the particular manner of my employing the same."[2]

If the *Diary* was intended to be for ever a secret,[3] this fact profoundly affects our view of its contents. From its pages we acquire a more intimate knowledge of Pepys than of any other personality of the past, but we know that the revelation is absolutely unconscious. There are no unrealities and no reserves; he stands to-day naked before a

[1] Lubbock, p. 36. [2] Pepysian MSS., No. 2554.

[3] A sarcastic reviewer of 1825 (*Westminster Review*, iv. 408) suggests that Pepys thought perpetual secrecy would be best secured by bequeathing the *Diary* to "that sepulchre of learning," the library of a small College, "as the safest depository for state secrets, and the sanctuary likely to be last invaded by the incursions of library inquirers;" but things have altered since his time.

world he never knew.[1] His "God forgive me" and "Blessed be God" are no hypocrisy, for he had no audience before which to pose. He is not a dramatist exploiting psychological material, but a faithful and true witness about himself, and it is this perfect sincerity, this absence of any trace of artificiality, that gives the *Diary* its charm. A recent writer on Montaigne[2] remarks that the pen is dictatorial, "It is always making ordinary men into prophets and changing the natural stumbling trip of human speech into the solemn and stately." But in the *Diary* Pepys is not the slave of his pen. It never suggests the prophet or betrays him into language that is stilted or unnatural; and he remains throughout the ordinary man, exhibiting the ordinary human qualities of kindliness, good sense, and humour. It is true that with these are associated an acuteness of observation beyond the ordinary, and a remarkable capacity for the thorough enjoyment of life.[3]

Owing partly to limitations of space, much has been omitted in the present volume, and in

[1] "J'ai toujours aimé les vêtements magnifiques et cependant j'apparais nu, plus nu que vous tous, nu avec mon habit de cour, avec ma perruque, mon beau manteau de velours, et mes souliers à boucles, intégralement nu" (Lucas-Dubreton, p. 14).

[2] *Times Literary Supplement*, January 31, 1924.

[3] We may apply to Pepys what Mr. Charles Whibley says of Disraeli, "The most precious of his gifts was his vitality; he lived with every sense and at every pore" (*Political Portraits*, 2nd series, p. 108).

particular the numerous references in the *Diary* to current politics, to the illnesses of Pepys and his wife, and to the more squalid aspects of his amours. The object of the work, published just 100 years after the *Diary* was first given to the world, is to provoke to the reading of the famous document itself, and to indicate its relation to the whole life of its author. The years 1660 to 1669 [1] are a mere fraction of Pepys's three-score years and ten, and in a sense the *Diary* is an indiscretion of his youth. That there are two Pepysian traditions was perceived by Stevenson : " He was a man known to his contemporaries in a halo of almost historical pomp, and to his remote descendants with an indecent familiarity like a tap-room comrade." [2] Our pleasure at being admitted to the circle of his intimates should not lead us to miss the halo, or to forget the distinguished public career.[3]

As the writer is engaged upon a larger life of Pepys, he has been fortunate enough to inherit the

[1] M. Lucas-Dubreton points out that it was precisely in these years that the principal comedies of Molière appeared (p. 19).

[2] *Familiar Studies*, p. 291.

[3] On this see Professor Wilbur C. Abbott, *The Serious Pepys* (*Yale Review*, April, 1914), and J. R. Tanner, *Samuel Pepys and the Royal Navy* (Lees Knowles Lectures for 1919).

material which the late Mr. Wheatley collected with the same object in view, and some of this has been utilised for the biographical part of the present volume. He cannot adequately express his gratitude for the generous kindness of Mr. Philip Norman, who has placed at his disposal his valuable unpublished monograph on the friendship between Pepys and Hewer, and has also allowed him to use his copies of the two pamphlets referred to on p. 239 below. Mr. Norman's unique knowledge of the topography of Old London has, in particular, been of the greatest service, and his researches will prove invaluable in connexion with the larger *Life*.

Thanks are also due to the Master and Fellows of Magdalene College, Cambridge, the owners of the copyright, for permission to quote freely from the *Diary*; to Mr. O. F. Morshead, the Pepysian Librarian, for kind and ready help; and to Mr. Stephen Gaselee, his predecessor in that office, for biographical material and for suggestions.

ALDEBURGH
September 6, 1924

“ Macaulay le juriste, confectionneur de dossiers, raconte qu'il eut une nuit un rêve affreux : sa petite nièce lui avouait qu'elle avait forgé le journal de Pepys . . . Donc il avait jugé sûr pièces fausses ; le bienheureux *Diary* n'était qu'un misérable papier apocryphe, indigne de foi, une supercherie à l'imitation d'Ossian ! Il fallait reviser le procès de Charles II et de sa cour. Il s'éveilla, en sueur, dans l'angoisse. . . . Dieu merci ! Dieu des historiens et des moralistes, merci ! Pepys est vrai, d'une indéniable vérité ; nous pouvons puiser chez lui à pleines mains, sans remords.”—*Lucas-Dubreton.*

CHAPTER I

The Earlier Life of Pepys

SAMUEL PEPYS was born on February 23, 1632-3.[1] The place of his birth was for long uncertain, but the discovery in the parish registers of St. Bride's Church, Fleet Street, of the record of the baptism on March 3 of "Samuell sonn to John Peapis wyef Margaret" now enables us to assign it definitely to the house in Salisbury Court, close to St. Bride's Churchyard, where John Pepys carried on the business of a tailor.[2] Here

[1] In Pepys's time the year reckoned for chronological purposes began on March 25, so dates falling between January 1 and March 24 belonged to 1632. These are indicated now, and were sometimes then, as 1632-3, but the difference of practice has been responsible for many errors.

[2] In the *Athenaeum* for September 4, 1915, Mr. W. H. Whittear shews that John Pepys's house ran back from Salisbury Court to St. Bride's Churchyard. The main part of the house was on the site now occupied by the White Swan public-house and the restaurant adjoining it on the south side; and the extension to the churchyard, probably the tailor's cutting-out room, was on ground now covered by Nos. 9 and 10 St. Bride's Avenue.

Samuel as a boy " carried clothes to " his father's customers.[1]

John Pepys had married beneath him, for his wife, whose surname is unknown, is described in the *Diary* as having been formerly " washmaid to my Lady Veere," but he himself came of a good family which had been connected for many generations with Cottenham in Cambridgeshire. The first name in their pedigree which is of interest to students of the *Diary* is John Pepys of Cottenham (*d.* 1589), who in 1579 acquired the manor of Impington, near Cambridge. This patriarch begat ten children, and four of these are important for the present purpose. (1) The eldest son, John Pepys (*d.* 1604), was the father of Sir Richard Pepys, appointed in 1654 a Baron of the Exchequer and soon after Lord Chief Justice of Ireland. (2) Another son, Talbot Pepys, who inherited the Impington estate, was Recorder of Cambridge; he died at the beginning of March 1665-6 at the age of 83.[2] (3) A daughter, Paulina, married Sir Sydney Mountagu, and was the mother of the first Earl of Sandwich, Samuel's patron. (4) Another son, Thomas " the Black," so called to distinguish him from a younger brother, Thomas " the Red,"

[1] *Diary*, March 11, 1667-8.

[2] His great-nephew Samuel visited him at Impington on July 15, 1661, and found him "sitting all alone, like a man out of the world ; he can hardly see, but all things else he do pretty livelyly."

was the father of John Pepys and the grandfather of Samuel. It was therefore the case that the Earl of Sandwich, the Lord Chief Justice of Ireland, and John Pepys the tailor owned a common grandfather. Thus there is no justification for an early reviewer of the *Diary*[1] who calls its author a *parvenu* ; but as he also speaks of him as "a very odious specimen of the Cockney," little weight need be attached to opinions proceeding from that quarter.

The references in the *Diary* to Samuel's boyhood are unilluminating. We learn that as a little child he had been carried in the arms of one of his father's servants into the two Temple Halls ; that he had assisted to beat the parish bounds on Ascension Day; and that at Durdans, near Epsom, he had been " very merry " when he was a small boy. There is a reference to " my nurse's house, Goody Lawrence," at Kingsland, " where my brother Tom and I was kept when young," and used to shoot with bow and arrows in the fields ; also to the King's Head Tavern at Islington, whither his father used to take them " to eat cakes and ale"; and to Horsley-Down, "where I never was since a little boy, that I went to enquire after my father, whom we did give over for lost coming from Holland." From a reference in the *Diary* of March 15, 1659-60, it may be inferred that

[1] *Blackwood* (1849), lxvi. 502, 503.

Samuel was sent for a time to the Grammar School at Huntingdon, which was not far from his uncle Robert's house at Brampton, and that he was there in 1644, when he was eleven years of age. From Huntingdon School he went to St. Paul's, where John Langley, the distinguished scholar, antiquary, and Puritan theologian, was at that time high-master. The sur-master was Samuel Cromleholme (the " Mr. Crumlum " of the *Diary*). Pepys visited him on March 9, 1664-5, when he had succeeded Langley as high-master, and, after the accustomed manner of schoolboys who have grown up, drastically revised his childish impressions. " Lord ! to see how ridiculous a conceited pedagogue he is, though a learned man, he being so dogmaticall in all he do and says." Of Samuel's career at St. Paul's we know nothing, except that he held a Robinson Exhibition, but he refers in the *Diary* now and again to the superiority of things as they were in his day. " We did spend our time and thoughts then otherwise than I think boys do now, and I think as well as methinks that the best are now ";[1] and the speeches on Apposition Day are " not so good as ours were in our time."[2] In spite of this lamentable decay of manners and scholarship, he gave the School £5 worth of books

Pepys left St. Paul's in 1650, and on June 21

[1] July 25, 1664. [2] February 4, 1662-3.

of that year he was entered at Trinity Hall, Cambridge, perhaps because his kinsman, John Pepys, LL.D., was a Fellow there. Before coming into residence, however, he migrated to Magdalene, and was admitted there as a sizar on October 1. The date of his first appearance at the University is fixed by a shorthand note in the *Diary* for December 31, 1664: "Went to reside in Magd. Coll. Camb. and did put on my gown first, March 5, 1650-1." A month later, on April 3, 1651, he was elected to a Spendluffe Scholarship. He did not matriculate until July 4, but in those days so long an interval between residence and matriculation was not unusual. On October 4, 1653, he became a Scholar on Dr. John Smith's Foundation, and in March 1653-4 he proceeded to the B.A. degree. Only a single episode in his Cambridge career still stands unsubmerged by the waters of oblivion,—an entry in the Magdalene College Registrar's book: "Oct. 21, 1653. Memorandum, that Peapys and Hind were solemnely admonished by myself and Mr. Hill for having bene scandalously overseene in drink[1] the night before; this was done in presence of all the Fellows then resident, in Mr. Hill's

[1] The expression "overseen in drink" = intoxicated, was in frequent use during the 17th century. The traditional "overserved with drink," which dates back to the Braybrooke editions and has been industriously copied by subsequent writers, is due to a misreading of the MS.

chamber. JOH. WOOD, *Registrarius.*" This was not his last visit to "Mr. Hill's chamber," as on February 25, 1659, he was "exceeding civilly received" and invited to "a very handsome supper" there, finding that in the discourse of the dons "there was nothing at all left of the old preciseness, . . . specially on Saturday nights." As Cambridge lay on the road to his father's house at Brampton, Pepys revisited it several times, and on October 8, 1667, he took round a small party consisting of his wife, her gentlewoman, and William Hewer, "and shewed them Trinity College, and St. John's Library, and went to King's College Chapel, to see the outside of it only." The next morning "the town musique did also come and play; but Lord! what sad music they made! . . . and so through the town, and observed at our College of Magdalene the posts new painted, and understand that the Vice-Chancellor is there this year. And so away for Huntingdon, mightily pleased all along the road to remember old stories."

On December 1, 1655,[1] Samuel Pepys married Elizabeth St. Michel, a pretty, portionless girl of 15. The diarist always kept the anniversary of his wedding-night on October 10, and ingenious

[1] The marriage certificate from the register of St. Margaret's, Westminster, is printed in Wheatley's edition of the *Diary*, vol. i. p. xxi. note 2.

attempts have been made to account for this discrepancy of dates. Even S. R. Gardiner turned aside from profounder historical studies to deal with this problem,[1] and his conjecture may be regarded as holding the field. He suggests that owing to the youth of the bride at the time when the marriage was registered,[2] she remained for some time longer with her mother, and did not join her husband until October 10, 1656, the day of commemoration in the *Diary*. This fits in with the most precise of the dates there given, for Pepys refers to October 10, 1661, as his *sixth* wedding-night. Mrs. Pepys was the daughter of Alexander Marchant de St. Michel, a French Protestant of good family, who had come over to England in the train of Henrietta Maria on her marriage with Charles I. He occupied the post of Gentleman Carver to the Queen, but as soon as his religion was known he lost the appointment. His conversion from Rome had already cost him the family property in France, and after various other misfortunes he settled at Bideford in Devonshire, where Elizabeth was born. Her mother was a daughter of Sir

[1] In a note contributed to the *Athenaeum*, 1900 (i.) p. 786.

[2] A closely parallel case is that of John Evelyn the diarist, who on June 27, 1647, married Mary Browne, a girl under thirteen, and in the following October, leaving her in Paris "under the care of an excellent lady and prudent mother," departed for England and was absent for more than a year and a half.

Francis Kingsmill and the widow of an Irish squire. Later on St. Michel lived for a time in Paris, but had returned to England not long before his daughter's marriage to Pepys.

Letters among the Carte Papers in the Bodleian Library at Oxford[1] shew that at some date earlier than March 11, 1655-6, Pepys had been provided with a home in the house of his kinsman Edward Mountagu at Whitehall, and was acting for him as a kind of steward, supervising his household and executing a number of small commissions. In a letter of that date his patron describes him as "my servant, Samuel Pepys." On November 27, 1656, Pepys, writing to Mountagu at Hinchingbrooke, explains that he has sent thither "swords and belts black and modish," caps, spurs, riding-coats, and "a paire of slippers";[2] and a year later he is discharging the same useful functions, despatching "one box of oranges, 2 raisors in a little box . . . some shittle cocks alsoe and 4 battledoares for the children."[3] He also superintended the removal of furniture, and supplied his patron with the news and talk of the town. In December 1657[4] he incurred

[1] See Sir C. H. Firth's article on "The Early Life of Pepys" in *Macmillan's Magazine*, lxix. (1894) 32.

[2] Carte MSS., lxxiii. 49.

[3] *Ib.* lxxiii. 177 (letter of December 10, 1657).

[4] *Ib.* lxxiii. 170, 187, 190 (letters of December 5, 22, and 26, 1657).

Mountagu's displeasure over the secret marriage of one of the maids, which was said to be due to his careless control and habit of staying out late at night; [1] but he was able to make his peace.

On March 26, 1658, Pepys underwent an operation for the stone.[2] This was performed by Thomas Hollier, or Hollyard, surgeon to St. Thomas's Hospital, who was living in Warwick Lane, and in order to be as near him as possible, the patient took rooms at Mrs. Turner's in Salisbury Court, where the operation took place. The anniversary was afterwards kept as a festival by him, and was celebrated with a dinner to which Mrs. Turner was always invited.

In June 1659 Pepys accompanied Edward Mountagu on board the *Naseby* when he went in command of a fleet to the Sound to arrange a peace between Sweden and Denmark; and it was then that the Admiral opened communications with the exiled King.[3] It has been usual to assign Pepys's appointment as clerk to Mr. George Downing, one of the Four Tellers of the

[1] Perhaps partly explained by the reference in the *Diary* to Wood's "in the Pell Mell, where heretofore in Cromwell's time we young men used to keep our weekly clubs" (July 5, 1665).

[2] For fuller information see Sir D'Arcy Power's article on "The Medical History of Mr. and Mrs. Samuel Pepys," printed in the Pepys Club *Occasional Papers*, 1903-14, p. 78.

[3] See *Diary*, November 7, 1660, and March 8, 1662-3.

Exchequer, to the end of 1659, and to regard it as a reward obtained for him by Mountagu's influence in recognition of his good service upon this expedition; but the occurrence among the Carte MSS.[1] of "an account of the plate, September 14, 1658" then left by Mountagu in Pepys's charge "in the great chest in the Exchequer," suggests that he was at that date already an Exchequer clerk; and in that case it is possible that his appointment should even be dated back to 1656, when Downing first took office. His duties were light, as we know from the *Diary*, and they need not necessarily have prevented his acting as Mountagu's agent; and it would have been no more difficult for him to obtain leave of absence to accompany his patron to the Sound than it proved to be at a later date when the fleet went to bring over the restored King.[2] But though Pepys continued to act for Mountagu after 1659, he was no longer living in his house, for we know that at the date of the beginning of the *Diary* on January 1, 1659-60, he was in a small house which he had rented in Axe Yard, on the south side of King Street, Westminster.

Only one other fact remains to be noticed about the early life of Pepys. It is clear from the *Diary* that he had served in the trained-bands, and continued to serve in Lord Sandwich's troop until it

[1] lxxiii. 201. [2] See p. 14 below.

was disbanded in November 1660. It is therefore somewhat surprising that he should have been so completely baffled by the military evolutions which he saw in Hyde Park on September 16, 1668. "Indeed, it was mighty noble, and their firing mighty fine, and the Duke of Monmouth in mighty rich clothes, but the well-ordering of the men I understand not."

CHAPTER II

The Beginning of the Diary

PEPYS'S *Diary* begins (as it ends) with a pious invocation. "Blessed be God, at the end of the last year I was in very good health, without any sense of my old pain, but upon taking of cold." The entries for the first two days of the year 1660 which follow this characteristic reference to his health, present in a microcosm almost the whole of the *Diary*. They include clothes ("my suit with great skirts"), a sermon, "the remains of a turkey," "a dozen bottles of sack," music, cards, the weather, politics, a loan of £10 from a friend, and the diarist's private accounts. It is true that there is nothing about women or plays; but the theatres did not re-open until the Restoration, and Pepys's first serious flirtation, that with Rebecca Allen, belongs to April 1661.

As a clerk in the Exchequer Pepys only received £50 a year, and although he was continuing his services to Mountagu, he and his wife lived in a humble way.[1] On the other hand, his duties allowed him plenty of leisure. For instance, on February 3, 1659-60, which may be regarded as a typical day, he spent part of the morning playing on the flageolet in St. James's Park; then, after a visit to the office, he took some friends and "shewed them the manner of the Houses sitting" and, after wine and anchovies at the Rhenish wine-house, "bespoke a shoulder of mutton at Wilkinson's to be roasted as well as it could be done." While waiting for dinner he took the party to see Whitehall, and after dinner he "left them and went to hear news." Towards evening they "went to take a turn in the Park," where the ladies ran races for a pot of ale. The evening finished with cards.

On January 16, 1659-60, Downing, who was then going into Holland, asked Pepys to accompany him, but gave him "little encouragement"; and three days later he told him that he "had a kindness" for him, and had got him to be one of the Clerks of the Council. Nothing came of this prospect of promotion, and the recipient of the offer shewed little gratitude for it. "I feared," he writes, "that his doing of it was but only to ease himself of the salary which he gives me."

[1] See *Diary*, January 16, 1659-60; and *cf.* the often-quoted entry of February 25, 1666-7, describing how he and his wife ("poor wretch!") lived in their "little room at my Lord Sandwich's."

It was not long, however, before a much better offer came in Pepys's way, for on March 6 Mountagu, the architect of his fortunes, asked him to go to sea with him as his secretary, with a salary at the rate of £200 a year. A deputy at the Exchequer was speedily arranged for; Mrs. Pepys was disposed of by being boarded out at a friend's house; on March 23 her husband, armed with a warrant appointing him Secretary to the Generals of the Fleet, went on board the *Swiftsure* in the Thames; and on April 2, 1660, he joined his chief in the *Naseby*. Here, after the leisure of the Exchequer, he found "infinity of business" in writing letters and orders; but there was also profit to be had from the gratuities given to the secretary by captains and others to whom he was in a position to do favours.

Life on board ship, where Pepys experienced nothing worse from the sea than finding himself "dizzy and squeamish," was very enjoyable, and on April 17 he writes: "So to sleep, every day bringing me a fresh sense of the pleasure of my present life." There was also much to interest him at Scheveningen and the Hague; and his impressions of the impending Restoration fully deserve the permanent record which he gave them. On May 17 he was presented to the King, "who seems to be a very sober man," and also to the Duke of York; and when on May 22 the King received his first salute from the fleet, the secretary, in a sudden access of loyalty, fired one of the guns himself, " but holding my head too much over the gun, I had almost spoiled my right eye." He thought the royal company dining by themselves " a blessed sight to see," and when the King "fell into discourse of his escape from Worcester," the tale of his perils and privations made him " ready to weep." There follows the famous account of the landing at Dover on May 25:

> [The King] " was received by General Monk with all imaginable love and respect at his entrance upon the land of Dover. Infinite the crowd of people, and the horsemen, citizens, and noblemen of all sorts. The Mayor of the town came and gave him his white staff, the badge of his place, which the King did give him again. The Mayor also presented him from the town a very rich Bible, which he took and said it was the thing that he loved above all things in the world. A canopy was provided for him to stand under, which he did, and talked awhile with General Monk and others, and so into a stately coach there set for him, and so away through the town towards Canterbury, without making any stay at Dover. The shouting and joy expressed by all is past imagination."

Mountagu was " almost transported with joy," and the diarist notes with satisfaction that when he had occasion to speak to the Duke of York on business he "called me Pepys by name."

The traveller returned to London on June 9 to stay with his father in Salisbury Court, and on the following day his wife joined him there. On June 22 he writes, "To bed, the first time since my coming from sea, in my own house, for which God be praised."

CHAPTER III

Clerk of the Acts

NINE days after Pepys returned from sea, his constant benefactor Mountagu told him, on June 18, 1660, that "he did look after the place of Clerk of the Acts" for him, and on June 23 he was able to say that he had obtained a promise of the appointment. On June 26 "one Mr. Watts," a merchant, offered Pepys £500 to "desist," but on June 28, feeling sure of his ground, he resigned his clerkship at the Exchequer, and on the following day he obtained his warrant[1] from the Duke of York, now Lord High Admiral of England. On June 29, however, it transpired that Thomas Barlow, who had been appointed to the office jointly with Dennis Fleming in 1638, was "yet alive, and coming up to town to look after his place." As Barlow was "a sickly man, and did not intend to execute the place himself," Pepys, to his great relief, succeeded in buying him

[1] The patent was duly signed on July 13.

out with an annuity of £100. On February 9, 1664-5, the news of Barlow's death reached his successor, "for which, God knows my heart," he writes, "I could be as sorry as is possible for one to be for a stranger by whose death he gets £100 per annum, he being a worthy, honest man."

As Clerk of the Acts Pepys was a Principal Officer of the Navy, the others being Sir George Carteret the Treasurer, Sir Robert Slyngesbie the Comptroller, and Sir William Batten the Surveyor. There were also two Commissioners of the Navy, Lord Berkeley and Sir William Penn, and these six made up the Navy Board,[1] the body of experts who administered the navy under the Lord High Admiral. Four of them were sailors and one—Lord Berkeley—a distinguished soldier; the Clerk of the Acts alone was without professional experience. A critic of the time might have complained with reason that Mountagu's influence had jobbed into the Board a person who was obviously unfit for the post. It was not long before the civilian element there was reinforced by the appointment as additional Commissioners[2] of

[1] Its full official title was "The Principal Officers and Commissioners of the Navy."

[2] There were also resident commissioners at the dockyards,—in 1660 at Chatham only, but in 1664 commissioners were appointed for Harwich and Portsmouth. They were "not obliged to a continual personal attendance jointly with the other Officers," and so did not sit on the Navy Board in London.

William Coventry in 1662 and Lord Brouncker in 1664, but Coventry had already had two years' experience of naval administration as Secretary to the Lord High Admiral, and Lord Brouncker was a man of science who took more than an amateur's interest in shipbuilding and in 1662 had built a yacht for the King. Other changes in the composition of the Navy Board during the period of the *Diary* were the appointment of Sir John Mennes as Comptroller on Slyngesbie's death in 1661 and of Colonel Thomas Middleton as Surveyor when Batten died in 1667. In 1665 Lord Berkeley was succeeded by Sir Thomas Harvey; and in 1667 Coventry resigned, his place being left vacant. In 1667 also Carteret was succeeded in the Treasurership of the Navy by the Earl of Anglesey, and when he was suspended in 1668 the office passed to Sir Thomas Osborne and Sir Thomas Littleton acting jointly.

In addition to a salary of £350 a year, the appointment of Clerk of the Acts carried with it the right to a house in the Navy Office in Seething Lane, so Pepys sold his lease of the house in Axe Yard for £41 to Mr. Dalton, "one of the wine-sellers to the King." On August 6, 1660, he received an offer of £1000 for his place, "which made my mouth water," but he resisted the temptation, and embarked upon what was to be a busy and diligent official life which must have contrasted strangely with the ample leisure of the Exchequer. As early as July 2, the day before the first meeting of the new Navy Board, he writes, " Infinite of business, that my heart and head and all were full."

At his entry upon his new office Pepys was profoundly ignorant of naval matters, but he at once began to equip himself with amazing energy for his post, exhibiting a fierce ambition to understand his business and a voracious appetite for new naval knowledge. As early as October 4, 1660, he is studying a ship-model and asking questions of a naval officer concerning " many things in a ship " that he " desired to understand." On November 30 he is displaying curiosity about " sea terms," and on March 13, 1660-1, he gets up early in the morning to read *The Seaman's Grammar and Dictionary*. On October 30, 1661, he visits Deptford on purpose to be shewn over " every hole and corner " of a ship. In June 1662 he is learning to measure timber, and practises with so much diligence that by August 3, 1663, he is enough of an expert to admonish the official timber-measurer at Chatham yard. For this " mathematiques " was necessary, and on July 4, 1662, he made a beginning with the multiplication-table. He studied " the nature and prices " of hemp and tar, and hired the mate of the *Royal Charles* to give him four lectures at his office " upon the body of a ship," " my interest still growing, for which God be praised." For this purpose the ship-model in the office was found useful, but on August 12 Anthony Deane the famous shipbuilder promised him a model of his own, " which will please me exceedingly, for I do want one of my own " ; and this was duly delivered on September 29. In June 1663 Deane gave him lessons on his method of drawing the lines of a ship, and on July 21 he presented him with a completed draught. This seems to have provoked Pepys to a resolution of learning something of the art of shipbuilding, " for I find it is not hard and very useful," [1] and this led to further instruction from the indispensable Deane.[2] He also visits Deptford to inform himself about stores; looks into " the nature of a purser's account and the business of victualling " ; learns " to understand the course of the tides " ; and decides to "allot a little time now and then " to reading some common law.

In the discharge of the ordinary duties of his office the diligence of the Clerk of the Acts was untiring. The shortest entry in the *Diary* suggests that he worked long hours : " At home and at the office all day. At night to bed " ; [3] but although

[1] April 2, 1664. [2] May 7, 1664.

[3] April 3, 1662. This may perhaps have suggested the entry which is said to have appeared in a caricature diary of Pepys as an undergraduate at Cambridge,—" Rose ; and so to bed."

the hours were long they were not regular, as required by the routine of a modern office in days when good artificial light is always available. In the summer Pepys was often up at 4 in the morning; but when the days began to shorten appreciably he rose at 5 and sat up later at night. In the winter he would lie in bed till 8, although occasionally we find such an entry as, "up pretty early, that is by seven o'clock, it being not yet light before or then."[1] By the end of March the earlier hours recommence;[2] in April he is up by 5; on June 1 he begins "again to rise betimes by 4 o'clock." On special occasions, when he had to go to Deptford or Woolwich on navy business, he would get up before 3 and make an early start. If troublesome matters had to be dealt with, Pepys would often stay at the office until midnight, and occasionally till one, two, three, or even four in the morning; but the entry for February 17, 1663-4, is exceptional. Pepys and Sir William Rider spend the evening over Mr. Wood's contract for masts. Rider leaves at midnight, but Pepys stays on:

[Hoping] "to save the King some more money, and out of an impatience to breake up with my head full of confused confounded notions but nothing brought to a clear comprehension, I was resolved to sit up and did till

[1] January 7, 1662-3.

[2] "Lay pretty long, that is till past six o'clock" (March 24, 1662-3).

now it is ready to strike 4 o'clock, all alone, cold, and my candle not enough left to light me to my owne house, and so, with my business however brought to some good understanding, and set it down pretty clear, I went home to bed with my mind at good quiet."

Mr. Wood had been in trouble with the Officers of the Navy already over a different matter, when they sent for him and told him their minds, "which he seemed not to value much."

The long hours at the office were relieved by days of comparative leisure, when he "lay long in bed," and after a short morning's work escorted Mrs. Pepys "to walk a little in St. James's Park"; and also by the "great comfort" which he derived from the knowledge that every day he understood "more and more the pleasure of following of business and the credit that a man gets by it." [1] This delight in his work appears again and again in the *Diary*. "Up, and all day at the office," he writes on May 6, 1665, "but a little at dinner, and there late till past 12. So home to bed, pleased as I always am after I have rid a great deal of work, it being very satisfactory to me." His love of pleasure sometimes leads him astray, and he has to fortify himself by a system of vows and penalties,[2] but "among so many lazy people" "the diligent man becomes necessary," [3] and he intended to be the necessary man in the navy.

[1] January 19, 1662-3. [2] See index, under "Vows."
[3] November 1, 1665.

That he achieved his purpose is suggested by a letter of November 12, 1669,[1] written during his absence in Holland and France by two of his colleagues to the Commissioners of Public Accounts to inform them that Mr. Pepys " is best able, from his constant attendance at the Board, to give an account " of their proceedings.

The physical vigour which enabled Pepys to work long hours at the office also manifested itself in another way. On March 24, 1663-4, he went by water to Greenwich, " walked very finely to Woolwich and there did very much business at both yards," walked back, " and so to Deptford and did the like there," then walked to Rotherhithe, " and so home to the office, where we sat late, and home weary to supper and to bed." Scarcely less energy was displayed by the women of his household, for on June 7, 1665, his wife and mother rose about two o'clock, " and with Mercer, Mary, the boy, and W. Hewer," went to Gravesend by water and did not return until five on the following morning.

Pepys has been called by one writer, " the best man of business of his time," [2] and has been credited by another with " a prodigious faculty of methodical arrangement."[3] For these qualities

[1] Historical MSS. Commission, *Eighth Report*, Pt. I. p. 131.

[2] *Dublin University Magazine*, xxxiv. (1849), 626.

[3] *Edinburgh Review*, xc. (1849), 548.

the office of Clerk of the Acts gave ample scope. On July 7, 1660, only four days after his first appearance at the Navy Board, he "began to take an inventory of the papers and goods and books of the office"; and on July 31 he was "doing things in order to the calculating of the debts of the navy." On April 16, 1662, he began an abstract of all the contracts made in the office since he came into it, and on July 7 he was putting new office books in order, "writing on the back-sides what books they be, and transcribing out of some old books some things into them." On January 9, 1662-3, he assigned a manuscript volume, "handsomely bound," to "things of the navy"; and on January 30 he writes, "And now I think I have a better collection in reference to the navy, and shall have by the time I have filled it, than any of my predecessors." This instinct for keeping memoranda and reducing everything to writing, led Pepys to transcribe and collect documents "against a black day" for the defence of himself and his colleagues if their conduct should be called in question; and in particular to keep a record of his proceedings before the Commissioners of Public Accounts.

If this methodical habit of sorting books and accumulating notes and memoranda stood alone, it might justify the writer of 1825 who was undiscerning enough to describe Pepys as a "laborious official drudge,"[1] but the *Diary* reveals less prosaic qualities, and among them a high capacity for administrative organisation. As early as October 24, 1662, he is to be found discoursing with the clerk of the cheque and the storekeeper at Deptford "about my late conceptions about keeping books of the distinct works done in the yards, against which," he adds, in the authentic spirit of the reformer, "I find no objection but their ignorance and unwillingness to do anything of pains, and what is out of their ordinary dull road, but I like it well and will proceed in it." He prevails on the authorities to adopt, with one modification, his "proposition" with regard to the methods of pursers; he invents "a new way of the call-book" in the yards, and a new form of book for the muster-masters; and he also draws up "new things" in the instructions for commanders. The same freshness of mind which made Pepys inventive on his own account, rendered him receptive to the ideas of other men, and his capacity for carrying things through converted mere suggestions into realised improvements. Thus in 1668 Mr. Francis Hosier the muster-master at Gravesend took "great pains in reducing to a method" the business of balancing the storekeepers' accounts. Pepys approved the scheme and carried it to the King and Council, and it was

[1] *Eclectic Review*, xxiv. (1825), 78.

eventually adopted by an Order in Council of his own drafting.[1]

His most important enterprise, however, in which he employed remarkable skill and diplomacy, was the "great letter" to the Duke of York on the "miscarriages" of the Navy Office, and his subsequent suggestions "for the better managing" of it. He had all the papers relating to this business bound up,[2] "it being that which shall do me more right many years hence than perhaps all I ever did in my life."[3] A full account of the episode from this collection has been given by the present writer elsewhere.[4] A point of interest which comes out in Pepys's defence of his own conduct as Clerk of the Acts is the enormous increase of business in the Navy Office during the second Dutch War of 1665 as compared with the first Dutch War of 1653; for the number of letters, orders, and contracts passing through the Navy Office was multiplied sixfold.

Pepys did not spend all his time in his office, for there were other duties attached to the Clerkship of the Acts which carried him abroad into the world of men and gave variety and interest

[1] March 7, 1668-9.

[2] The volume is No. 2242 in the Pepysian Library.

[3] May 8, 1669.

[4] *Catalogue of Pepysian MSS.* (Navy Records Society's Publications) i, 28-32.

to his life. He went a good deal on 'Change to discuss with the merchants the prices of commodities required in the navy; with his colleagues he visited the Duke of York once a week to take his instructions as Lord High Admiral; and he paid frequent visits of inspection to the dockyards down the River. It was on one of these expeditions that Pepys first realised at Deptford his own official importance: "Never till now did I see the great authority of my place, all the captains of the fleet coming cap in hand to us."[1] At Chatham on April 8, 1661, he encountered the ghost of Kenrick Edisbury, a former Surveyor of the Navy, but it turned out to be his pillow, which he had flung from him, standing upright in the light of the moon. This busy official also found time for diversion of a different kind. On January 21, 1663-4, he paid a shilling "to stand upon the wheel of a cart, in great pain, above an hour," to see an execution. On April 25, 1664, he attended a prize-fight, "with good pleasure enough." On September 4, 1663, Pepys and his wife saw "a goose with four feet and a cock with three" at Bartholomew Fair, and on August 14, 1666, they witnessed a bull-baiting, "but it is a very rude and nasty pleasure."

The office of Clerk of the Acts brought Pepys

[1] January 12, 1660-1.

within range of other promotion, at first of the lesser and then of the more important kinds. On July 23, 1660, he was sworn in as deputy for Mountagu, now Lord Sandwich, for one of the Clerkships of the Privy Seal, with the obligation of taking duty a month at a time in rotation with the other clerks. This ("blessed be God") brought him in at first about £3 a day. He served for six months (August and December 1660; April, August, and December 1661; and April 1662), but his absences from the Navy Board were resented by his colleagues, and, as the profits were declining, he concluded that the appointment was "little worth," and resigned it on August 17, 1662. With the office he must have lost a privilege which he valued, for we read that on Sunday April 20, 1662, he attended service at the King's Chapel at Whitehall "where I challenged my pew as Clerk of the Privy Seal and had it."

On September 24, 1660, Pepys and Batten were sworn in as Justices of the Peace for Middlesex, Essex, Kent, and Hampshire, the counties in which the principal dockyards were situated, "with which honour I did find myself mightily pleased, though I am wholly ignorant in the duty of a justice of peace." On February 15, 1661-2, Pepys was admitted a Younger Brother of the Trinity House, Lord Sandwich being at that time

Master;[1] and on March 16 the Duke of York "took very civil notice" of him in St. James's Park. On April 30, 1662, when on an official visit to Portsmouth, he was made a burgess of the town. "It cost me a piece in gold to the Town Clerk, and 10s. to the Bayliffes," and 6s. for drink for the Mayor and Corporation.

In November 1662 the King issued a Commission for the Affairs of Tangier, and by Lord Sandwich's interest Pepys was placed upon it. He was informed of the design beforehand on August 19, and with characteristic thoroughness at once began to get up the subject. The Commission commenced its sittings on December 1, and Pepys attended regularly, although he was disgusted with the want of "true integrity" about its proceedings, "so that I am almost discouraged from coming any more to the Committee, were it not that it will possibly hereafter bring me to some acquaintance of great men."[2] He complains later that things are "poorly and brokenly" done, and that Prince Rupert will do nothing but swear and laugh, though Ashley "looks near into the King's business."

A charter establishing a Corporation for the Royal Fishing, dated April 8, 1664, included

[1] Historical MSS. Commission, *Fifteenth Report*, Appendix, Pt. II. pp. 157-8.

[2] January 27, 1662-3.

Pepys among the 36 members of the Company, with the Duke of York as Governor,—another appointment which he owed to the friendship of Lord Sandwich. On September 5 he was elected on a standing Fishery Committee which he attended with regularity,—but he found the proceedings of Lord Craven as Chairman "very confused and very ridiculous."

The first Treasurer of the Tangier Commission was Thomas Povey, whom Pepys thought an absurd person, and no more fit for that employment than "he is to be King of England," being of "poor parts and great unfitness for business." Pepys himself had been growing in repute on the Commission, and had come to regard Tangier as "one of the best flowers in my garden"; so when on March 17, 1664-5, Povey, whose accounts had been getting more and more muddled, suggested that he should take over the Treasurership, the idea was not unacceptable. The Duke spoke warmly in support of Pepys, and on March 20 his appointment was approved at the Commission "with great content and allowance beyond expectation." On April 19, 1665, it passed the Privy Seal, and on June 5 the new Treasurer presented his first statement of accounts "with great acceptation, and so had some good words and honour by it." But his predecessor, who had shewn in office "fatal folly and neglect," had been shrewd enough to attach to his surrender the condition that he should continue to take half the profits. From this time forward, Tangier plays an important part in the activities of the pluralist Clerk of the Acts.

In the spring and summer of 1665 the victualling system broke down, and Pepys had his own ideas about the proper way to reform it. On October 6 he was busy drawing up a "letter by way of discourse to the Duke of Albemarle" giving his "conception how the business of the victualling should be ordered," "wherein," he writes, "I have taken great pains, and I think I have hitt the right if they will but follow it." On October 14 his proposal was "read before the King, Duke, and the Caball with complete applause and satisfaction." A feature of the scheme was the appointment of a Surveyor-General of Victualling, with subordinates in each victualling-port; and on October 19 Pepys wrote to Coventry and modestly offered himself for the post. His suggestion was accepted, the salary being fixed at £300 a year, but as the new office was created for the war only, he resigned it on July 28, 1667.

Pepys's final promotion gave him "occasion of much mirth," for on March 13, 1668-9, he received a commission as captain of the *Jersey*, in order to enable him to sit upon a court-martial to enquire into the loss of the *Defiance*; "and there I did manage the business . . . And so I did lay the law open to them, and rattle the masters-attendant out of their wits almost; and made the trial last till seven at night, not eating a bit all the day." This display of zeal led to an invitation to assist at another court-martial (where "I confess I was pretty high"), but the proceedings of the commanders were "so devilishly bad" that he could endure them no longer, "but took occasion to pretend business at the Office, and away."[1]

The *Diary* is a mine of information about the routine of the Navy Office, the abuses in naval administration and the attempts to remedy them, and the appalling consequences of want of money; but these have been dealt with elsewhere,[2] and the present volume is concerned only with matters personal to Pepys. It will be enough to say that in his office of Clerk of the Acts he reveals himself as a most capable public servant. He is a candid critic of his colleagues, but a tower of strength to them in times of office trouble and a staunch defender of the Navy Board against attacks from outside. As the skilled draughtsman of the Office he prepared the documentary defences, and on two occasions at least he proved himself capable of effective speech. On October 22, 1667, the Principal Officers were summoned to answer in

[1] April 1 and 3, 1669.

[2] *Catalogue of Pepysian MSS.* (General Introduction), vol. i.

the Commons, before a Committee of the whole House, to a charge of neglecting the defences of the Medway. "None of my brethren said anything but me there," writes Pepys with pardonable pride, "but only two or three silly words my Lord Brouncker gave"; and he succeeded in fully satisfying the House. Some months later, on March 5, 1667-8, the Officers were again on their defence at the Commons' bar over the business of tickets, the House being full and prejudiced. The Clerk of the Acts spoke for more than three hours, —"most acceptably and smoothly," he writes, "without any hesitation or losse, but with full scope, and all my reason free about me, as if it had been at my own table." No vote was taken that day, for "my speech being so long, many had gone out to dinner and come in again half drunk"; but the orator was overwhelmed with congratulations. "Everybody that saw me almost come to me . . . with such eulogys as cannot be expressed," and some one called him another Cicero,—"for which the Lord God make me thankful! and that I may make use of it not to pride and vain-glory."

To the incense of praise Pepys was peculiarly susceptible, and he collected into the *Diary* flattering notices of himself with all the zest of the popular actress of fiction. His story is one of a steady rise in life due to unremitting diligence and a capital business head, and he follows his own upward progress with the keenest interest. As early as August 20, 1662, he notes that Coventry told Lord Sandwich that he "was indeed the life" of the Navy Office, "so that on all hands, by God's blessing," he writes, "I find myself a very rising man." He walks "with great confidence" among the courtiers at Whitehall, and takes pride in the number of enquiries after him when he had the nettle-rash. He has his crest put on his wine-bottles. Meeting an old acquaintance whose talk he used to "adore," he thinks him "but an ordinary man," and his son's nose "unhappily awry." He is proud to see himself accepted in good company and thought better than he is.[1] The Lord Mayor is "very respectfull" to him, the Duke of Albemarle "mighty pleasant," and the Lord Chancellor strokes him on the head. His credit in the Office grew daily.[2] Coventry "did largely owne his dependance" there upon Pepys's care;[3] Albemarle told him that he was "the right hand of the navy";[4] and when on January 28, 1665-6, the King came to him "of himself" and said: "Mr. Pepys, I do give you thanks for your good service all this year, and I assure you I am very sensible of it," he went to bed "in a great

[1] November 24, 1664. [2] December 31, 1664.
[3] March 15, 1664-5. [4] April 24, 1665.

delirium" of joy. In the midst of all these compliments, however, a discordant note was struck. In August 1667 James Carcasse, one of the four clerks of the Ticket Office, whose dismissal for irregularities had been mainly secured by the action of Pepys, gave out that he intended to hang him, at which the Clerk of the Acts was both surprised and pained. But in 1668 he was still collecting testimonials and hoping that they would not make him proud.

CHAPTER IV

Mrs. Pepys

ELIZABETH ST. MICHEL brought to Pepys "a comely person."[1] Lord Sandwich thought her "a great beauty,"[2] and paid her special attention; and his heir went so far as to court her, "even to the trouble of his lady."[3] Like other pretty women, she was fond of dress, and her husband encouraged her. He writes on Sunday, May 4, 1662: "I walked to Gray's Inn to observe fashions of the ladies, because of my wife's making some clothes," and when "her new suit of black sarcenet and yellow petticoat" saw the light on Whit Sunday a fortnight later, he thought it "very pretty." On ceremonial occasions the business of dressing appears to have absorbed a great deal of time, for when Mrs. Pepys expected to start at five o'clock in a coach and four to dine with the Carterets at Cranbourne, she found it

[1] February 4, 1664-5. [2] June 15, 1663.
[3] November 10, 1668.

necessary to rise "between three and four of the clock in the morning to dress herself."[1] But later on, on Christmas Day 1668, shc "poor wretch! sat undressed all day, till ten at night, altering and lacing of a noble petticoat."

Mrs. Pepys's careful husband was sometimes troubled by what he regarded as her extravagance. In their early days, when money was hard to come by, she spent £5 on a petticoat of "a most fine cloth of 26*s*. a yard, and a rich lace,"—"at which I was somewhat troubled, but she doing it very innocently I could not be angry."[2] But Pepys was disposed to be rather mean with his wife, and on November 9, 1661, Lady Sandwich, who was a good friend to them both, took him to task. She "did mightily urge me to lay out money" upon her, "which I perceived was a little more earnest than ordinary, and so I seemed to be pleased with it, and do resolve to bestow a lace upon her." On consideration, however, he followed Lady Sandwich's advice, and gave her £20 "to lay out in clothes against Easter for herself."[3] Later on, when Pepys became well-to-do, his wife was allowed to gratify her tastes more freely, and she was on occasion very splendid. On May Day 1669 he came home from the office at noon to dinner and found her

[1] February 25, 1665-6. [2] August 18, 1660.
[3] February 9, 1661-2.

"extraordinary fine, with her flowered tabby gown" "now laced exceeding pretty, and indeed was fine all over." She prevailed on him with difficulty to put on his own fine suit "of flowered tabby vest and coloured camelott tunique," with "the gold lace at the hands," and thus attired, the couple took the air in their own coach, "with our new liveries of serge, and the horses' manes and tails tied with red ribbons, . . . and green reines, that people did mightily look upon us; and the truth is, I did not see any coach more pretty, though more gay, than ours, all the day." A month later the *Diary* had come to an end, and before the close of the year Elizabeth Pepys was in her grave.

Pepys himself had a passion for neatness, but his wife was incurably untidy, and this was a frequent cause of domestic friction. Her clothes were "carelessly laid up" and she left "her things lying about." On May 2, 1663, he came "to some angry words" with her "about neglecting the keeping of the house clean, I calling her beggar and she me pricklouse, which vexed me." On one occasion she was 7*s.* out in her monthly accounts, "which did occasion a very high falling out between us, I indeed too angrily insisting upon so poor a thing, and did give her very provoking high words," which "she took very stomachfully."[1]

[1] February 28, 1664-5.

Mrs. Pepys was not only untidy, she was also ignorant and ill-educated and could not spell properly,—but this does not appear to have annoyed her husband to the same extent. He took infinite pains to improve her mind, buying "a pair of globes" for her instruction, giving her lessons in arithmetic, and reading "a lecture to her in geography" after dinner, "which she takes very prettily, and with great pleasure to her, and me to teach her."[1] On May 7, 1665, she began to learn drawing and painting; but this essay in art proved so attractive to the pupil that Pepys was troubled to see his wife "minding her paynting and not thinking of her house business."[2]

A real bond between husband and wife was supplied by music. As early as August 28, 1660, Pepys began to teach her "some scale in music," and found her "apt beyond imagination." On October 1, 1661, she began to learn singing from Mr. Goodgroome, her husband's own singing-master, but the lessons were soon dropped. In the autumn of 1666 she began to learn again, and took "mighty pains" and was "proud that she shall come to trill";[3] but after a month of it he writes disconsolately on March 1, 1666-7, "Her ear is so bad that it makes me angry, till the poor wretch cried to see me so vexed at her. . . . She

[1] January 6, 1663-4. [2] May 3, 1666. [3] February 7, 1666-7.

hath a great mind to learn, only to please me, and therefore I am mighty unjust to her in discouraging her so much; but we were good friends, and to dinner." In the end, Mrs. Pepys's perseverance triumphed, and she pleased her husband by singing well in part-songs, "which is a comfort to my very heart."[1] On May 6, 1667, he writes, she "do begin to give me real pleasure with her singing." Pepys was rendered more favourably disposed to her deficiencies by the appalling performance of Betty Turner, who was "a beast" "as to singing, not knowing how to sing one note in tune, . . . worse than my wife a thousand times, so that it do a little reconcile me to her."[2] With instrumental music Mrs. Pepys was more successful, "for though her eare be bad, yet I see she will attain any thing to be done by her hand."[3] On November 20, 1666, an arrangement was made with Mr. Gregory, "an able and sober man," to teach her to play the viol, and on February 28, 1666-7, she began to learn the flageolet. By September 11, 1667, she could play anything upon it "almost at first sight, and in good time."

On April 25, 1663, Mrs. Pepys began to learn dancing, "but I fear will hardly do any great good at it," wrote her husband, "because

[1] April 18, 1667. [2] January 22, 1667-8.
[3] September 11, 1667.

she is conceited [1] that she do well already, though I think no such thing." Two days later he adds, "I fear I have done very ill in letting her begin to learn to dance," and on May 21 he arrives at the conclusion that she is being spoiled. By "this occasion of dancing and other pleasures" she "finds other sweets besides pleasing of me, and so makes her that she begins not at all to take pleasure in me or study to please me as heretofore." This did not prevent his learning to dance himself, as "a thing very useful for a gentleman"; [2] and a day came [3] when Pepys's own office was swept and garnished for a dance which lasted till "almost three in the morning"; "and so to bed, . . . my mind mightily satisfied with all this evening's work, and thinking it to be one of the merriest enjoyment I must look for in the world, . . . only the musique did not please me," the four fiddlers "not being contented with less than 30*s*."

The married life of Pepys and his wife was more than ordinarily full of quarrels and reconciliations, but there can be no doubt that the union was one of true affection on both sides. On October 24, 1662, when they had been living together for just six years, he writes, "We have

[1] *I.e.*, "she is of opinion"; the word here has not the modern implication.

[2] May 4, 1663.

[3] January 24, 1666-7.

been for some years now, and at present more and more, a very happy couple, blessed be God." On December 17 he refers to her "dear company and talk," and when she was away at Brampton he describes himself as "sad for want of my wife, whom I love with all my heart."[1] At dinner at the Deanes he "sat with little pleasure" because she was at home alone, and hurried back to dine with her over again.[2] The *Diary* for April 14, 1661, describes a touching scene, when Pepys flung out of his father's house "in a discontent, but she, poor wretch, followed me as far in the rain and dark as Fleet Bridge to fetch me back again, and so I did." When she had the toothache, and "her face miserably swelled," he "sat up with her, talking and reading and pitying her";[3] and when he was himself in trouble at the Navy Office, thinking of resignation and unable to sleep, he got his wife to talk to him to comfort him.[4]

Some of their differences were over quite trumpery matters. It is perhaps characteristic of both that the first record in the *Diary* of Pepys being angry with his wife was over half-a-crown which she had put away in a paper box and "had forgot where she had lain it"; but he concludes, "we were friends again, as we are always."[5]

[1] June 15, 1663.
[2] September 26, 1663.
[3] December 20, 1667.
[4] March 5, 1667-8.
[5] October 24, 1660.

No doubt she was sometimes irritating. Pepys refers to her long-winded stories[1] and "silly discourse,"[2] and says that she is not to be trusted with liberty, "for she is a fool."[3] He was sometimes annoyed by her manner of dressing, and more than once they quarrelled on this account. On May 29, 1667, he was "horrid angry" about her costume, and refused to go out with her, and on June 4 it "grew to high words between us"; but Pepys hit on the ingenious device of reading Boyle's *Hydrostatics* aloud, and letting her "talk till she was tired."

Poor Mrs. Pepys did not always escape personal chastisement. On April 5, 1664, "she answering me some way that I did not like, I pulled her by the nose. . . . The poor wretch took it mighty ill." On December 19, "she giving me some cross answer, I did strike her over her left eye such a blow as the poor wretch did cry out and was in great pain, but yet her spirit was such as to endeavour to bite and scratch me." In spite of an application of butter and parsley, the state of the eye sent Pepys alone to church on Christmas Day. On July 12, 1667, another tempestuous scene took place:

"So home, and there find my wife in a dogged humour for my not dining at home, and I did give her a pull by the nose and some ill words, which she provoked me to by

[1] May 12, 1666. [2] August 6, 1666. [3] June 17, 1668.

something she spoke, that we fell extraordinarily out, insomuch that I going to the office to avoid further anger, she followed me in a devilish manner thither, and with much ado I got her into the garden out of hearing, to prevent shame, and so home, and by degrees I found it necessary to calme her, and did, and then to the office, where pretty late, and then to walk with her in the garden, and so to supper, and pretty good friends, and so to bed with my mind very quiet."

Mrs. Pepys was not the only recipient of this form of marital correction, for on September 13, 1667, Pepys noted that Mrs. Lowther "hath got a sore nose, given her, I believe, from her husband, which made me I could not look upon her with any pleasure."

Some of the more serious differences between Pepys and his wife arose out of jealousy, to which he, at any rate, was peculiarly prone. It was in vain that he reasoned with himself and called himself a fool. "My devilish jealousy," he writes on May 26, 1663, "makes a very hell in my mind, which the God of Heaven remove, or I shall be very unhappy."[1] He was jealous of Captain Holmes "in his gold-laced suit"; of Pembleton the dancing-master, "a pretty neat black man"; of William Hewer his trusted clerk; and even of William Penn the Quaker, the founder of Pennsylvania! Mrs. Pepys, on her side, thought her husband was too much taken up with her waiting gentlewomen, was very

[1] *Cf.* January 11, 1663-4.

jealous of Mrs. Knipp the actress, who winked at him in the theatre, and objected to "la belle Pierce," the wife of Dr. James Pearse the surgeon, whose "beautiful company" Pepys enjoyed too much.

Jealousy may be evidence of affection, and Pepys was both affectionate and jealous; but he was not a faithful husband. It is not to his discredit that he was susceptible to the charm of women,—"A strange slavery that I stand in to beauty, that I value nothing near it,"[1] "so that indeed I am not, as I ought to be, able to command myself in the pleasures of my eye."[2] At the French church he was "much pleased with the three sisters of the parson, very handsome, especially in their noses";[3] and at St. Olave's he developed a possessive admiration for Mrs. Lethulier, "my fat brown beauty of our parish, . . . a very noble woman."[4] His judgment was, however, always discriminating, and he was sometimes devastating in his criticisms. At the Lord Mayor's dinner on October 29, 1663, he went away early, "being wearied with looking upon a company of ugly women." He endeavours to do justice to "the faire Mrs. Margaret Wight, who is a very fine lady, but the cast of her eye, got only by an ill habit, do her much wrong, and her

[1] September 6, 1664. [2] April 25, 1666.
[3] December 11, 1664. [4] December 3, 1665.

hands are bad; but she hath the face of a noble Roman lady";[1] and he carefully distinguishes between "two neighbour's daughters," the elder, "a long red-nosed silly jade," and the younger, "a pretty black girle, and the merriest sprightly jade that ever I saw."[2] On September 30, 1666, he fails to find in church "one handsome face," "as if indeed there was a curse . . . upon our parish"; and on April 21, 1667, when he takes his wife to the afternoon service at Hackney, he goes chiefly to see "the young ladies of the schools, whereof there is great store, very pretty." On May 26 he repaired to St. Margaret's, Westminster, where "I did entertain myself with my perspective glass up and down the church, by which I had the great pleasure of seeing and gazing at a great many very fine women."

This appreciation of female beauty led to a number of flirtations, pursued in the strenuous manner of the 17th century, but innocent enough for all that. We learn from an entry of February 3, 1664-5, that Pepys fined himself "12*d.* a kiss after the first," but meeting the lady with the Roman profile, "who indeed is a very pretty lady," he "did adventure upon a couple," and paid the fine. Affairs which began with innocent freedoms sometimes developed into something more serious. There were also entanglements

[1] June 1, 1666. [2] June 6, 1666.

with ladies of easy virtue, and there was at least one most discreditable episode in which David, taking advantage of his official position, sent Uriah the Hittite to sea. These matters are usually entered in the *Diary* in a jargon compounded of various languages,[1] which in some curious way appealed to Pepys's fancy, although it can scarcely have made the secrecy of the record more impenetrable. But through it all Pepys preserved a kind of fundamental decency. Free discourse "wearied" him, and he had a wholesome distaste for the lower forms of vice.

Mrs. Pepys appears to have been entirely ignorant of her husband's misdeeds until the swift development of the final tragedy which was to wreck for a time the happiness of their married life. On October 25, 1668, "which occasioned the greatest sorrow to me that ever I knew in this world," his wife, "coming up suddenly," discovered her husband and Deb Willet, her gentlewoman, in a compromising situation.[2] The story is too poignant to be told in an abbreviated

[1] For instance, on January 2, 1666-7, he entertained a guest at the Rose Tavern, and because her character was not above suspicion he thought it necessary to describe their proceedings thus: "We did biber a good deal de vino, et je did give elle twelve soldis para comprare elle some gans for a new anno's gift."

[2] The description in Wheatley's edition of the *Diary* does not appear to justify Mrs. Pepys's indignation, but a suppressed passage puts quite a different complexion upon the incident.

form. After painful scenes, in which the wife became "frantick" and the husband wept, a kind of peace was patched up on November 19 by the faithful Hewer, who also "did cry like a child." The *Diary* for that day ends in an agony of repentance and supplication: "I do, by the grace of God, promise never to offend her more, and did this night begin to pray to God upon my knees alone in my chamber, which God knows I cannot yet do heartily; but I hope God will give me the grace more and more every day to fear Him, and to be true to my poor wife." This solemn promise Pepys failed to keep.

The relations of the pair continued for a time to be unhappy. Mrs. Pepys insisted upon her husband being accompanied everywhere by William Hewer, "who goes up and down with me like a jaylour,"[1] "for she do plainly declare that she dares not trust me out alone";[2] and on December 21, when Hewer was not available, he suffered the final indignity of going out in the custody of the boy Tom. From time to time his wife would "rip up old faults,"[3] and once she threatened him "with the tongs red-hot at the ends."[4] He found her "mighty dogged," and wept to himself for grief.[5] She was not able to

[1] November 23, 1668.
[2] November 20, 1668.
[3] January 10, 1668-9.
[4] January 12.
[5] January 21.

forget his "late unkindness," but "now and then hath her passionate remembrance of it, as often as prompted to it by any occasion."[1] Meanwhile he was in constant terror lest his fresh meetings with Deb Willet should be discovered; but the episode ended on May 7, 1669, near the close of the *Diary*, with "private vows last night in prayer to God Almighty."

[1] January 31.

CHAPTER V

The Family

THROUGHOUT the *Diary* Samuel's attitude towards his own relations is affectionate but discriminating. "I do condemn myself mightily," he writes on September 5, 1664, "for my pride and contempt of my . . . kindred that are not so high as myself"; but he was under no illusions about the real position of the family, which was "never considerable."[1] He thinks it "a sad consideration how the Pepyses decay,"[2] and notes, perhaps with a mental reservation with regard to himself, that it had been their "very bad fortune . . . never to marry an handsome woman, excepting Ned Pepys."[3] But to the members of this plain and inconsiderable family he always shewed himself a loyal friend.

MR. AND MRS. JOHN PEPYS, SENIOR

Samuel was a good son. On December 12, 1660, when he was none too well off, he refused to

[1] February 10, 1661-2. [2] April 26, 1664. [3] July 29, 1667.

allow his father to repay a loan of £6, for "it went against me to take it of him and therefore did not, though I was afterwards a little troubled that I did not." In September 1664 he looked out some of his old clothes for his father and sent his mother 20*s*.; and when she came on a visit to him in May 1665 he equipped her with a new suit, "which makes her very fine."[1] In June 1666 he undertook to make an annual allowance to his father of £30, "at which the poor man was overjoyed and wept";[2] and when he left for the country Samuel gave him "some money to buy him a horse" and sent £20 to his mother and sister.[3] On March 2, 1666-7, he paid out of his own purse a legacy of £50 due from his Uncle Robert's estate, in order to save his father, who was legally liable; and on December 5, 1667, "not for want but for good husbandry," six pairs of old shoes were despatched to Mr. Pepys senior, "yet methought it was a thing against my mind to have him wear my old things."

There were frequent quarrels between the parents, due to the unhappy disposition of the elder Mrs. Pepys, who had grown "pettish" and was "unsufferably foolish and simple."[4] Samuel was also troubled to see his father "so much decay of a suddain, as he do both in seeing

[1] May 14. [2] June 17. [3] June 20. [4] May 31, 1661.

and hearing";[1] but this did not prevent him from obtaining from Lord Sandwich, with a fine contempt for the public interest, the refusal for his decaying parent of the post of Yeoman Tailor of the Wardrobe.[2] This did not actually fall in until October 28, 1667, when the son resolved "that my father shall not be troubled with it, but I hope I shall be able to enable him to end his days where he is, in quiet." The reference is to Brampton near Huntingdon, for by the death of his elder brother Robert on July 5, 1661,[3] a small estate there passed to Samuel's father, with a charge of £30 a year on it for the benefit of Samuel himself.[4] The elder Pepys settled there in August,[5] followed soon after by his wife and daughter.[6] The house, which still stands by the main road not far from Huntingdon, is a 16th century building of the farm-house type, with a late 17th century addition, although "some inharmonious developments dating from the Victorian era disfigure the south front";[7] but the income from the land was only about £80 a year.[8]

[1] May 19, 1661. [2] June 3, 1661.

[3] He was "taken with a dizziness in his head," followed by "fits of stupefaction."

[4] H. B. Wheatley, *Pepysiana*, p. 9.

[5] *Diary*, August 31, 1661. [6] *Ib.* September 5, 1661.

[7] Mr. Philip Norman's MS. [8] *Diary*, June 17, 1666.

During the early part of 1667 both parents were very ill, and Mrs. Pepys senior was "declared by the doctors to be past recovery." The devoted son at once wrote "an affectionate and sad letter" to his father. On March 25 he heard that his mother's death was hourly expected, and that night he dreamed a dream. The record of it is singularly touching, and true to the life of dreams; and two days afterwards the news came that she had died on the day of his dream. On April 10 he received a better report of his father, and on April 13 he writes characteristically, "I long to have him in town, . . . for I would fain do all I can that I may have him live, and take pleasure in my doing well in the world." The projected visit took place in May, but was cut short in June by the appearance of the Dutch in the Medway. From this point the *Diary* has little to say about Samuel's father. The final reference of December 23, 1668, is to an arrangement negotiated by his son with the landlord of the house in Salisbury Court by which he was liberated from the lease.

THOMAS PEPYS

When Mr. John Pepys senior retired to Brampton, the tailor's business was taken over by Samuel's younger brother Tom.[1] Samuel had

[1] Born June 18, 1634.

"great fears that he will miscarry for want of brains and care,"[1] but he did all he could to help him, giving him a good deal of his custom, and talking of a plan for buying tallow for the navy and assigning the profit to Tom.[2] He also threw himself with energy into the business of finding him a wife, and embarked upon various negotiations which for ceremonious complexity would not have disgraced a minor German court. Several proposals broke down, however, over the size of the bride's portion, and one over that of Tom's house, while one of the chosen could not "fancy" Tom because of the "bad imperfection in his speech." For a time the business prospered, and on June 14, 1663, Samuel thought that his brother was growing "a very thriving man." But Tom, who had already borrowed £20 of him, came to Samuel on August 29 for £20 more, and could give no proper account of his financial position; and on October 21 the diarist records a considered opinion,—that "he is very sluggish, and too negligent ever to do well at his trade."

The troubles with Tom were nearly over. In January 1663-4 he was taken ill, and was said to be "in a deep consumption," and on March 15 he died; which put his brother "into a present very great transport of grief and cries." He was

[1] August 31, 1661. [2] April 21, 1662.

buried three days later in "the middle isle" of St. Bride's Church, and the funeral was attended by nearly 150 mourners, who had "six biscuits a-piece, and what they pleased of burnt claret." After the ceremony the family "fell to a barrell of oysters, cake, and cheese," being "too merry for so late a sad work. But, Lord! to see how the world makes nothing of the memory of a man an houre after he is dead!"[1] Tom's affairs were left in some disorder, and his liabilities exceeded his assets by £90. His brother was "cruelly vexed" at being asked to pay his debts.

JOHN PEPYS, JUNIOR

Between Tom Pepys and his brother Samuel there was only a difference in age of a little more than a year; but John Pepys, the youngest of the family,[2] was more than eight years Samuel's junior, and this accounts for the parental attitude towards him indicated in the *Diary*.

Like Samuel, John was educated at St. Paul's School, and passed thence with a leaving Exhibition to Cambridge.[3] On February 25, 1659-60, he was admitted a sizar at Christ's College,[4] and a year later he was chosen "Schollar of the

[1] March 18, 1663-4. [2] Born November 26, 1641.

[3] *Diary*, February 8, 1659-60.

[4] He had been first entered as a sizar at Magdalene, May 26, 1659.

House."[1] In August 1662[2] he was offered the moderatorship of his year, but Samuel dissuaded him from accepting it; and in 1663 he proceeded to the B.A. Degree.[3] At the beginning of August, John came to stay with his brother, who seized the opportunity to examine him upon Descartes, "and I perceive he has studied him well, and I cannot find but he has minded his book and do love it"; but two days after John broke down in Aristotle, and Samuel pronounced him "not so thorough a philosopher" as he took him for. From this point there is to be traced in the *Diary* a certain dissatisfaction with John. In a moment of irritation his brother "called him asse and coxcomb";[4] he complained that he loitered away his time; and on September 24 he was despatched to Cambridge again with "a most severe reprimand," "with great passion and sharp words."

The relations between the two brothers were not improved when, six months later, Samuel discovered among Tom's papers some letters from John "speaking very foule words" of him,[5] and it was long before he could bring himself to forgive him. Nevertheless, the family spirit was

[1] February 27, 1660-1.

[2] August 9, 1662.

[3] "I have news this day from Cambridge that my brother hath had his bachelor's cap put on" (*Diary*, January 27, 1662-3).

[4] August 20, 1663.

[5] March 19, 1663-4.

strong enough within Samuel to induce him to endeavour to procure for his erring brother a *mandamus* for a Fellowship,[1] and to bestow upon him some of his old clothes;[2] but no reconciliation took place until April 28, 1666, when John was about to proceed to the M.A. Degree and to take orders. On September 8 John came to see his brother, who was "very kind to him" and gave him "40*s*. for his pocket"; and a longer visit in October sent Samuel to his tailor's "to speak for a cloak and cassock for my brother, . . . and I will have him in a canonical dress, that he may be the fitter to go abroad with me."[3] On October 7 he writes, "I made my brother in his cassocke to say grace this day, but I like his voice so ill that I begin to be sorry he hath taken this order upon him."

As in spite of Samuel's efforts on his behalf,[4] no spiritual promotion came in John's way, he abandoned the clerical career and became an official. On March 30, 1670, his brother "Mr. Pypes," who had already recommended him by letter as a man of "sobriety, diligence, and education,"[5] appeared in person before the Trinity House with a letter of recommendation from the

[1] April 27, 1664. [2] September 4, 1664.

[3] September 27, 1666. [4] February 21, 1665-6.

[5] S.P. to Sir R. Brown, March 26, 1670 (printed in Lord Braybrooke's edition of the *Diary*, 1854, iv. 201).

Duke of York, and John Pepys was elected Clerk to the Corporation in the room of Mr. Askew deceased.[1] When Samuel became Secretary of the Admiralty in 1673, John Pepys and Thomas Hayter succeeded him as joint Clerks of the Acts. He died in 1677, leaving a debt of £300 due to the Trinity House, which his brother paid.

PAULINA PEPYS

Samuel's sister Paulina was seven years and a half younger than himself and a year older than John.[2] Her brother thus describes her appearance on May 31, 1666,—"a pretty good-bodied woman, and not over thicke, as I thought she would have been, but full of freckles and not handsome in face." In November 1660 it had been arranged that she should come to live with him as a servant, and "Pall," "with many thanks did weep for joy."[3] She arrived on January 2, 1660-1; but after six months' trial Samuel was "troubled to hear how proud and idle Pall is grown," and "resolved not to keep her."[4] After reprimanding her in her father's presence, which "brought down her high spirit,"[5] he despatched her to Brampton on September 5, 1661, "crying ex-

[1] Historical MSS. Commission, *Eighth Report*, Part I. and Appendix, p. 254.

[2] She was born on October 18, 1640.

[3] November 12, 1660. [4] July 23, 1661. [5] August 25, 1661.

ceedingly," with 20*s.* and "good counsel how to carry herself to my father and mother." The relations between brother and sister continued to be strained, for when Samuel visited Brampton in October 1662, though he gave her 10*s.* he shewed her no kindness, "for I find her so very ill-natured that I cannot love her, and she so cruel a hypocrite that she can cry when she pleases."[1] On January 4, 1662-3, when it was suggested that Pall should return to them as Mrs. Pepys's waiting gentlewoman, the idea was rejected, although it was "a very great trouble" to Samuel that he should have a sister "of so ill a nature" that he was "forced to spend money upon a stranger when it might better be upon her, if she were good for anything."

His sister's marriage involved Pepys in negotiations as prolonged and ceremonious as that of his brother Tom. When reviewing his position on the last day of the year 1663, he noted that "she grows now old, and must be disposed of one way or other." The result was a succession of suitors, with prodigious haggling in ale-houses over the amount he was prepared to give as her marriage portion. Captain Grove; Philip Harman the upholsterer (who demanded £500 as long as Pepys would only give £450 and rose to £800 as soon as he agreed to £500: "this I do not like"); and

[1] October 14, 1662.

Benjamin Gauden, the son of Dennis Gauden the victualler, appeared one after the other upon the scene. The last was discarded because Sir William Warren the timber merchant pointed out that a family connexion between the Clerk of the Acts and the Victualler of the Navy would render the former suspect in all his dealings.[1] A definite arrangement was eventually made for "a match in the country" with a Mr. Ensum, "one that hath seven score and odd pounds land per annum in possession, and expects £1000 in money by the death of an old aunt."[2] He looked for a portion of £600, and Pepys compromised with him for £500 down and £100 more on the birth of the first child,[3] but in December 1666 Mr. Ensum died. On receiving the news, his prospective brother-in-law referred to him contemptuously as "a clowne,"[4] and offered his sister's hand to William Hewer, who, though much flattered by the proposal, "says he hath no intention to alter his condition."[5] Pepys then coquetted with the idea of offering Pall to his old school-fellow Richard Cumberland, who had formerly been a Fellow of Magdalene,[6] having "a mighty mind to have a relation so able a man and honest, and so old an acquaintance"; but no active steps were taken,

[1] April 2, 1666. [2] March 19, 1665-6. [3] June 17, 1666.
[4] December 12, 1666. [5] January 16, 1666-7.
[6] In 1691 he was made Bishop of Peterborough by William III.

and by way of contrast another proposal, which came through Roger Pepys of Impington, was for "one Barnes,"[1] "a great non-conformist,"[2] whose father had married a Pepys. Of this also we hear nothing more, and on February 27, 1667-8, Paulina Pepys married John Jackson, "a plain young man, handsome enough for Pall, one of no education nor discourse, but of few words, and one altogether that I think will please me well enough."[3] The portion was to be £600, with a jointure of £60 a year.[4] The young couple went to live at Ellington in Huntingdonshire,[5] and there their first child was born. When Samuel saw his sister three months after her marriage, he still maintained his rôle of critic. He noticed that she was growing fat, though "comelier than before," and had become "a mighty pert woman."[5]

THE ST. MICHELS

The parents of Mrs. Pepys, and her brother Balthazar St. Michel ("Brother Balty") and his wife, are frequently mentioned in the *Diary*. The family was in extreme poverty, and their daughter was so ashamed of their condition that she would

[1] June 12, 1667.
[2] February 4, 1663-4.
[3] February 7, 1667-8.
[4] February 10, 1667-8.
[5] See May 24, 1668.

not let her husband know where they lived.[1] Later on,[2] he discovered that they were in Long Acre, an "ill-favoured place."[3] Mrs. St. Michel was given to begging of her daughter on Monday mornings, when she knew that Pepys would be away from home attending the Duke of York;[4] but he did not object to her taking her mother "some apples, neat's tongues, and wine,"[5] and when her father was ill he sent him 20*s*.[6] On March 29, 1667, Balthazar St. Michel told Pepys that "his purse, and 4*s*. a week which his father receives of the French church, is all the subsistence his father and mother have, and that about £20 a year maintains them"; to which their son-in-law adds the comment, "If it please God, I will find one way or other to provide for them, to remove that scandal away." In June 1667 St. Michel senior went abroad, Pepys sending him "three Jacobuses in gold, having real pity for him and her"; and in January 1667-8 both the parents were in Paris. "I could be willing to do something for them," writes their son-in-law, "were I sure not to bring them over again hither."[7] Before the end of the year, however, Mrs. St. Michel, at any rate, was back in England, and her daughter was visiting her at Deptford.

[1] June 5, 1663.
[2] See February 17, 1663-4.
[3] February 22, 1663-4.
[4] March 28, 1664.
[5] January 9, 1664-5.
[6] September 12, 1665.
[7] January 28, 1667-8.

Alexander St. Michel was one of those amiable visionaries on whom poverty seems entailed. On May 2, 1663, in association with Dr. John Colladon, he had obtained a profitless patent for curing smoky chimneys; and on July 7, 1665, another patent was granted to him for "an invention or way for to keep the water that is in ponds wherein people wash their horses, . . . wholesome, sweet, and with little or no mud in the bottom, as also a way for the moulding, grinding, or rubbing of bricks in any form or shape whatsoever fit for the internal and external ornament of any buildings." In 1667 he offered to shew the King "that he can draw up all submerged ships; can prevent others from being submerged; has discovered King Solomon's gold and silver mines, much vaster than those discovered by Columbus and now much fuller than they were in that King's time."[1] In a letter to his brother-in-law, dated February 8, 1673-4,[2] giving an account of the family history, Balthazar St. Michel describes his father as "full of whimsies, and propositions of perpetual motion, etc., to kings, princes, and others, which soaked his pocket and brought all our family so low, by his not minding anything else,

[1] The patents are printed in H. B. Wheatley, *Samuel Pepys and the World he lived in*, pp. 241-50.

[2] Printed in John Smith, *Life, Journals, and Correspondence of Samuel Pepys*, i. 146.

spending all he had got, and getting no other employment to bring in more."

Balthazar St. Michel, although on January 4, 1663-4, Samuel had pronounced him "idle, and out of all capacity . . . to earn his bread," succeeded in carving out for himself a respectable career in the navy. On December 3, 1662, he married Esther Watts, "a most little and yet, I believe, pretty old girl, not handsome nor has anything in the world pleasing, but they say she plays mighty well on the base violl."[1] At first she proved "very unquiet,"[2] but afterwards Pepys pronounced her "a pretty discreet young thing, and humble."[3] In February 1663-4 the couple went into Holland to seek their fortune, and Samuel presented "Balty" with 10*s*. and "a close-bodied light-coloured cloth coat, with a gold edgeing in each seam that was the lace of my wife's best pettycoat that she had when I married her";[4] but they returned the next year, after painful experiences, and applied to Pepys for his assistance for a living.[5] The good brother-in-law soon succeeded in procuring for Balty admission to the Duke of Albemarle's Guards, and "to be put as a right-hand man, and other marks of special respect."[6] A few months later he obtained for

[1] December 18, 1662.
[2] December 21, 1663.
[3] June 26, 1665.
[4] See February 10, 1663-4.
[5] July 25, 1665.
[6] December 4, 1665.

him a better appointment, "only hazardous,"[1]—that of a muster-master at sea. It was worth £100, "besides keeping him the benefit of his pay in the Guards."[2] Mrs. Pepys's "roguish brother"[3] had now become a "good serious man,"[4] and although he admitted that he "could be willing fairly to be out of the next fight,"[5] he acquitted himself so well in his profession as to be reported to the Duke of York as the best muster-master in the fleet.[6] In October 1666 he had a serious illness, attributed to the conduct of his wife, who was charged by Mrs. St. Michel the elder "with going abroad and staying out late, and painting in the absence of her husband";[7] but by the end of the year he had recovered. Pepys complained that he spent too much time upon the adornment of his person,[8] and did not lay up anything,[9] but he obtained for Balty another sea appointment as muster-master and deputy-treasurer of Sir John Harman's fleet going to the West Indies.[10] Before he sailed, Samuel read him and his wife an impressive lecture on the necessity of thrift,[11] and arranged for the profits of the deputy-treasurership to be paid to Mrs. Pepys for the benefit of their father and mother.[12]

[1] March 25, 1666. [2] April 28, 1666.
[3] February 3, 1663-4. [4] April 3, 1666. [5] July 16, 1666.
[6] January 16, 1666-7. [7] September 20, 1666.
[8] February 20, 1666-7. [9] February 26, 1666-7.
[10] March 27, 1667. [11] March 29, 1667. [12] April 4, 1667.

Balty continued to hold the office of muster-master; and the last entry in the *Diary* concerning him relates to the permission granted him by the Duke of York to discharge the duties by deputy, "in his new employment which I design for him about the storekeepers' accounts."[1] From this point his career in the navy was assured. In 1673 we find him occupying the important post of muster-master at Deal;[2] and on April 19, 1686, he became resident Commissioner of the Navy at Deptford and Woolwich.[3] Esther St. Michel died in February 1686-7, and on January 29, 1688-9, he married Margaret Darling as his second wife.[4] He was still living at the time of Pepys's death in 1703, and he and his daughter Mary both received mourning rings.

[1] February 10, 1668-9.
[2] *Catalogue of Pepysian MSS.* ii. 25.
[3] *Ib.* i. 85.
[4] Wheatley, *Pepysiana*, p. 19.

CHAPTER VI

The Household

THE progress of Pepys in wealth and position can be measured by comparing his household staff at the beginning and end of the *Diary*. In the little house in Axe Yard in 1660 he kept only one servant. In the official residence in the Navy Office in 1669 the establishment appears to have included a cook, a chambermaid, a "middle-mayd,"[1] and a boy attired in a livery of green lined with red.[2] For a long time also Mrs. Pepys had a waiting gentlewoman.[3] William Hewer, Pepys's clerk, was an inmate of the house until the family grew "mighty out of order" through his "corrupting the mayds by his idle talke and carriage,"[4] and on November 14, 1663, he departed "weeping" to lodgings.

[1] April 5, 1669.

[2] November 22, 1668.

[3] In succession, Mrs. Gosnell, Mary Ashwell "a merry jade," Mary Mercer, Barker, and Deb Willet.

[4] October 31, 1663.

It is clear from the *Diary* that domestic difficulties are not peculiar to the present time. As early as October 30, 1661, Pepys laments "the inconvenience that do attend the increase of a man's fortune by being forced to keep more servants, which brings trouble." Mrs. Pepys was inclined to quarrel with the maids, and her husband's peace was sometimes much disturbed. In the summer of 1663, in particular, the *Diary* records a series of disasters. In July she and her gentlewoman, Mary Ashwell, fell out when they were staying at Brampton, and at the end of August she returned to her parents.[1] The cook had already left "in a huff,"[2] and an old servant had come in to take her place, but she at once began "to have her drunken tricks," and left on the next day, leaving "the house all in dirt and the clothes all wet." "Goody Taylour" was then brought in "to do the business . . . till another comes," and the dinner was fetched from a cook-shop. Two days later,[3] "a good likely girl" named "Jinny," "a parish child of St. Bride's, of honest parentage and recommended by the churchwarden," was engaged, but this paragon, having been provided with new clothes, ran away the same night. On the following day she was brought back by "a bedel of St. Bride's parish," and the clothes recovered, but the girl herself was

[1] See August 25, 1663. [2] See August 17, 1663. [3] August 20.

not invited to remain. A new cook, "we having no luck in maids now-a-days,"[1] "fell sick" and went home, having only stayed four days. An entry of August 17 is scarcely surprising,—"Came home, . . . where I find a sad distracted house, which troubles me."

Upon this there followed an interval of "perfect content and quiett,"[2] and at the end of 1664 the diarist claimed to have "a pretty and loving quiett family . . . as any man in England." But the halcyon days were nearly over, and fresh trouble was hard at hand. On January 5, 1664-5, Mrs. Pepys gave the cook notice, although her husband, after hearing both sides, found his wife "much in fault";[3] and on March 6 the chambermaid left "with the greatest ingratitude." On March 30, 1666, the cook went off "of her owne accord," being one that "would not bear being told of any faulte in the fewest and kindest words." On April 24 a girl who had come on the previous day to be under the cook, discovered "that London do not agree with her," and "packed up her things to be gone home again." On April 25 a successor was engaged, but she went home the same day. On May 1 the cook took to her bed with an attack of ague, and was away for ten days. For twelve months after this

[1] September 10, 1663. [2] December 31, 1663.
[3] January 31, 1664-5.

there was an interval of comparative peace, and then the cook took to drink, "and, when her mistress told her of it, would be gone, and so put up some of her things and did go away of her own accord, nobody pressing her to it."[1] There was trouble because the maids let in their acquaintances to "talk and prate with them"[2] in the kitchen, and Pepys almost made up his mind to dismiss one of them for leaving the door open, "though it do so go against me to part with a servant that it troubles me more than anything in the world."[3] On July 10, 1667, the kitchen-maid left, "declaring that she must be where she might earn something one day and spend it and play away the next."

Incidentally, the *Diary* throws light on the habits of the age, and especially upon the strictness of domestic discipline. On December 1, 1660, at a time when the Pepyses had only one maid, the entry for the day begins, "This morning, observing some things to be laid up not as they should be by the girl, I took a broom and basted her till she cried extremely, which made me vexed." On February 19, 1664-5, Pepys made his wife, "to the disturbance of the house and neighbours, to beat our little girle, and then we shut her down into the cellar, and there she lay all night." Mrs. Pepys found her gentlewoman Barker "to have

[1] May 18, 1667. [2] May 6, 1667. [3] May 11, 1667.

been abroad, and telling her so many lies about it, that she struck her,"[1] and Pepys himself kicked the cook for leaving the door open, "and was seen doing so by Sir W. Pen's footboy, which did vex me to the heart, because I know he will be telling their family of it, though I did put on presently[2] a very pleasant face to the boy, and spoke kindly to him, as one without passion, so as it may be he might not think I was angry, but yet I was troubled at it."[3]

On two occasions Pepys boxed William Hewer's ears, but most of his disciplinary energy was reserved for the castigation of his footboy, William Wayneman, a youth of some force of character. On November 2, 1661, his master "did extremely beat him" for letting off some gunpowder which he was carrying loose in his pocket and "finding him in a lie about the time and place that he bought it." On December 26, 1661, the Pepyses and Penns were in an alehouse, partaking of cakes and ale, and after the meal was over the boy was called in to finish the remains. It was then discovered that "he had called for two cakes and a pot of ale for himself, at which," writes Pepys, "I was angry, and am resolved to correct him for it." On February 28, 1661-2, his master recited to him his delinquencies up to date, and then "whipped him soundly, but the rods were

[1] May 12, 1667. [2] *I.e.*, immediately. [3] April 12, 1667.

so small that I fear they did not much hurt to him, but only to my arm, which I am already, within a quarter of an hour, not able to stir almost." On June 21, 1662, Pepys whipped him for lying till he himself was "not able to stir," and eventually obtained an admission of his faults, but "I confess," he adds, "it is one of the greatest wonders that ever I met with, that such a little boy as he could possibly be able to suffer half so much as he did to maintain a lie. . . . So to bed, with my arm very weary." On January 12, 1662-3, the incorrigible Wayneman "struck down Creed's boy in the dirt, with his new suit on." The victim of the assault was "in a pitifull taking and pickle," but "I basted my rogue soundly." In the end Will Wayneman had to leave, since punishment made him "never the better, he is grown so hardened in his tricks, which," says Pepys with true discernment, "I am sorry for, he being capable of making a brave man." [1] Tom Edwards, Wayneman's successor, required less discipline, but he succeeded in inflicting the same sufferings on his master. On January 20, 1665-6, he loitered on a message, whereupon "I become angry, and boxed my boy when he came, that I do hurt my thumb so much that I was not able to stir all the day after, and in great pain."

[1] April 24, 1663.

On special occasions the servants were required to keep very early hours. On November 19, 1660, Mrs. Pepys sat up till two in the morning "that she may call the wench up to wash." Later on, a bell was hung "by our chamber door to call the mayds."[1] It failed to rouse them, but, writes Pepys, "I will get a bigger bell." This was effective, and by its means Mrs. Pepys called up the maids to their washing at one o'clock in the morning.[2] On July 29, 1663, Pepys, rising at six, found the cook "not gone to bed yet, but was making clean of the yard and kitchen." On July 7, 1666, the servants did not get to bed till one in the morning; and on Christmas Eve their mistress sat up till four "seeing her mayds make mince-pies."

On the other hand, the household was admitted to a much greater degree of familiarity than has since become customary. It is true that Pall, when she came to live with her brother as a servant, was not permitted to "sit down at table" with him,[3] and Mary Ashwell was rebuked for making herself "equal with the ordinary servants of the house";[4] but in other respects class lines were not sharply drawn. Sarah the chambermaid, "a tall and a very well-favoured wench,"[5] left because

[1] October 3, 1663. [2] October 26, 1663.
[3] January 2, 1660-1. [4] June 10, 1663.
[5] November 28, 1661.

she could not get on with Mrs. Pepys, but Pepys himself observed " so much goodness and seriousness in the mayde " that " if she had anything in the world," he would have considered her as a wife for his brother Tom.[1] At Christmas 1664, for three nights in succession, Mrs. Pepys presided over the " gambolls " of her household, which included cards and blindman's buff kept up till four in the morning.[2] Pepys himself retired to rest, leaving his " wife and people " to their sports, " but without any great satisfaction to myself therein." On Twelfth Night Mrs. Pepys " designed " so much " mirthe " " to end Christmas with among her servants " that they did not go to bed at all.[3]

On November 3, 1663, when he put on his first periwig, the maids were called in to see it, and were " mightily troubled " at his parting with his own hair. On Sunday November 15, 1663, after supper, family prayers were preceded by " hearing of the mayds read in the Bible," and soon after Pepys included among his vows an undertaking " to say prayers in my family twice in every week." [4]

[1] December 16, 1662.
[2] December 26, 1664.
[3] January 6, 1664-5.
[4] January 12, 1663-4.

CHAPTER VII

Neighbours and Friends

DURING the period of the *Diary* Pepys does not seem to have many intimate friends, but he was a social being and had hosts of acquaintances. It is true that in a moment of irritation he assumes the cynic and writes, " But Lord ! to see to what a poor content any acquaintance among . . . the people of the world, as they now-a-days go, is worth ; for my part I and my wife will keep to one another and let the world go hang, for there is nothing but falseness in it," [1]—but this attitude of mind was not natural to him.

The acquaintances with whom he was most closely and frequently brought into contact were his colleagues of the Navy Office who occupied adjoining houses and gardens. With the " two Sir Williams," Batten and Penn, he was at daggers drawn. Sir William Batten, the Surveyor, was a naval officer of experience and on the whole

[1] March 5, 1666-7.

painstaking and upright; but Pepys's view of him is coloured by the hostility between their wives. He thought that Lady Batten and her daughter looked "something askew" upon his wife because she did not "buckle to them,"[1] and there was "no great friendship" between the families.[2] On April 5, 1662, he depreciated him to Carteret, and when on May 26 Batten failed to be elected as Master of the Trinity House, Pepys confessed himself "not a little pleased, because of his proud lady." On July 4 he talked to Sir William Warren from 12 to 4 "without eating or drinking all day," and one of their subjects of conversation was "Sir W. Batten's corruption." On July 25, however, there was a reconciliation, the manner of which reflects much credit upon Batten. "This morning Sir W. Batten came in to the office and desired to speak with me; he began by telling me that he observed a strangeness between him and me of late, and would know the reason of it. . . . At last he desired the difference between our wives might not make a difference between us, which I was exceedingly glad to hear." The feud between the ladies, however, continued in full force. On November 5, 1662, Lady Batten complained to Pepys that his wife had spoken "unhandsomely" of her, and that one of the maids had mocked her over the garden wall. He

[1] August 25, 1661. [2] February 14, 1661-2.

"schooled" the offender, but the incident rankled, and on Sunday December 28 Mr. and Mrs. Pepys took occasion to go out of church before Lady Batten, "which I believe will vex her." On March 10, 1662-3, there was another "fray" with Lady Batten, "about my boy's going thither to turn the watercock with their maydes' leave, but my Lady was mighty high upon it and she would teach his mistress better manners, which my wife answered aloud that she might hear, that she could learn little manners of her." It is not long after this that we find Pepys discoursing with Commissioner Pett on Batten's "corruption and folly,"[1] and eagerly recording the statement of the storekeeper at Chatham, "how basely Sir W. Batten has carried himself to him, and in all things else like a passionate dotard, to the King's great wrong."[2]

From the date of their reconciliation in 1662, the personal relations between the two husbands were ostensibly friendly. Pepys was "kind" even to Lady Batten,[3] and he went so far upon one occasion as to lead her "through the streets by the hand to St. Dunstan's Church";[4] while after a time Mrs. Pepys so far forgot the past as to partake of lobsters and prawns at the Rhenish winehouse with her ancient foe.[5] A little later, Pepys played

[1] April 8, 1663. [2] May 13, 1663. [3] July 29, 1663.
[4] August 9, 1663. [5] May 2, 1665.

billiards at Sir William Batten's house and won 8*s*.[1] "It is pretty to see," he writes on June 18, 1665, "how we appear kind one to another, though neither of us care 2*d*. one for another." But it is not at all to Pepys's credit, that while thus maintaining an appearance of friendship, he missed no opportunity of vilifying Batten behind his back. In conversation with other people he is constantly referring to his "corruption," his "suspicious dealings," his "rogueries," "knavery," and "cheats." When Batten was dangerously ill, Pepys wrote, on February 7, 1664-5, "I am at a loss whether it will be better for me to have him die, because he is a bad man, or live, for fear a worse should come"; and on May 7, 1667, he calls him "a malicious fellow." Yet his death, after two days' illness, on October 5, 1667, troubled Pepys and his wife "mightily, partly out of kindness, he being a good neighbour, and partly because of the money he owes me."

If Pepys disliked Batten, he positively hated Penn the distinguished seaman, who was also his colleague upon the Navy Board. At first he found him "a very sociable man" and "a merry fellow," but on June 3, 1662, there was a dispute in the Office on the claim of the Clerk of the Acts to draw all contracts which made bad blood between them, and from this time forward, although they

[1] August 14, 1665.

continued to meet and dine together, the tide of private vituperation in the *Diary* flows fast. "I hate" him "with all my heart for his base treacherous tricks," writes Pepys on July 5, 1662, "but yet I think it not policy to declare it yet." Later on, Penn is called "a counterfeit rogue," an "asse," "a coxcomb," "a false knave," "a perfidious rogue," and "rotten-hearted." On March 20, 1666-7, he aggravated his offences by giving the Pepyses "a bad nasty supper, which makes me not love the family." On June 6, 1667, the Penns gave a dinner-party out of compliment to Pepys's father, and the invitation was accepted, "though I know them as false as the Devil himself." After the entertainment the guest writes, "Here as merry as in so false a place, and where I must dissemble my hatred, I could be." On September 6, 1667, Pepys discoursed to Mrs. Turner in a coach, all the way to Walthamstow, "touching the baseness of Sir W. Pen and sluttishness of his family."

For the charges against Penn in his official capacity there seems to have been little foundation. Pepys admits elsewhere[1] that he was "a bred seaman," who had done service in the war, though "a man of very mean parts." He thought him "the first man in England" for the Comptroller's office, "though I love him not, nor do desire to

[1] October 10, 1664.

have him in,"[1] and allowed him "merit of his own" that made him fitter than any one else for a command at sea;[2] but his personal animosity continued unabated until the termination of Penn's membership of the Navy Board. He joined Gauden in the victualling, and on March 30, 1669, invited all his colleagues to a "parting dinner," "which I am glad of, I am sure," wrote Pepys, "for he is a very villain."

For the Comptroller Sir John Mennes, the Clerk of the Acts felt only a good-natured contempt. At first he found him "a fine gentleman and a very good scholler,"[3] and noted subsequently that he was an admirer of Chaucer.[4] He thought him "the best mimique" he ever saw, "and certainly would have made an excellent actor."[5] But Mennes, though he had been a capable seaman in his day, had outlived his usefulness, and the uncomplimentary remarks about him in the *Diary* are better justified than in the cases of Batten and Penn. Pepys resents his inefficiency and calls him "a doting coxcomb";[6] "though I believe in my mind the man in general means well."[7] "Like an old dotard, he is led by the nose" by Batten,[8] and

[1] August 22, 1666.
[2] March 26, 1668.
[3] November 8, 1661.
[4] June 14, 1663.
[5] January 2, 1665-6.
[6] January 10, 1662-3.
[7] May 22, 1663.
[8] June 23, 1663.

does everything "like a fool."[1] On March 12, 1663-4, he was "vexed to see how Sir J. Minnes deserves rather to be pitied for his dotage and folly than employed at a great salary to ruin the King's business." But when, on August 20, 1666, he was said to be dying, Pepys was troubled "mightily," "for he is a very harmless honest gentleman, though not fit for the business."

Another colleague was Lord Brouncker, the first President of the Royal Society. The *Diary* describes him as "a rotten-hearted false man" like Penn,[2] but speaks highly of his ability, calling him "the best man of them all" in the Office,[3] although, according to Clifford, he "did mind his mathematics too much."[4]

Sir George Carteret, the Treasurer of the Navy, has been described by Clarendon as "a worthy and most excellent person, ... the most generous man in kindness and the most dexterous man in business ever known"; a man of "honesty and discretion," and one of the best seamen of England.[5] This is confirmed by Coventry, who told Pepys that he was "a man that do take the most pains, and gives himself the most to do business, of any man about the Court, without any desire of pleasure or divertisements,"—"which," adds his auditor, "is

[1] October 14, 1663. [2] January 29, 1666-7.
[3] August 25, 1668. [4] March 29, 1669.
[5] Quoted in the *Dictionary of National Biography*, ix. 208.

very true."[1] But his education had been defective, and Pepys speaks of his "perverse ignorance,"[2] even going so far as to call him "a passionate and ignorant asse."[3] In 1665 Pepys was charged with the duty of arranging a match between Carteret's son Philip and Lord Sandwich's daughter "Lady Jem,"[4] and from this time the relations between them were most friendly. The family shewed him great kindness, and on the day of the wedding Lady Carteret "do also now call me cozen, which I am glad of."[5] On April 12, 1667, he writes, "I do take the Vice-Chamberlain[6] for a most honest man."

The only member of the Navy Board for whom Pepys had nothing but praise is Mr., afterwards Sir William, Coventry. Evelyn calls him "a wise and witty gentleman,"[7] and the *Diary* shews how warmly Pepys was attached to him. A month after Coventry's first appearance at the Office he writes, "My heart rejoices to see Mr. Coventry

[1] October 30, 1662. [2] June 22, 1663. [3] April 1, 1665.

[4] Lady Jemima Mountagu. Pepys had not only to negotiate the marriage, but to bring to the point a shy and tongue-tied bridegroom, and to instruct him in the proper deportment of a lover, "to take the lady always by the hand to lead her," and to "make these and these compliments" (July 16, 1665).

[5] July 31, 1665.

[6] In addition to the Treasurership of the Navy, Sir George Carteret held the office of Vice-Chamberlain of the Household.

[7] Evelyn's *Diary*, October 11, 1659.

so ingenious and able and studious to do good";[1] and he became "still in love more and more with him for his real worth."[2] He attached immense importance to Coventry's good opinion, and "would not be thought a lazy body" by him, "by being seen . . . to walk up and down doing nothing";[3] and he spent Sunday afternoon in the office writing orders, that he "might not appear negligent to Mr. Coventry."[4] After he had left the Navy Board for the Treasury, Pepys continued to consult him and to make enthusiastic entries about him; and when the Principal Officers attended the Duke of York for their usual weekly business he mourned his absence. "But, Lord! methinks both he and we are mighty flat and dull over what we used to be when Sir W. Coventry[5] was among us."[6] He is no enemy to anybody, "but is severe and just, as he ought to be where he sees things ill done."[7] Coventry's disgrace and imprisonment in 1669 struck Pepys "to the heart";[8] "to serve him I should, I think, stick at nothing."[9]

Of Pepys's unofficial friends the two most distinguished were Sir William Petty and John

[1] July 11, 1662. [2] November 20, 1662.
[3] January 4, 1662-3. [4] January 11, 1662-3.
[5] He was knighted on March 3, 1664-5.
[6] September 10, 1667. [7] October 5, 1667.
[8] March 4, 1668-9. [9] March 31, 1669.

Evelyn his brother diarist. He writes of the former as one "who in discourse is, methinks, one of the most rational men that ever I heard speak with a tongue, having all his notions the most distinct and clear";[1] and the *Diary* is full of references to Evelyn's "excellent discourse." The first allusion to him is under date May 1, 1665, when Pepys and a party of friends, on their way back from dining at Colonel Blount's house at Charlton, stopped at Deptford and called at Sayes Court, "but it being dark and late, I staid not." On May 5, he and his colleagues, paying an official visit to Deptford, went "after dinner to Mr. Evelyn's," and "he being abroad, we walked in his garden, and a lovely noble ground he hath indeed." The diarists must have met already at the Royal Society, to which Pepys had been admitted in the previous February, but on September 10 they supped together at Captain Cocke's, when Evelyn appeared in an unaccustomed light. The news of Lord Sandwich's success against the Dutch inspired that correct and dignified personage with "such a spirit of mirth" that he made the company "die almost with laughing." On September 27 the two were alone together in Evelyn's coach, and Pepys conversed with him "touching all manner of learning," and found him "a very fine gentleman."

[1] January 27, 1663-4.

On October 24 the diarists met again at dinner "and there merry"; and from this point the friendship ripened steadily. Pepys paid several visits to Sayes Court and was shewn all his host's treasures: "a most excellent person he is, and must be allowed a little for a little conceitedness, but he may well be so, being a man so much above others."[1] On January 3, 1665-6, Evelyn sent Pepys a draft of his "infirmary and project for Chatham,"[2] and on January 29 there was more "excellent discourse" between them on "the vanity and vices of the Court." On Sunday April 29, 1666, "he and I walked together in the garden" at Sayes Court "with mighty pleasure, he being a very ingenious man; and the more I know him the more I love him."

On January 20, 1667-8, Evelyn sent Pepys a "Prospect of the Medway while the Hollander rode master in it,"[3] and in his letter of acknowledgment, dated February 8, Pepys refers to the gloomy reflections induced by his own share in "that miscarriage," such as "have given me little less disquiet than he is fancied to have who found his face in Michael Angelo's

[1] November 5, 1665.

[2] John Evelyn to S.P., printed in Evelyn's *Diary and Correspondence* (Murray, 1871), p. 641. They afterwards discussed it in Lord Brouncker's coach on January 29.

[3] Appendix to Lord Braybrooke's edition of the *Diary* (1854), iv. 196.

Hell."[1] The familiarity of this correspondence makes it all the more remarkable that none of these interviews and transactions are mentioned in Evelyn's *Diary*; but Evelyn was more than twelve years older than Pepys, and the friendship on his side may have ripened more slowly. Indeed, the first reference to him is not until June 10, 1669, ten days after Pepys's own *Diary* had come to an end. On February 19, 1670-1, however, he pays him the handsome compliment of associating him with the great Christopher Wren as "two extraordinary ingenious and knowing persons."

[1] *Ib.* iv. 197. The reference is to the appearance of Biagio da Cesena in the picture of the Last Judgment.

CHAPTER VIII

Food and Clothes

SAMUEL PEPYS, who approached life " with all the gusto of a boy," took a boyish interest in what he had to eat and drink.

His choice ranged over a vast and varied field. Many of the dishes are, of course, familiar in modern cookery, although it is surprising to find that such antiquity can be assigned to " sasages " and buttered eggs. At Mr. Bernard's, on November 14, 1661, he encountered " a pie of such pleasant variety of good things as in all my life I never tasted " ; and on Sunday February 15, 1662-3, Pepys and his wife sat down to three ducks and two teal for dinner,—and then found the afternoon sermon dull ! On September 6, 1664, he attempted some housekeeping on his own account, and " took occasion to buy a rabbit " at a poulterer's, " but it proved a deadly old one when I came to eat it." He was particularly fond of oysters. On February 27, 1663-4, he writes,

"Before dinner we had the best oysters I have seen this year, and I think as good in all respects as ever I ate in my life: I ate a great many." Lobsters also occupied a high place in his esteem. On April 17, 1661, he and three friends accounted for a barrel of oysters and two lobsters; and on May 18, 1666, he went to bed early, "not very well, having eaten too much lobster at noon at dinner." He enjoyed "a good sullybub" at Commissioner Pett's at Chatham; and he was inclined to be greedy over cream. Anchovies and olives were frequently taken with wine, and he ascribed an attack of nettle-rash to over-indulgence in "Dantzic-girkins."[1] On November 4, 1663, Mrs. Pepys was busy making "marmalett of quince," and on September 21, 1660, Pepys and three friends disposed of above 200 walnuts at a sitting. Vegetables are not often referred to, although "sparagus" and carrots are mentioned, but not potatoes. Soup only appears once, although on one occasion "a mess of good broth" is taken before going to bed.

Besides the more familiar dishes, the *Diary* mentions others which are now almost unknown—pickled sturgeon; a neat's udder; a hog pudding of Lady Batten's making; "a good hog's harslet,[2] a piece of meat I love"; "a lamprey pie (a most rare pie)"; neat's feet and mustard; a cygnet; a

[1] February 9, 1662-3. [2] Part of the entrails.

swan pie; a Spanish olio; and "a poor Lenten dinner of coleworts and bacon." In the 17th century venison played a more important part than it does now, and it was a frequent gift among friends. In particular, the diarist often refers with appreciation to the venison pasty, although the one provided by "coz. Snow" on October 17, 1661, for the entertainment of the Pepys family, "proved a pasty of salted pork." Samphire was a favourite pickle; the dried roe of the mullet, called *botargo*, was eaten with bread and butter to provoke thirst;[1] and one hostess provided nettle porridge for her guests.[2]

At one point Pepys registers his social progress in terms of food. On August 17, 1660, he entertained a guest on very homely fare,—"nothing but a dish of sheep's trotters"; but on November 3, 1661, he notes a landmark on his upward path: "At night my wife and I had a good supper by ourselves of a pullet hashed, which pleased me much to see my condition come to allow ourselves a dish like that." About three weeks later,[3] he refers to a "good surloyne of rost beefe" as "the first that ever I had of my own buying since I kept house." The reference on October 24, 1662, to "a most excellent dish of tripes of my own directing, covered with mustard,

[1] June 5, 1661. [2] February 25, 1660-1.
[3] November 21.

. . . of which I made a very great meal," should perhaps be regarded as the record of a relapse.

Tobacco is mentioned several times in the *Diary*, but it does not appear to have played any important part in the life of Pepys or his friends. On November 3, 1665, he sees commanders on board ship taking tobacco, and on July 30, 1666, he records the fact that the Duke of Albemarle chewed it when his ship was going into action with De Ruyter. On August 18, 1667, he notes that when one of the horses in the coach in which he was riding had a fit of the staggers, a cure was effected by the coachman, who "blew some tobacco in his nose." He also observed its beneficial results in the case of Mr. Chetwynd, who "by chewing of tobacco is become very fat and sallow, whereas he was consumptive."[1] But there is no evidence that Pepys ever smoked, and the only entry about taking tobacco in another form is of quite an exceptional character. On June 7, 1665, when the Plague was raging in London, he writes,

> "This day, much against my will, I did in Drury Lane see two or three houses marked with a red cross upon the doors, and 'Lord, have mercy upon us' writ there; which was a sad sight to me, being the first of the kind that, to my remembrance, I ever saw. It put me into an ill conception of myself and my smell, so that I was forced to buy some roll-tobacco to smell to and chaw, which took away the apprehension."

[1] June 29, 1661.

Readers of the *Diary* cannot fail to notice the frequent irregularity of the hours of meals, and the vast quantity of food consumed, especially at dinner.

Breakfast is occasionally mentioned,[1] often as an extra meal taken before, or in the course of, a journey; but it does not appear to have been a regular institution. On September 9, 1661, Pepys and others "had a good slice of beef or two to our breakfast" in the King's Privy Kitchen, but this was clearly an exceptional opportunity; and so also was the slice "of roast beef off the spit" at Sir William Batten's which made both host and guest late for morning service on Sunday February 24, 1666-7. In August 1662 Pepys was staying at Chatham on business, and on Sunday the 3rd he rose early in the morning and walked to the Dockyard, where Commissioner Pett met him and, after shewing him "his garden and fine things," gave him "a fine breakfast of bread and butter and sweetmeats and other things with great choice, and strong drinks." With only two or three exceptions,[2] the other references are all

[1] The statement in Wheatley's *Pepysiana* (p. 95), that there was no breakfast in Pepys's day, can scarcely have been intended to be taken literally.

[2] The breakfast at the Swan on cold chine of pork referred to on December 29, 1662, is really an early dinner; as also the meal taken before his brother Tom's funeral on March 18, 1663-4.

associated either with travelling by land or water or with life on board ship. The entertainment at Mr[s]. Batelier's on August 26, 1668, when "they danced all night long, with a noble supper, and about two in the morning the table spread again for a noble breakfast, beyond all moderation," clearly falls into a category by itself.

Although breakfast was not an institution, this cannot be said of the "morning draught." This refreshment, although usually taken at the tavern, was not always alcoholic. It might take the form of whey at the "wheyhouse," or "a pot of chocolate." On September 22, 1660, Pepys took a pickled herring with his morning draught, and on June 21, 1661, he "ate some gammon of bacon, etc.," thus converting it into what was practically a breakfast.

The principal meal of the day was dinner, generally eaten about noon, but on April 21, 1666, Pepys was so busy at the office that he could only get home about three, "to clap a bit of meate in my mouth, and so away." On August 14, 1663, "the time having outslipt me and my stomach," he did not get his dinner until nearly four; and on one or two occasions he did not dine at all. But the fare, when it came, was abundant. On November 23, 1663, Pepys, who was then alone, sat down to "a good goose and a rare piece of roast beef"; on Sunday July 3, 1664, he and his wife had "the remains of yesterday's venison and a couple of brave green geese"; and on New Year's Day 1664-5 they had "a good venison pasty and a turkey" to themselves, "without any body so much as invited by us, a thing unusuall for so small a family of my condition," but, he adds, "we did it, and were very merry." Supper was a lighter meal, and was sometimes omitted altogether when the dinner had been on a more than usually oppressive scale.

It was not until January 20, 1661-2, that Pepys began to buy wine in bulk. He went into partnership with three friends to import two butts of sherry from Cadiz, "and mine was put into a hogshead, and the vessel filled up with four gallons of Malaga wine"; but on August 27, 1662, he sold this compound to Sir William Batten, "and am glad of my money instead of wine." He had already tasted some "strange and incomparable good clarett of Mr. Rumball's,"[1] one of the officers of the Wardrobe, and on March 3, 1662-3, he broached a tierce of claret which had found its way into his own cellar, but three months later[2] he found that the cellar door had been left unlocked and more than half the claret had disappeared, which made him "deadly mad." The loss was the more painful as he was developing a taste for claret, having found "a sort of French

[1] October 29, 1660. [2] June 2, 1663.

wine, called Ho Bryan,[1] that hath a good and most particular taste that I never met with."[2] On December 3, 1663, an unknown friend sent him a runlet of tent from Portsmouth, and in the following February[3] a purser came to see him bearing 12 bottles of sack. On July 7, 1665, Pepys furnishes an inventory of the contents of his cellar, "taking notice to what a condition it hath pleased God to bring me that at this time I have two tierces of claret, two quarter casks of canary, and a smaller vessel of sack; a vessel of tent, another of malaga, and another of white wine, all in my wine cellar together; which I believe none of my friends of my name now alive ever had of his owne at one time."

The *Diary* mentions muscadine, Florence wine, Rhenish wine, Bristol milk, and "some new sort of wine lately found out, called Navarre wine, which I tasted, and is, I think, good wine."[4] It also refers to metheglin or mead; "a can of good julep"; wormwood wine; "syder"; purl; mum; horse-radish ale, supposed to be good for the stone; and to several kinds of ale well known in Pepys's time, Margate ale, Lambeth ale, China ale, Alderman John Bide's ale at Mile End Green, and College beer at Eton, "which is very good." Strong waters were also in request, and various

[1] Haut Brion. [2] April 10, 1663.
[3] February 1, 1663-4. [4] February 10, 1668-9.

home-made decoctions,—raspberry sack, elderberry spirits, and "very good red wine" of Lady Batten's "own making in England."[1]

On September 25, 1660, the diarist tasted tea for the first time, and on the authority of "Mr. Pelling the potticary" he afterwards[2] approved the administration of it to Mrs. Pepys as a remedy for "her cold and defluxions," although he preferred "a dish of coffee" for himself when he suffered from the same complaint. On one occasion he drank a pint of orange juice with sugar in it,—not as a remedy but on its own merits,—and pronounced it "very fine drink."

In the earlier part of his career Pepys drank too much, and his triumph over this tendency is one of the most creditable episodes in his life.

The habits of thc age were all against him. At the Salutation Tavern "we staid and drank till Mr. Adams began to be overcome," is an early entry[3] which finds many counterparts. On June 1, 1660, the captain of the *Naseby* came on board "quite fuddled," and told Pepys that the Vice-Admiral, Rear-Admiral, and he had been drinking all day, thus doing something to justify Prince Rupert's fiery protest, "God damn me, if they will turn out every man that will be drunk, they must turn out all the commanders in the fleete."[4]

[1] December 13, 1660. [2] June 28, 1667.
[3] March 5, 1659-60. [4] January 2, 1667-8.

On March 8, 1660-1, the "high company" dining with the Lieutenant of the Tower sat drinking all the afternoon. On the day of the King's Coronation, April 23, 1661, Pepys "wondered to see how the ladies did tipple"; and on November 18, when dining with friends, he notes "that there was a young parson at the table that had got himself drunk before dinner, which troubled me to see." These scruples did not prevent him from taking a malicious pleasure in making his "uncle Thomas and aunt Bell" "almost foxed with wine till they were very kind,"[1] or finding it good sport to see a sober man like his physician, Mr. Hollier, "a little fuddled, and so did talk nothing but Latin and laugh," although he adds, "he was not drunk to scandal."[2]

For the first two years of the *Diary* Pepys was learning by experience the evils of over-drinking. On January 18, 1660-1, he complained to Hollier of the decay of his memory, and was advised to drink less. He found that wine made his head ache and rendered him unfit for business, so he made good resolutions which suffered the usual fate. On May 14, 1661, he prays God that he may be able to leave it off; three weeks later[3] he goes to bed "very near fuddled" with excess of claret. On Sunday September 29 he omits prayers, "being now so out of order that I durst

[1] August 11, 1663. [2] March 31, 1668. [3] June 5.

not read" them "for fear of being perceived by my servants in what case I was"; and a similar catastrophe occurred on Sunday, November 10, but this time in consequence of over-indulgence in canary. Good resolutions were not enough, and on the last day of the year, when he made his customary survey of his position, he wrote, "I have newly taken a solemn oath about abstaining from plays and wine, which I am resolved to keep." As the oath finally took shape, it came to be based upon the ingenious idea of enlisting a lesser vice to destroy a greater. Pepys was careful about money and he attached money penalties to the breaches of his vow, thus fining himself into sobriety.

The benefits of this method of reformation were soon felt. After less than a month's practice of it, he wrote, "Thanks be to God, since my leaving drinking of wine, I do find myself much better and do mind my business better, and do spend less money, and less time lost in idle company."[1] It is true that a little later he began to waver, finding "reason to fear that by my too sudden leaving off wine I do contract many evils upon myself";[2] but he persevered, drinking no wine at the tavern, and forbearing all healths, though sometimes allowing himself a little latitude on special occasions. One of the obligations attached

[1] January 26, 1661-2. [2] February 17, 1661-2.

to the vows was that they were to be read over every Sunday, and, after discharging this duty in the Temple Garden on Sunday August 17, 1662, Pepys writes, " It is a great content to me to see how I am a changed man in all respects for the better since I took them, which the God of Heaven continue to me and make me thankful for." When from time to time the vows expired, he would take " a liberty " and " then fall to them again " ; and it must be admitted that there were occasional backslidings. He also made exceptions which he regarded as justifiable, holding hypocras to be no breach of his vow, " it being, to the best of my present judgement, only a mixed compound drink and not any wine : if I am mistaken, God forgive me ! but I hope and do think I am not."[1] He allowed himself " a cup of good drink " during plague-time,[2] but this was " taken notice of by envious men " to his disadvantage, and a rumour got about the Court that he had " come to be a great swearer and drinker,"[3] so Pepys renewed his vows and fell back upon beer. In 1667 he adopted the practice of drinking burnt wine,—" an evasion, God knows, . . . (but it is an evasion which will not serve me now hot weather is coming, that I cannot pretend, as indeed I really have done, that I drank it for cold),

[1] October 29, 1663. [2] September 15, 1665.
[3] September 27, 1665.

but I will leave it off, and it is but seldom, as when I am in women's company, that I must call for wine, for I must be forced to drink to them."[1] On October 8, 1667, he went down into the cellars at Audley End "and drank of much good liquor," which led him to develop a brief and sudden partiality for strong waters; but from this time to the end of the *Diary* we hear nothing of over-indulgence in wine. The battle so courageously fought had been fairly won, and Pepys had become a moderate drinker.

The diarist was profoundly interested in his fellow-creatures, and he enjoyed entertaining and being entertained. "Mightily pleased," he writes on February 23, 1665-6, "to find myself in condition to have these people come about me and to be able to entertain them, and have the pleasure of their qualities, than which no man can have more in the world." His first dinner-party, held at Lord Sandwich's lodgings on January 26, 1659-60, was mainly for the benefit of relations,—"my father, my uncle Fenner, his two sons, Mr. Pierce, and all their wives, and my brother Tom,"—but the fare was abundant. They had "a dish of marrow bones; a leg of mutton; a loin of veal; a dish of fowl, three pullets and two dozen of larks all in a dish; a great tart, a neat's tongue, a dish of anchovies; a dish of prawns and cheese."

[1] March 26, 1667.

The subsequent improvement in Pepys's social position can be measured by comparing this comparatively humble effort at the beginning of the *Diary* with a much more magnificent entertainment described near the end of it.[1] The company consisted of Lord Sandwich, his son and heir Lord Hinchingbrooke, Lord Peterborough, Mr. Sydney Mountagu, Sir Charles Harbord, and Sir William Godolphin. The diarist does not enumerate the articles of food, but his account of the whole proceeding gives an impression of costly splendour. After the host had greeted his guests,

> "and some time spent in talk, dinner was brought up, one dish after another, but a dish at a time, but all so good; but above all things the variety of wines, and excellent of their kind, I had for them, and all in so good order that they were mightily pleased and myself full of content at it; and indeed it was, of a dinner of about six or eight dishes, as noble as any man need to have I think; at least all was done in the noblest manner that ever I had any, and I have rarely seen in my life better anywhere else, even at the Court. . . . Thus was this entertainment over, the best of its kind, and the fullest of honour and content to me that ever I had in my life; and shall not easily have so good again."

Whether he was entertaining or being entertained, Pepys cared more for "excellent good table-talke" than for meat and drink. The heavy official dinners, at the Clothworkers' Hall, at the Trinity House, and with the Lord Mayor, were

[1] January 23, 1668-9.

not altogether to his taste, although he appreciated the compliment of the invitation. "So to Trinity House," he writes on October 5, 1664, "and there I dined among the old dull fellows"; and again on February 15, 1664-5, "At noon with Creed to dinner to Trinity House, where a very good dinner among the old sokers." On February 9, 1665-6, he dined with the Lieutenant of the Tower, "where strange pleasure they seem to take in their wine and meate, and discourse of it with the curiosity and joy that methinks was below men of worthe." He found more congenial company at his first Royal Society club supper, on February 15, 1664-5, where he met men "of most eminent worth" and enjoyed "excellent discourse till ten at night."

As a diner-out Pepys was disposed to be critical. He finds fault with Aunt Wight's hands, and "her greasy manner of carving,"[1] and when he enjoyed the hospitality of Mr. Cutler the merchant, "his old mother was an object at dinner that made me not like it."[2] He resents the Duke of Albemarle's "sorry company," with "dirty dishes, and a nasty wife at table, and bad meat, of which I made but an ill dinner."[3] He is "sick" of the Pearses' "damned sluttish dinner," and absconds to see a play.[4] He objects to being fed entirely upon

[1] April 22, 1663. [2] December 17, 1665.
[3] April 4, 1667. [4] September 16, 1667.

"pigeon-pyes" at the Lowthers', although he finds some compensation in the tricks of a juggler after dinner, "such as my wife hath since seriously said that she would not believe but that he did them by the help of the Devil."[1] And for the housekeeping of his enemy Sir William Penn, Pepys has no good word to say. On one occasion "the dishes were so deadly foule" that he "could not endure to look upon them";[2] and on another they set before him "a damned venison pasty that stunk like a devil."[3] His sage reflection, "strange to see how a good dinner and feasting reconciles everybody,"[4] was not made upon this occasion.

It has been suggested that Pepys's interest in his clothes was due to the fact that he was a tailor's son, but his treatment of the subject in the *Diary* does not support this view. His observations do not shew any special technical knowledge of tailoring; and it was his desire to maintain his dignity in the world, and not any professional interest in clothes as such, that led him to "go handsome" and to walk up and down the New Exchange with Mr. Creed "talking mightily of the convenience and necessity of a man's wearing good clothes."[5] One of his earliest investments was in "a pair of

[1] May 24, 1667. [2] January 17, 1663-4.
[3] August 1, 1667. [4] November 9, 1665.
[5] September 12, 1664.

silk stockings of a light blue" with which he was "much pleased." When he became Clerk of the Acts he indulged in an orgy of new garments,—a "fine camlett cloak with gold buttons, and a silk suit, which cost me much money, and I pray God to make me able to pay for it";[1] a "jackanapes coat with silver buttons";[2] a "velvet coat (the first that ever I had) and a velvet mantle";[3] and a short cloak was converted into a black cloth coat "to walk up and down in."[4] In October 1663, after a period of comparative economy, he resolved upon going in "better plight," and gave a large order to his brother Tom,—a cloth cloak "lined with velvet and other things modish, and a perruque"[5]; "two new cloth suits, black, plain both"; "a new shagg gowne, trimmed with gold buttons and twist, with a new hat, and silk tops for my legs"; "and also perriwiggs."[6] The best black cloth suit was subsequently "trimmed with scarlett ribbon, very neat."[7] The bill came to £55. At the same time he laid out £12 in clothes for his wife. Of subsequent suits, the most impressive are, one of coloured cloth with the cloak lined with plush, "which is a dear and noble suit, costing me about £17,"[8] and "two rich silk suits"

[1] July 1, 1660.
[2] July 5, 1660.
[3] August 21, 1660.
[4] September 23, 1660.
[5] October 21, 1663.
[6] October 31, 1663.
[7] November 29, 1663.
[8] October 30, 1664.

which proved so splendid that Pepys was constrained to order a plain ordinary silk suit also.[1]

The Plague and the Fire introduced a period of economy in clothes, but on May 1, 1669, we meet the "flowered tabby vest and coloured camelott tunique" with gold lace at the hands referred to above,[2] which was so fine that for some time its proprietor was "afeard to wear it,"[3] and when he appeared in it in the Park the gold lace at the sleeves attracted so much attention that he resolved to have it taken off.[4] This splendour of attire is foreign to modern ideas, but at one point the experience of the centuries meets. We learn that on April 22, and again on July 15, 1666, Pepys "walked wearily" and "in great pain" from wearing new shoes that were too tight for him.

Some light is thrown by the *Diary* on the fashions of the day. On October 7, 1660, Pepys changed his long black cloak for a short one, "long cloaks being now quite out," and on October 13, 1661, he left off "half skirts." He appears to have sympathised with Lady Wright's view concerning "the great happiness . . . there is in being in the fashion."[5] In June 1662 "close knees" were coming in, and "I think they will be very convenient."[6] On November 30 Pepys wears a muff for the first time, appropriating a "last year's

[1] June 1, 1665. [2] P. 39 above. [3] May 2, 1669.
[4] May 10, 1669. [5] December 3, 1661. [6] June 12, 1662.

muffe" belonging to his wife, and buying her a new one. On Sunday May 10, 1663, he puts on "a black cloth suit, with white lynings under all, as the fashion is to wear, to appear under the breeches"; and on August 17 he acquires a "new low-crowned beaver according to the present fashion made." In the matter of periwigs the Clerk of the Acts was well ahead of the Court, for he began to wear one on November 3, 1663, the Duke of York following suit on February 15, 1663-4, and the King in the following April. On April 8, 1664, he bought a cane to walk with.

On October 7, 1666, the King declared in Council "his resolution of setting a fashion for clothes," "to teach the nobility thrift." Pepys saw the Duke of York try on the new vest on October 13; the King himself began to wear it on October 15; and on October 17 the Court was "all full of vests." Pepys himself wore it for the first time to church on Sunday November 4, with a belt and silver-hilted sword, "and I like myself mightily in it, and so do my wife." In 1668 shoulder-belts came in,[1] and on April 30, 1669, he had his silver-hilted sword gilded.

On his mother's death, Pepys provided mourning for the whole household,[2] and it cost him £50.[3]

[1] May 17, 1668. [2] March 27, 1667. [3] April 6, 1667.

CHAPTER IX

Sermons

DURING the earlier years of the *Diary* Pepys was a regular attendant at church. He went as a rule to his own parish church, St. Olave's, Hart Street, where the Officers of the Navy had the privilege of a special pew; [1] but he sometimes indulged in a peripatetic survey of churches, "going from one church to another and hearing a bit here and a bit there." [2] His love of music often took him to the King's Chapel at Whitehall to hear the anthem. As official business increased upon him he often assigned Sunday to his private accounts, to arrears of public business, or to writing up his diary; but

[1] On August 19, 1660, Pepys, Batten, and Penn went to the churchwardens "to demand a pew, which at present could not be given us, but we are resolved to have one built." With great promptitude, the erection of a gallery was begun on August 29, and it was used for the first time on November 11. The gallery was removed when the church was restored in 1870-1, but the memorial to Pepys put up in 1884 is on the wall where it was formerly situated.

[2] March 16, 1661-2.

to the last he remained a connoisseur of sermons, and he may be regarded as a fair specimen of the critical layman of the time.

No less than 316 sermons are mentioned in the *Diary*,—116 of them with approval, 130 with varying degrees of condemnation, and the remaining 70 without comment. Many of them are labelled with a single epithet, and of these there is a rich variety. Terms of praise are "good," "eloquent," "honest," "able," "gallant," "excellent," "very fine," "painful" (in the sense of painstaking), "pungent," "learned," "admirable." Sermons which he disliked are characterised as "lazy," "poor," "silly," "dry and tedious," "cold," "indifferent," "sorry," "idle," "bad," "common," "impertinent" (in the sense of irrelevant); "sad and long," "ordinary," "simple," "most pitiful," "drowsy," "flat and dead." Under the infliction of one of these he "read over the whole book of the story of Tobit";[1] and when on Sunday July 5, 1663, "an old doting parson preached," Pepys and the Battens "in spite to one another, kept one another awake; and sometimes I read in my book of Latin plays, which I took in my pocket." On several other occasions he slept out the sermon.

In his fuller descriptions of sermons and preachers Pepys could be sufficiently pungent. The

[1] February 5, 1659-60.

occupants of the pulpit are variously described as "a dull formal fellow," "a very silly fellow," "a very sorry fellow,' "a confident young coxcomb," "a most insipid young coxcomb," "a sleepy presbyter," and "a dull flat presbyter." On July 8, 1660, the Bishop of Chichester "made a great flattering sermon" before the King, "which I did not like that clergy should meddle with matters of State." On one occasion,[1] "a stranger preached like a fool"; on another,[2] on board the *Swallow*, he heard "our navy chaplain preach a sad sermon, full of nonsense and false Latin," but the preacher gratified at least one of his hearers by praying "for the Right Honourable the Principal Officers." Not long before, Pepys had experienced similar satisfaction at Impington Church, when "at our coming in the country-people all rose with so much reverence," and the officiating clergyman began the service with "Right Worshipful and dearly beloved."[3] One preacher annoyed him with "a great deal of false Greek,"[4] and the Dean of Rochester offended his taste by explaining from the pulpit that the effect of the Fire had been to reduce the City "from a large folio to a decimo-tertio."[5] On December 23, 1666, he was afflicted by "a vain fellow with a periwigg"; and on June 14, 1668, "a vain pragmatical fellow

[1] March 31, 1661. [2] April 27, 1662. [3] August 4, 1661.
[4] August 2, 1663. [5] September 9, 1666.

preached a ridiculous affected sermon " that made him angry.

At first Pepys formed a high opinion of Dr. Milles the rector of his parish. He calls him " a very good minister,"[1] and credits him with " as excellent a sermon . . . against drunkenness as ever I heard in my life";[2] but his desertion of his parish during the Plague did not endear him to his people, and on June 3, 1667, he appears in the *Diary* as " a lazy fat priest." Dr. Milles was the victim of one of the diarist's most biting criticisms: on February 10, 1666-7, he " made an unnecessary sermon upon Original Sin, neither understood by himself nor the people." And if the rector of the parish failed to satisfy him, for the curate or " lecturer " he entertained an unmeasured contempt. He is referred to as a " simple Scot," who preached " most tediously ";[3] as " a simple, bawling young Scot";[4] and as " our ordinary silly lecturer."[5] On June 21, 1663, he writes, " So to church, and slept all the sermon, the Scot, to whose voice I am not to be reconciled, preaching." Indeed, the performances of this unfortunate young man came to serve as a standard for measuring demerit, for on October 18, 1663, " a simple coxcomb preached worse than the Scot."

[1] August 19, 1660. [2] February 24, 1660-1.
[3] October 26, 1662. [4] April 5, 1663. [5] July 8, 1666.

On the other hand, Pepys was very appreciative of really good preaching. He thought Peter Gunning's [1] sermons "excellent"; and on April 23, 1665, he heard a "most plain, honest, good, grave sermon" from "the famous young Stillingfleete," [2] whom the bishops believed to be "the ablest young man to preach the Gospel of any since the Apostles." More appreciative still is the reference to a sermon preached at St. Olave's, Hart Street, on January 20, 1666-7, by Robert Frampton: [3]

"Coming home I to church, and there, beyond expectation, find our seat and all the church crammed, by twice as many people as used to be, . . . so to my great joy I hear him preach, and I think the best sermon for goodness and oratory, without affectation or study, that ever I heard in my life. The truth is, he preaches the most like an apostle that ever I heard man; and it was much the best time that ever I spent in my life at church."

[1] At the beginning of the *Diary* Peter Gunning was in charge of the Chapel of Exeter House in the Strand. He afterwards became in succession Master of Corpus Christi College, Cambridge, Master of St. John's, Bishop of Chichester, and Bishop of Ely.

[2] At this time Edward Stillingfleet was only 30 years of age. He had recently been appointed one of the King's chaplains, and the sermon was preached in Whitehall Chapel. They were almost contemporaries at Cambridge, for Stillingfleet was elected to a Fellowship at St. John's the year before Pepys took his B.A. degree. In 1678 he became Dean of St. Paul's, and in 1689 Bishop of Worcester.

[3] In 1673 he was appointed Dean, and in 1680 Bishop, of Gloucester.

At Hinchingbrooke, on May 24, 1668, Pepys heard Lord Sandwich's chaplain preach "a very good and seraphic kind of sermon, too good for an ordinary congregation"; and a discourse by George Gifford, the rector of St. Dunstan's-in-the-East, delivered at St. Olave's on August 23, 1668, particularly pleased him. He thought it "a very excellent and persuasive, good and moral sermon," and the preacher "shewed, like a wise man, that righteousness is a surer moral way of being rich than sin and villainy."

The time usually allotted to the sermon was an hour, measured presumably by the hour-glass in the pulpit, and Pepys complains when this was exceeded.[1] On April 2, 1662, on the occasion of the Spital Sermon, "it being a Presbyterian one, it was so long, that after above an hour of it we went away, and I home and dined." He notes it as something extraordinary that the Bishop of London[2] should give the final blessing to the congregation in St. Paul's, "which was, he being a comely old man, a very decent thing, methought."[3] It is curious to find Pepys, on August 9, 1663, taking down the heads of the sermon in Latin with what looks very like an anticipation of the fountain-pen,—"a silver pen" given him by Mr. Coventry "to carry inke in."[4]

[1] February 8, 1662-3.
[2] Humphrey Henchman.
[3] February 28, 1663-4.
[4] August 5.

CHAPTER X

Books

THE famous collection of nearly 3000 volumes[1] in the Pepysian Library at Magdalene College, Cambridge, was the fruit of long experience, and its accumulation was, for the most part, the work of Pepys's later life. But in the *Diary* the tastes of the collector are already beginning to disclose themselves. As early as May 15, 1660, he bought three books at the Hague " for the love of the binding," and in the following November[2] he spent 14*s.* on decorating a new Bible with silver bosses.

In 1665 traces begin to appear of a definite library policy. On January 18, 1664-5, Pepys gave " thorough direction " for the " new binding of a

[1] On the Library generally see Mr. F. Sidgwick's Introduction to *Bibliotheca Pepysiana*, Part II. ("Early Printed Books"). It contained 2,971 volumes in 1705, and seven have since disappeared. The purchase or gift of about 150 is recorded in the *Diary* (*ib.* p. iv).

[2] November 2, 1660.

great many of" his "old books, to make" his "whole study of the same binding within very few"; and when the work was finished he thought his study "a beautifull sight."[1] On July 23, 1666, he took counsel with "Sympson the joyner,"—"he and I with great pains contriving presses to put my books up in, they now growing numerous"; and he found the result to his "most extraordinary satisfaction."[2] Arrangements were made with a bookbinder to gild the backs of all the books in the new presses alike;[3] and Pepys then numbered each with a paper label,[4] and laid the foundation of a catalogue by "reducing the names of all" his "books to an alphabet."[5] At the beginning of 1668 he adopted the principle, to which he afterwards adhered, of weeding out his books from time to time, "being resolved to keep no more than just my presses will contain."[6] On February 16, 1667-8, another catalogue was begun,

[1] February 10, 1664-5.

[2] August 24, 1666. There is some uncertainty about the number of these presses. One of them came home on August 17, 1666, and on August 24 "comes Sympson to set up my other new presses," but on January 10, 1667-8, "my two presses" only are mentioned. The library could not have been as large then as it became later, but it seems probable that all the presses now in the Pepysian Library were made at some time or other by "Sympson the joyner."

[3] August 31 and September 28, 1666.

[4] December 20, 1666. [5] December 25, 1666.

[6] February 2, 1667-8; *cf.* also January 10,

and one of the last entries in the *Diary*[1] relates to his setting his brother John to work upon a catalogue during his absence abroad.

With this passion for fine exteriors, and pleasure in well-ordered shelves, is associated in Pepys a love of books for their own sake. He makes futile resolutions not to buy them, but they draw him like a magnet. His system of vows is made to cover expenditure upon them, and on August 10, 1663, he congratulates himself on the fact that " whereas before, my delight was in a multitude of books, . . . I am become a better husband and have left off buying." Three months later, he was ordering Rushworth and Scobell " etc.,"—" which I will make the King pay for as to the Office, and so I do not break my vow at all."[2] He made £2 or £3 for himself out of this dubious transaction, spending it all upon other books;[3] " and do see how my nature would gladly return to laying out money in this trade." On February 22, 1663-4, he bought some maps of cities in violation of his vow, and promptly fined himself 5*s*. for the benefit of the poor-box; but by June 27 he was backsliding again, and this time nothing is said about a fine. On August 19, 1667, he writes that he cannot refrain from reading, " though I have all the reason in the world to

[1] May 24, 1669. [2] November 23, 1663.
[3] December 10, 1663.

favour my eyes," and a little later we find him buying books freely. And Pepys missed no opportunity of reading the books which he bought. On his journeys by river to the dockyards at Deptford and Woolwich he was frequently accompanied by a book. On December 27, 1665, "it being a very fine, clear, dry night," he walked home over the fields "by light of linke," reading all the way. And on January 9, 1666-7, when dining "alone on a rabbit" at an ordinary, a work on the proceedings of Parliament relieved his solitude.

As would naturally be the case before the days of specialisation, when knowledge was conceived as all one, Pepys's selection of books covered a great variety of subjects. Theology was well represented, being usually but not always reserved for Sunday reading. In this he included ecclesiastical history and biography, and Fuller was his favourite Sunday author. His *Church History* was a standing dish, as also the *Worthies of England*; and it was from Fuller's *History of the Holy War* that Pepys broke off, on Sunday November 3, 1661, in order to "try to make a song in the praise of a liberall genius (as I take my own to be) to all studies and pleasures." He also read Stillingfleet, and Walton's *Life of Hooker*, and the *Works of King Charles the Martyr*, which he thought "a noble book."

History proper included Rushworth, "a most excellent collection,"[1] and "a book the most worth reading for a man of my condition, or any man that hopes to come to any publique condition in the world, that I do know";[2] "the lives of Henry 5th and 6th, very fine," in Speed's Chronicle;[3] Cavendish's life of Wolsey, "a good book";[4] a life of Cromwell, "to his honour as a soldier and politician, though as a rebell";[5] the history of Algiers, "a very pretty book";[6] Alvarez Semedo's *History of China*, "a most excellent book with rare cuts";[7] Foxe's *Book of Martyrs*; Heylin's *Life of Laud*, "a shrewd book, but that which I believe will do the Bishops in general no great good but hurt, it pleads for so much Popish";[8] the life of Julius Caesar; and Chamberlayne's *Angliae Notitia*, "which promises well and is worth reading."[9]

Legal proceedings always interested Pepys, and this led him to purchase books on Law. While walking to Deptford and back, he read a "civill and ecclesiasticall law-book";[10] and he derived much pleasure from the writings of Chief Justice Coke, pronouncing his Pleas of the Crown, in

[1] December 25, 1663.
[2] December 26, 1663.
[3] March 2, 1666-7.
[4] June 3, 1667.
[5] August 11, 1667.
[6] December 18, 1667.
[7] January 14, 1667-8.
[8] September 16, 1668.
[9] January 30, 1668-9.
[10] May 16, 1666.

particular, "very fine noble reading."[1] Philosophy was represented by Hobbes's *Leviathan*, "which is now mightily called for";[2] and Art by Evelyn's *Sculptura*. Under Science, three works greatly impressed Pepys:—"Dr. Power's book of discovery by the microscope," the first English work on that subject; "Boyle's book of colours," containing "many fine things worthy observation,"[3] although "so chymical that I can understand but little of it, but understand enough to see that he is a most excellent man";[4] and Boyle's *Hydrostatics*, which he read "with extraordinary content," admiring it "as a most excellent piece of philosophy."[5]

Pepys also eagerly bought and read plays and poetry. He read Chaucer "with great pleasure,"[6] and also Abraham Cowley, Waller, and Dryden's *Annus Mirabilis*; but he thought *The Siege of Rhodes* "the best poem that ever was wrote,"[7] and read it going to Mortlake by water on Sunday afternoon "with great delight."[8] He altogether failed, however, to appreciate *Hudibras*. He bought a copy for 2*s.* 6*d.*, and found it "so silly an abuse

[1] June 23, 1667. [2] September 3, 1668. [3] May 26, 1667.

[4] June 2, 1667. [5] July 24, 1667.

[6] November 21, 1666. Pepys does not mention Milton, perhaps a dangerous name. "Il restera à la porte du seul poème epique de l'Angleterre; Milton jouait de l'orgue dans une inaccessible cathédrale" (J. Lucas-Dubreton, p. 246).

[7] October 1, 1665. [8] August 5, 1666.

of the Presbyter Knight going to the warrs " that he was ashamed of it, and sold it at once to a friend for 18*d.*[1] Finding later on that " all the world " was crying it up " to be the example of wit," he reluctantly bought another copy.[2] He failed, however, to make anything of it ; " I cannot, I confess, see enough where the wit lies." [3]

As Pepys was enough of a linguist to read French easily, and even to understand a friar preaching in Portuguese in the Queen's Chapel " with his cord about his middle," [4] he was a purchaser of foreign books, and especially French and Spanish.[5] Among the former, he acquired a work " which I did think to have had for my wife to translate," [6] but upon examination it proved to be of such a character that he burned it, " that it may not stand in the list of books nor among them, to disgrace them if it should be found," [7] taking

[1] December 26, 1662. [2] February 6, 1662-3.

[3] December 10, 1663. A French writer on Pepys accounts for this : " Butler a le sens du ridicule et le gôut de l'irrespect ; de là l'incompréhension pepysienne" (J. Lucas-Dubreton, p. 242).

[4] March 17, 1666-7.

[5] See an article by Mr. Stephen Gaselee on " The Spanish Books in the Library of Samuel Pepys " (Bibliographical Society's *Transactions*, Suppl. No. 2, 1921). There are 185 separate works, including 70 ballads bound together, and 26 comedies, mostly on moral and religious subjects.

[6] January 13, 1667-8. It was *L'Escole des Filles*, by Helot, burned at the foot of the gallows in 1672.

[7] February 8, 1667-8.

the precaution of reading it through first himself one Sunday morning, as "not amiss for a sober man once to read over to inform himself in the villainy of the world." [1]

Among Pepys's purchases, Music is of course well represented, and he acquired a number of books of a miscellaneous character on subjects which happened to interest him, such as Heraldry, Witchcraft, and Prophecy. On February 18, 1665-6, he bought Francis Potter's "Interpretation of the Number 666,"—"a booke writ about twenty years ago in prophecy of this year coming on, 1666, explaining it to be the marke of the beast,"—and on this he concludes that "certainly this year of 1666 will be a year of great action, but what the consequences of it will be, God knows!" On Christmas Day, 1667, he even condescended to a shocker,—"The History of the Drummer of Mr. Mompesson," "which is a strange story of spies, and worth reading indeed." On the other hand, he acquired Harrington's *Oceana*, Florio's translation of Montaigne's *Essays*, and Evelyn's book "against Solitude." [2] Nor did he altogether neglect the Classics. On June 13, 1662, he was up by 4 o'clock in the morning to read Cicero's *Second*

[1] February 9, 1667-8.

[2] "Public Employment, and an Active Life, and all its appanages, preferred to Solitude": see Evelyn's *Diary*, February 15, 1666-7.

Oration against Catiline, "which pleased me exceedingly"; and on December 22 he was reading Ovid's *Metamorphoses* with his wife. On June 21, 1663, he rose early to read the Latin Grammar, "which I perceive I have great need of."

We also hear of his own first attempt at authorship. On January 30, 1663-4, he writes:—

"This evening, being in a humour of making all things even and clear in the world, I tore some old papers,—among others, a romance which (under the title of 'Love a Cheate') I begun ten years ago at Cambridge; and at this time reading it over to-night I liked it very well, and wondered a little at myself at my vein at that time when I wrote it, doubting that I cannot do so well now if I would try."

CHAPTER XI

Music [1]

Pepys's critics have called him commonplace,—a type of the average man; but, if there were no other evidence to the contrary, he is redeemed from the commonplace by his love of music. On this subject he speaks with positive passion. On December 6, 1665, finding himself in "the best company for musique" he ever was in, he wishes that he "could live and die in it," and he spent the night "in extasy almost." "Musique is the thing of the world that I love most;" [2] it is "all the pleasure I live for in the world." [3] And on February 27, 1667-8, he reaches the climax of devotion, writing of the "wind-musique" in the *Virgin Martyr*,

> [It is] "so sweet that it ravished me, and indeed in a word, did wrap up my soul so that it made me really sick, just as I have formerly been when in love with my wife; that

[1] For fuller information, see Sir Frederick Bridge, *Samuel Pepys, Lover of Musique* (1903).

[2] July 30, 1666.

[3] February 12, 1666-7.

neither then, nor all the evening going home and at home, I was able to think of any thing, but remained all night transported, so as I could not believe that ever any musick hath that real command over the soul of a man as this did upon me."[1]

One of the diarist's chief musical pleasures was singing in the company of friends. One of the earliest entries in the *Diary*[2] shews him repairing with some musical acquaintances to the Green Dragon on Lambeth Hill after the noon-day dinner, "and there we sang all sorts of things," and "staid there till nine o clock, very merry, and drawn on with one song after another till it came to be so late." At first, Sundays were devoted to Psalms and "holy things," but later on, friends came regularly to the house on that day and the programme was no longer so limited. On Sunday October 29, 1665, Pepys and his friend Mr. Hill the merchant talked music until midnight and continued the next day, with "excellent company and good singing," until the same hour. Pepys complains that the voice of one of his guests is "quite spoiled," but "when he begins to be drunk he is excellent company."[3] Even when he was alone, or with his family, Pepys

[1] Compare Richard Hooker's praise of music, as affecting "that very part of man which is most divine," and carrying us "as it were into extasies, filling the mind with an heavenly joy, and for the time in a manner severing it from the body" (*Ecclesiastical Polity*, edition of 1620, pp. 258-9).

[2] January 16, 1659-60.

[3] October 30, 1665.

was accustomed at all times and in all places to break into song. He formed a habit of "humming" the trillo to himself.[1] He sings in his cabin on board ship; upon the leads of his house in the moonlight; in the garden in the dark; walking in the fields; sitting under a tree in the Park; on the water going down to Erith alone; in Mr. Hales's studio while he is painting Mrs. Pepys as St. Catharine; and in the coach on his way back from Cambridge. On May 5, 1666, "it being a fine moonshine," Pepys, his wife, and Mary Mercer sang from 11 to 12 in the garden "with mighty pleasure to ourselves and neighbours, by their casements opening; and so home to supper and to bed."

The taste for music and the capacity for producing it were widely spread in Pepys's day. Even under the Puritan régime it was possible to sing in a coffee-house "variety of brave Italian and Spanish songs, and a canon for eight voices."[2] The Cock alehouse provided a harp and a violin for the delectation of diners, and there was music at the Globe. At one ordinary the landlord's wife sang and played so well that Pepys "staid a great while and drunk a great deal of wine";[3] at another, "to our dinner we had a fellow play well upon the bagpipes and whistle like a bird

[1] June 30, 1661. [2] February 21, 1659-60.
[3] May 7, 1661.

exceeding well."[1] At the Bear at Cambridge "musique (with a bandore for the base)" gave him a "levett" early in the morning;[2] the barber's boy played the violin while he was having his hair cut;[3] and some citizens of Epsom, "met by chance," sang four or five parts excellently:—"I have not been more pleased with a snapp of musique, considering the circumstances of the time and place, in all my life anything so pleasant."[4] Mrs. Pepys's waiting gentlewomen were all expected to sing, and "boy Tom," who had been a choir-boy in the Royal Chapel, possessed a thorough knowledge of music and could sing anything at sight.

Unlike many amateurs, Pepys was not content with vocal music but played with skill on several instruments. At the beginning of the *Diary* he played the lute, going so far as to string it on a Sunday, for which he prayed God to forgive him.[5] After the end of 1660, however, it is not referred to except to record the fact that Lord Lauderdale hated it; but as he told Pepys that "he had rather hear a cat mew than the best musique in the world, and the better the musique the more sicke it makes him," this *obiter dictum* did not carry great weight.[6] For some time he made a practice

[1] May 17, 1661.
[2] October 15, 1662.
[3] July 22, 1663.
[4] July 27, 1663.
[5] October 21, 1660.
[6] July 28, 1666.

of rising " pretty betimes " and playing the viol before going to the office. The flageolet also was a favourite instrument. On February 9, 1659-60, Pepys played on it in a drinking-house near Temple Bar, while waiting for a dish of poached eggs. Going to the Hague on May 14, 1660, he travelled with " two very pretty ladies, very fashionable and with black patches, who very merrily sang all the way and that very well "; and this encouraged him to take out his flageolet and " pipe " to them. Four days later he played to the echo at the House in the Wood at the Hague " to great advantage." In his earlier days Pepys possessed a triangle, on which he taught Mary Ashwell to play, " and made her take out a Psalm very well, she having a good ear and hand."[1] He also purchased a recorder, " which I do intend to learn to play on, the sound of it being, of all sounds in the world, most pleasing to me."[2]

Other instruments are also referred to in the *Diary*, and notably the " harpsichon." " Old Mrs. Crisp " performed upon it,[3] and it was used to accompany songs. Pepys sometimes heard good music from it, but once he found himself in the grip of the conventions, for when Mrs. Turner's daughter played, "Lord! it was enough to make any man sick to hear her; yet I was

[1] May 3, 1663. [2] April 8, 1668.
[3] March 17, 1659-60.

forced to commend her highly."[1] On another occasion he was less considerate. "Mr. Temple's wife," he tells us,[2] "after dinner, fell to play on the harpsicon till she tired everybody, that I left the house without taking leave, and no creature left standing by her to hear her." For himself he preferred to buy "a little espinette," as it took up less room:[3] it cost him £5. For a time he entertained the idea of getting an organ, but one he found to be only a toy and another was too big for his house. He was "mighty earnest to have a pair" at St. Olave's, and had "almost a mind to give them a pair, if they would settle a maintenance on them for it";[4] but there is no record of such a gift having been made. He thought the bagpipes "mighty barbarous musick," and the guitar at the best "but a bawble"; but he liked the dulcimer when well played, and also found pleasure in the trump-marine.

Pepys paid much attention to the theory of music. On January 14, 1661-2, he began to take lessons in composition from John Berkenshaw.[5] For a course extending over a month or five weeks the fee was £5, "which is a great

[1] May 1, 1663. [2] November 10, 1666.

[3] April 4, 1668. [4] April 21, 1667.

[5] Evelyn calls him "that rare artist, who invented a mathematical way of composure very extraordinary, true as to the exact rules of art, but without much harmony" (*Diary*, August 3, 1664).

deal of money and troubled me to part with it." [1] On September 17, 1665, he drew a music scale with a view to practising composition, and on October 15, while waiting for the barber, he composed "a duo of counterpoint" according to Berkenshaw's rule. In the early part of 1668 he tried to invent "a better theory of musique than hath yet been abroad," [2] expecting that it "will come to something that is very good," [3] and finding great satisfaction in it.[4]

The *Diary* only claims four songs as Pepys's own, and it is uncertain how large a part was played in their composition by helpful friends. He calls "Great, good, and just" "my song," [5] and it has been generally held that he composed it, although the possessive may be interpreted in a different sense. The view that "my song" only means a song that he was accustomed to sing, finds support from an entry of February 11, 1661-2: "At night begun to compose songs, and begin with 'Gaze not on Swans,'" as if this were his first composition. In this musical achievement Mr. Berkenshaw appears to have played a considerable part.[6] On December 6, 1665, Pepys

[1] February 24, 1661-2. [2] March 20, 1667-8.

[3] March 23, 1667-8. [4] April 6, 1668. [5] January 30, 1659-60.

[6] February 24 and March 14, 1661-2. Although he depended a good deal upon professional assistance, Pepys objected to the intrusion of a professional musician into a meeting of amateurs, "for it spoils, methinks, the ingenuity of our practice" (July 29, 1664).

spent the afternoon in setting to music the song of Solyman to Roxalana in the second part of Davenant's *Siege of Rhodes*:

"Beauty retire, thou doest my pitty move";

and on the 9th he sang it to his friend Mr. Hill, "which he likes, only excepts against two notes in the base." Later on, he taught it to Mrs. Knipp the actress, who made it "go most rarely." Modern musicians have agreed with its author's judgment: "a very fine song it seems to be."[1] There are two settings in the Pepysian Library,—one the original, written by Pepys himself, and painted into Hales's portrait of him in the National Portrait Gallery, and the other as amplified later, possibly by the Italian musician Morelli.[2] Sir Frederick Bridge has pointed out[3] that the wrong one has been ascribed to Pepys in Wheatley's edition of the *Diary*.[4] On April 5, 1666, he began setting to music Ben Jonson's song, "It is decreed," but this was not finished until December 19, when Mr. Hingston the organist was called in to provide a bass. The author seems to have preferred it to "Beauty retire."[5] On November 30, 1667, Pepys tried to "make a piece" by his "eare and viall" to "I wonder what the grave"; but there is nothing to shew that it was ever completed and written down.

[1] February 23, 1665-6.
[2] See p. 222 below.
[3] On pp. 99-100 of his book.
[4] Facsimile inserted in December 6, 1665.
[5] August 22, 1666.

CHAPTER XII

Plays[1]

PEPYS found in the theatre one of the major pleasures of his life. During the nine years and five months of the *Diary* he went there 351 times and, as Sir Sidney Lee has pointed out, these figures are affected by the fact that "for more than twelve months of that period the London playhouses were for the most part closed, owing to the Great Plague and the Fire." He saw in the theatre a standing temptation, leading to extravagance and the neglect of his official business, but he found it too strong for him. "Hence," he writes on September 25, 1661, "much against my nature and will, yet such is the power of the Devil over me I could not refuse it, to the Theatre, and saw *The Merry Wives of Windsor* ill done." The result was that plays, like wine, were soon brought within the ambit of his vows of abstinence.

[1] For fuller information, see an article by Sir Sidney Lee on "Pepys and Shakespeare" in the *Fortnightly Review* for 1906.

These vows are first referred to on October 21, 1661: "And so against my judgment and conscience (which God forgive, for my very heart knows that I offend God in breaking my vows herein) to the Opera"; but all this remorse did not prevent his attending the theatre pretty regularly until the close of the year. His backslidings were frequent, and one of the uncovenanted plays was so bad that he wished he had kept his vow. "But however, as soon as I came home I did pay my crown to the poor's box, according to my vow, and so no harm as to that is done, but only business lost and money lost and my old habit of pleasure wakened, which I will keep down the more hereafter."[1] He tries to satisfy his conscience by ingenious sophistries, holding that his oath did not apply to the new Theatre Royal because at the time of swearing "it was not then in being."[2] On January 2, 1663-4, he bound himself by a new vow of extraordinary complexity,—"that I will not see above one in a month at any of the publique theatres till the sum of 50*s*. be spent, and then none before New Year's Day next unless that I do become worth £1000 sooner than then, and then am free to come to some other terms." Pepys feared at the time that he was binding himself too strictly, and it was not long before he began to find fresh

[1] October 20, 1662. [2] May 8, 1663.

expedients for evading the letter of his obligations. In August 1664 he went to four plays,—one in his own right; one at the expense of Sir William Penn, which he held to be no breach of his vows; one by appropriating Mrs. Pepys's "time of the last month, she not having seen any then, so my vowe is not broke at all, it costing me no more money than it would have donc upon her had she gone both her times that were due to her";[1] and one by getting Mr. Creed to "give my wife and me a play this afternoon, lending him money to do it, which is a fallacy that I have found now once to avoyde my vowe with, but never more to be practised I swear."[2] On September 28, 1664, he saw an extra play at Lord Rutherford's expense, "so that with a safe conscience I do think my oathe is not broke, and judge God Almighty will not think it otherwise."

In the following year the Plague put an end to this form of indulgence, and it was not until December 7, 1666, that Pepys began going to plays again, with his cloak about his face for fear of being seen. In the latter part of April 1667 there was an orgy of plays,—one every day for a week,—because the Duke of York and Sir William Coventry, the two people whose good opinion he was most anxious to retain, were away at Portsmouth.[3] On August 12 another orgy

[1] August 8, 1664. [2] August 13, 1664. [3] April 18, 1666-7.

began, and he went to the theatre every week-day except one for a fortnight, which left him with his "belly now full with plays." This led to a renewal of his oaths, followed by further relapses, and after Christmas 1667 he began to go freely to the theatre, nothing more being heard of vows of abstinence.

Sir Sidney Lee has pointed out that Pepys represents the average playgoer. His appreciation of a play is much affected by things not really relevant to it. He is rendered receptive by the comfort of his seat, the prettiness of the actresses, and the freedom of his mind from domestic and business cares. What he most enjoys is character-acting, which always appeals to the average man, and he reserves his highest praise for Ben Jonson's comedies of manners and the heroic tragedies of Massinger and Beaumont and Fletcher. He calls Ben Jonson's *Alchymist* "a most incomparable play,"[1] and describes *The Silent Woman* as "the best comedy . . . that ever was wrote."[2] On the other hand, the pure poetry and passion of Shakespeare, except when supported by scenery, songs, and dances, leave him cold. *Twelfth Night* he thought one of the weakest plays that ever he saw on the stage; *The Merry Wives of Windsor* did not please him at all, "in no part of it";[3] *Romeo and Juliet* was the worst play he

[1] June 22, 1661. [2] September 19, 1668. [3] August 15, 1667.

ever heard in his life;[1] *Midsummer Night's Dream* was insipid and ridiculous, though "I saw, I confess, some good dancing and some handsome women, which was all my pleasure";[2] and *The Taming of the Shrew* was "mean"[3] and "silly."[4] On the other hand, *Macbeth* was "a most excellent play for variety"[5] and *Othello* "a mighty good play," though "a mean thing" compared to Sir Samuel Tuke's *Adventures of Five Hours*,[6] a work described by Sir Sidney Lee as "a trivial comedy of intrigue." The only play of Shakespeare's which Pepys really appreciated was *Hamlet*, and that was partly due to the superb acting of Betterton. He learned "To be or not to be" by heart and then had it set to music;[7] and this rendering is still to be found in a book of manuscript music in the Pepysian Library. It must be remembered that *The Tempest* and *Macbeth* as Pepys saw them were only adaptations, and *The Taming of the Shrew* a particularly bad adaptation. It is to his credit that he took no pleasure in the merely indecent. The plays of Dryden, Etherege, and Sedley struck him as simply silly.

A good deal of light is thrown by the *Diary* on the Restoration stage. Pepys witnessed the re-

[1] March 1, 1661-2.
[2] September 29, 1662.
[3] April 9, 1667.
[4] November 1, 1667.
[5] December 28, 1666.
[6] August 20, 1666.
[7] November 13, 1664.

placement of boys by women in women's parts, a great development of scenic machinery, and the musical accompaniment of plays. An entry of February 12, 1666-7, relating to the improvements claimed by Killigrew, runs thus:—

> "He tells me . . . that the stage is now by his pains a thousand times better and more glorious than ever heretofore. Now, wax-candles, and many of them; then, not above 3 lbs. of tallow: now, all things civil, no rudeness anywhere; then, as in a bear-garden: then, two or three fiddlers; now, nine or ten of the best: then, nothing but rushes upon the ground and every thing else mean; and now, all otherwise."

Pepys himself observes the great increase in the number of citizens, 'prentices, and "mean people" in the half-crown pit, and regards it as evidence of "the vanity and prodigality of the age." [1] Everybody ate oranges in the theatre at *6d.* apiece,[2] and sometimes they were flung at the performers.[3] One gentleman "of good habit," "eating of some fruit in the midst of the play, did drop down as dead, being choked; but with much ado Orange Moll did thrust her finger down his throat and brought him to life again." [4]

Some of the diarist's remarks about the stage are characteristically artless and disarming. He reflects on "the vanity and pride" of actors; how

[1] January 1, 1667-8. [2] March 26, 1668.
[3] January 15, 1668-9. [4] November 2, 1667.

strange the players are to one another after the play is done;[1] and how the women paint.[2] A visit to stageland behind the scenes leads him to comment on the theatrical wardrobe,—"how fine they shew on the stage by candle-light, and how poor things they are to look now too near hand."[3] On October 19, 1667, one of Lord Orrery's plays was nearly wrecked by the reading on the stage of a letter disclosing the plot,—"which was so long, and some things . . . so unnecessary" that the audience began to laugh and hiss. Soon after,[4] the play was "mightily bettered" by the letter being printed "and so delivered to every body at their going in." On December 28, 1667, the diarist was "mightily" pleased "to see the natural affection of a poor woman, the mother of one of the children brought on the stage: the child crying, she by force got upon the stage and took up her child and carried it away." On one occasion even the careful Pepys fell a victim to a box-office trick. "I was prettily served this day at the playhouse-door, where, giving six shillings into the fellow's hand for us three, the fellow by legerdemain did convey one away, and with so much grace faced me down that I did give him but five that, though I knew the contrary, yet I was

[1] April 7, 1668. [2] October 5, 1667.
[3] March 19, 1665-6. [4] October 23.

overpowered by his so grave and serious demanding the other shilling that I could not deny him, but was forced by myself to give it him." [1]

[1] February 24, 1667-8.

CHAPTER XIII

Science

A NOTABLE characteristic of Pepys's mind was "the most indiscriminating, insatiable, and miscellaneous curiosity."

He was interested in the ways of living creatures,—Captain Holmes's baboon, which "already understands much English," and "might be taught to speak or make signs";[1] Dr. Williams's dog, which had killed and buried above 100 cats;[2] the Lancashire serpents "that do feed upon larks," catching them by ejecting poison "up to the bird";[3] "the strength of hawkes, which will strike a fowle to the ground with that force that shall make the fowle rebound a great way from ground, which no force of man or art can do";[4] the Duke of York's bird from the East Indies, which "talks many things and neyes like

[1] August 24, 1661. [2] September 11, 1661.
[3] February 4, 1661-2. [4] August 6, 1663.

the horse";[1] gold-fish "kept in a glass of water, that will live so for ever";[2] and the geese in St. James's Park. He was intrigued by the problem why "negros drowned look white and lose their blackness";[3] and by the practice of Sir George Carteret's farmers, who gave their calves "a piece of chalke to licke, which they hold makes them white in the flesh within."[4] For this grave public official any kind of monstrosity had an irresistible fascination,—a strange birth at Salisbury; the "most prodigious bigness for their age" of two children from Ireland;[5] the "strange sight" of the bearded woman in Holborn;[6] and the giantess "who is but twenty-one years old, and I do easily stand under her arms."[7] On May 12, 1668, he saw a mummy in a merchant's warehouse at Islington, and was fortunate enough to secure a bone for himself.

Inventions of all kinds attracted him,—the pumping-engines in St. James's Park; Mr. Spong's smoke-jack, "very pretty"; "a gun to discharge seven times, the best of all devices that ever I saw, and very serviceable, and not a bawble";[8] "a very pretty weather-glass for heat and cold";[9]

[1] April 25, 1664.
[2] May 28, 1665.
[3] April 11, 1662.
[4] August 1, 1665.
[5] July 8, 1667.
[6] December 21, 1668.
[7] January 4, 1668-9.
[8] July 3, 1662.
[9] March 23, 1662-3.

Colonel Blount's "new chariot, made with springs"; Cornelius van Drebbel's "instrument to sink ships";[1] and Sir Samuel Morland's "late invention for casting up of sums of £ *s. d.*, which is very pretty but not very useful."[2] He was also curious about processes,—"the manner of assaying of gold and silver,"[3] of peeling hemp, of "going about of draining of fenns,"[4] and of sawing marble.[5] He takes pleasure in seeing cabinet-makers at work,[6] and stands from 3 in the afternoon till 8 at night watching his coach being varnished.[7] On December 22, 1665, "I to my Lord Bruncker's, and there spent the evening by my desire in seeing his Lordship open to pieces and make up again his watch, thereby being taught what I never knew before; and it is a thing very well worth my having seen, and am mightily pleased and satisfied with it."

This curiosity, specialised in a particular direction, accounts for the claim of Pepys to be regarded as a man of science. Long before his admission to the Royal Society, he had frequented the company of the "virtuosoes." As early as January 23, 1660-1, he visited Gresham College, then their headquarters, and "found great company of

[1] November 11, 1663.
[2] March 14, 1667-8.
[3] May 19, 1663.
[4] October 29, 1663.
[5] February 24, 1663-4.
[6] February 11, 1666-7.
[7] April 30, 1669.

persons of honour there." On May 23, 1661, he met Mr. Jonas Moore the mathematician at the Rhenish wine-house, "and there he did by discourse make us fully believe that England and France were once the same continent, by very good arguments"; and the same day at the Lord Mayor's he "had very good discourse with Mr. Ashmole, wherein he did assure me that frogs and many insects do often fall from the sky ready formed." A week later,[1] over wine and anchovies, he discoursed with Mr. Greatorex "of many things in mathematics." On April 28, 1662, Dr. Clerke offered to bring him into the "college of virtuosoes," as the Royal Society was then called, and to shew him some anatomy, "which makes me very glad"; and on February 27, 1662-3, he attended two lectures on the human body at Chyrurgeon's Hall. On October 5, 1664, he "had very fine discourse" with Henry Oldenburg, "the Secretary of the Virtuosi of Gresham College"; and on January 9, 1664-5, he saw the newly incorporated Royal Society bring their Charter-book to be signed by the Duke of York as a Fellow, the King's name appearing there as Founder.

On February 8, 1664-5, "Samuel Pepys, Esq. was proposed candidate by Mr. Povey," and on February 15 "Mr. Pepys was unanimously

[1] June 2, 1661.

elected and admitted";[1] but the entries relating to him in the records of the Royal Society are singularly meagre. On March 8 he was desired to visit Major Holmes to enquire into "the late performances of the pendulum watches" in his voyage to Guinea, and on March 15 he made his report to the Society.[2] On March 22 he was asked to follow the matter up by procuring "the journals of those masters of ships who had been with Major Holmes in Guinea and differed from him in the relation concerning the pendulum watches";[3] but no further report was presented. On the same day "Mr. Pepys was desired to bespeak a man at Deptford for diving," and on June 7 he had to be "reminded of the diver for the diving experiments this season."[4] On January 11, 1667-8, his name appears on a list of Fellows to be solicited by the President for a contribution to the building of the proposed Royal Society College,[5] and on April 2 he records the success of the operation: he was "forced to subscribe," and "did give £40."[6] Pepys did not belong to the class of skilled experimenters whose names appear frequently in the records of the Society, and he was probably too busy to act as a collector of the miscellaneous random infor-

[1] Thomas Birch, *The History of the Royal Society* (1756), ii. 13.
[2] *Ib.* ii. 21, 23. [3] *Ib.* ii. 26. [4] *Ib.* ii. 55. [5] *Ib.* ii. 238.
[6] *Diary*, April 2, 1668.

mation which was so eagerly accumulated in those days when scientific investigation had yet to become systematic.

Shortly before Pepys was elected a Fellow, the Royal Society had interested itself in the effects of tobacco. On January 18, 1664-5,[1] Mr. Boyle had stated at a meeting "that he had been informed that the much drinking of coffee produced the palsy," and the Bishop of Exeter said "that himself had found it dispose to paralytical effects." Another Fellow then "affirmed that he knew two gentlemen, great drinkers of coffee, very paralytical"; but Dr. Whistler was not disposed to throw the responsibility upon coffee, and "suggested that it might be inquired whether the same persons took much tobacco." This seems to have led Mr. Daniel Coxe to embark on an investigation, and on May 3, 1665, he read a paper to the Society giving an account of "the effects of tobacco-oil distilled in a retort, by one drop of which given at the mouth he had killed a lusty cat."[2] Pepys was present at the reading of the paper, and at the same time "saw a cat killed

[1] Birch, ii. 9.

[2] *Ib.* ii. 42; *cf.* also ii. 386 *n*, where a letter of June 28, 1669, gives a circumstantial account of the self-starvation of "Mrs. Jane Naunton, a maiden lady about 23 . . . very fat of body . . . having appetite and digestion, both of solids and liquids, beyond what is usual with those of her qualifications," adding that she was a taker of tobacco.

with the Duke of Florence's poyson." From the time of his election he was a frequent attendant at the meetings of the Society, encountering men "of most eminent worth," hearing "very noble discourse," and witnessing "fine experiments,"— "but I do lacke philosophy enough to understand them, and so cannot remember them."[1] But an experiment which he did not forget to record was one on transfusion of blood, which "did give occasion to many pretty wishes, as of the blood of a Quaker to be let into an Archbishop, and such like."[2]

On November 30, 1667, Pepys attended an election of officers at Arundel House, which "Mr. Henry Howard of Norfolke" had placed at the disposal of the Royal Society, "they being now disturbed at Gresham College,"[3] and "was near being chosen of the Council, but am glad I was not, for I could not have attended, though above all things I could wish it, and do take it as a mighty respect to have been named there." At the dinner which followed he heard Dr. Wilkins discourse "of the universal speech"; and on April 2, 1668, he experimented with an ear-trumpet, to his "great content." These interests persisted until the end of the *Diary*. Three weeks before it was closed,[4] Pepys and his wife were walking

[1] March 1, 1664-5. [2] November 14, 1666.
[3] January 7, 1666-7. [4] May 4, 1669.

with Lord Brouncker in their garden at the Navy Office " and by and by comes Mr. Hooke, and my Lord and he and I into my Lord's lodgings, and there discoursed of many fine things in philosophy to my great content, and so home to supper and to bed."

CHAPTER XIV

Art

EARLY in the *Diary* Pepys describes himself as taking great pleasure in pictures.[1] On the day on which he heard that the salary of the Clerk of the Acts was to be £350 he bought "two fine prints of Ragotti from Rubens,"[2] and this was the first of a series of judicious purchases which included "brave vellum covers to keep pictures in."[3] It became necessary for him to bring this form of self-indulgence into his system of vows,[4] but finding in a warehouse on Cornhill "great plenty of good pictures, God forgive me! how my mind run upon them." He ended by buying £10 worth, proposing to evade the obligations of his oath by making the King "one way or other pay for them, though I saved it to him another way."[5] He admired Lely's work, and

[1] January 23, 1660-1. [2] July 7, 1660.
[3] January 14, 1661-2. [4] May 9, 1662.
[5] December 26, 1663.

especially his portrait of Lady Castlemaine, "which is a most blessed picture";[1] but he found the painter "a mighty proud man" and "full of state." He also praises Huysmans, and thought a picture by Simon Verelst, the Dutch flower-painter, "worth going twenty miles to see."[2] The paintings in the King's closet at Whitehall were "most incomparable," "such variety of pictures and other things of value and rarity that I was properly confounded, and enjoyed no pleasure in the sight of them, which is the only time in my life that ever I was so at a loss for pleasure in the greatest plenty of objects to give it me."[3] He often walked up and down the Whitehall galleries "spending time upon the pictures."

As his financial position improved, Pepys began to spend more freely upon prints for his portfolios and pictures for his house. He hung one room with maps,[4] invested in a number of prints of cities, and imported from France "many excellent prints" by Robert Nanteuil the French engraver.[5] At the beginning of 1669 he commissioned Henry Dankers the landscape-painter to paint in four panels of his dining-room "the four houses of the King, White Hall, Hampton Court,

[1] October 20, 1662. [2] April 11, 1669.
[3] June 24, 1664. [4] April 27, 1666.
[5] January 25, 1668-9.

Greenwich, and Windsor."[1] The painter began upon Greenwich, and his patron made a special journey thither to verify the accuracy of the performance.[2] Rome was eventually substituted for Hampton Court.[3]

Pepys was an admirer of great houses and stately surroundings. He thought the statues at Arundel House "a brave sight";[4] he admired Hatfield House,—"the chapell with brave pictures, and above all the gardens, such as I never saw in all my life";[5] and he thought Clarendon House, then in building, "the finest pile I ever did see in my life, and will be a glorious house."[6] He was also much impressed with the "fine monuments" in St. Saviour's, Southwark,[7] and saw the tombs in Westminster Abbey "with great pleasure."[8]

Of the Pepys portraits,[9] those by Savill and Hales were painted during the *Diary* period. Pepys began sitting to Savill on November 27, 1661, and Mrs. Pepys on December 13. The pictures, "which do not much displease us,"[10] cost £6 altogether, and 36s. for the two frames.[11]

[1] January 20 and 22, 1668-9. [2] March 16, 1668-9.
[3] March 31, 1669. [4] May 30, 1661. [5] July 22, 1661.
[6] January 31, 1665-6. [7] July 3, 1663. [8] September 12, 1664.
[9] See the papers by Mr. Lionel Cust and Mr. Samuel Pepys Cockerell in the Pepys Club *Occasional Papers*, 1903-14.
[10] December 30, 1661. [11] January 16, 1661-2.

On February 22, 1661-2, they were hung in state in the dining-room, and Pepys was sufficiently pleased with them to sit again for his picture " in little." This was finished on May 3, 1662, and cost £3.

Savill was a painter of no special note, and as soon as he became a man of substance Pepys flew higher. On September 21, 1664, and again on May 31, 1665, he refers to his intention to have Mrs. Pepys painted by Huysmans, but this does not appear to have been carried out, although Mr. Lionel Cust is inclined to assign to Huysmans the fine portrait at Magdalene of Pepys himself, hitherto attributed to Lely, and probably painted soon after the *Diary* came to an end. He eventually selected John Hales, whom Mr. Cust describes as " an imitator of Lely " but " a quite creditable performer " ; and on February 15, 1665-6, Hales began to paint Mrs. Pepys " like a St. Katharine," following the prevailing fashion adopted in compliment to the Queen. At quite an early stage Pepys, " with great content," perceived that it would be " a very brave picture."[1] After visiting the studio with a frequency which must have been irritating to the artist, he writes on March 8, " her face and necke, which are now finished, do so please me that I am not myself almost, nor was not all the night after in writing

[1] February 19, 1665-6.

of my letters, in consideration of the fine picture that I shall be master of." The portrait was inspected on March 15, "a most pretty picture, and mighty like my wife": he paid the artist £14 for it, "and the truth is, I think he do deserve it." On March 17 Pepys began to sit for his own portrait; "he promises it shall be as good as my wife's, and I sit to have it full of shadows, and do almost break my neck looking over my shoulder to make the posture for him to work by." An "Indian gowne" was hired for him "to be drawn in,"[1] and he was represented holding in his left hand his song, "Beauty retire."[2] The artist had painted in a "landskipp" as a background, but Pepys insisted on this being "done out, and only a heaven made in the roome of it."[3] He was "mightily pleased" with the result, and paid another £14 with a cheerful mind, although he insisted upon an alteration to Mrs. Pepys's hand.[4] Both pictures were brought home in a coach on May 16. Pepys's own portrait was afterwards engraved.[5] On June 6 Hales began to paint Mr. Pepys senior, and this also was a success. "It joys my very heart," wrote the devoted son on June 13, "to thinke that I should have his picture so well done, who, besides that he is my father, and a man that loves me and hath ever done so,

[1] March 30, 1666. [2] April 11, 1666. [3] April 20, 1666.
[4] August 28, 1668. [5] See July 14, 1668.

is also at this day one of the most carefull and innocent men in the world." The price of this portrait was £10.

On July 6, 1668, Mrs. Pepys began to sit to Samuel Cooper, "the great limner in little," and the result was "a noble picture, but yet I think not so like as Hales's is."[1] For this her husband paid £30; and £8 3*s.* 4*d.* for a gold case to put it in.

On February 10, 1668-9, Pepys's head was cast in plaster, "most admirably like,"[2] and the *Diary* furnishes a detailed account of how it was done.

[1] July 18, 1668. [2] February 15.

CHAPTER XV

Money

THE financial position of Pepys during the greater part of the period of the *Diary* can be accurately ascertained from his scrupulously-kept monthly accounts. These begin on January 29, 1659-60, when he found himself "to be worth £40 and more, which I did not think, but am afraid that I have forgot something." After May 31, 1667, these fell into arrear, but the figures for that date shew him to be now worth £6,900. We learn from the entry for December 31, 1666, that in 1665 his income was £3,560 and his expenditure £509. The corresponding figures for 1666 were £2,986 and £1,154, "which is a sum not fit to be said that ever I should spend in one year, before I am master of a better estate than I am." This progressive prosperity was the occasion of many pious ejaculations. For instance, on December 31, 1663, he reaches £800, "for which the good God be pleased to give me a thankful heart and a mind careful to preserve this and increase it." On July 31, 1664, he writes,

"To my great joy, and with great thanks to Almighty God, I do find myself most clearly worth £1,014, the first time that ever I was worth £1,000 before, which is the height of all that ever I have for a long time pretended to.... So with praise to God for this state of fortune that I am brought to as to wealth ... I home to supper and to bed, desiring God to give me the grace to make good use of what I have and continue my care and diligence to gain more."

On August 2, 1665, he found himself "really worth £1,900, for which the great God of Heaven and Earth be praised."

Part of this money was invested at interest, but large accumulations of cash were kept in the house. On September 27, 1664, Pepys had nearly £1,000 there. On August 28, 1665, there was £1,800 in the house in an iron chest, and as he was about to move his household to Woolwich because of the Plague, this caused him some anxiety. He thought of taking it with him, but reassured himself with the consideration that no one would think that he could be such a fool as to leave it behind, and therefore it would be quite safe.[1] On July 6, 1666, he had £2,000, "whereof £1,000 in gold," "but the fear of being robbed ... was very great, and is still so, and do much disquiet me."[2] Nevertheless, the sum was subsequently increased by another £1,000,[3] some of it being

[1] September 14, 1665. [2] July 7, 1666. [3] July 23, 1666.

public money, probably held on account of Tangier. On October 24 he considered the propriety of distributing it for safety, "dividing what I have, and laying it in several places, but with all faithfulness to the King in all respects." [1] We hear nothing more of this proposed distribution, which may have taken the form of investment; but in June 1667, when the Dutch came up the Medway, Pepys made a girdle, "by which, with some trouble, I do carry about me £300 in gold about my body, that I may not be without something in case I should be surprised." [2] On the same day, "at two hours' warning," he despatched his wife and father to Brampton "with about £1,300 in gold in their night-bag," with instructions to bury it in the garden, and he sent another £1,000 after them by Mr. Gibson. Four months later, on October 10, Pepys went himself to dig the money up at night with the aid of a dark lantern:—

"But, Lord! what a tosse I was for some time in that they could not justly tell where it was; that I begun heartily to sweat, and be angry that they should not agree better upon the place, and at last to fear that it was gone: but by and by poking with a spit, we found it, and then begun with a spudd to lift up the ground. But, good God! to see how sillily they did it, not half a foot under ground, and in the sight of the world from a hundred places, if any body by accident were near hand, and within sight of a neighbour's window, and their hearing also, being

[1] October 31, 1666. [2] June 13, 1667.

close by.... [At first] there was short above a hundred pieces, which did make me mad.... So W. Hewer and I out again about midnight, for it was now grown so late, and there by candle-light did make shift to gather forty-five pieces more."

The next day another thirty-four pieces were discovered, and the treasure was carried safely back to London. Another guinea was found later on.

In his early days Pepys was a borrower.[1] At the end of 1661 he was afraid to cast up his accounts, and his "trouble of mind" over the purchase of "a pair of tweezers" for 14*s*. shews that he was practising a rigid economy;[2] but by the end of October 1662 he was beginning to save money, "though it be but a little." He then became an investor, beginning with a loan to Lord Sandwich of £500, afterwards increased to £700;[3] but this was a risky undertaking, and he blessed God when the debt was reduced.[4] On April 21, 1665, he placed £350 at 10% in the hands of John Andrews, the victualling-contractor for Tangier, and a reference of August 15, 1665, shews that he had then nearly £1,000 "in the King's hands." On February 1, 1665-6, he had £2,000 on call with Sir Robert Viner the goldsmith, but on March 29, 1666, he had "no mind

[1] August 31, 1661. [2] June 20, 1662.
[3] August 24, 1663. [4] February 10, 1664-5.

to have it lie there longer,"[1] and on April 3 he transferred nearly the whole of it[2] to Sir William Warren the timber merchant, for the purchase of prizes. At the end of June 1666 Pepys began to concentrate his resources, "for a great turne is to be feared in the times"; but at the beginning of 1667, when things were looking better, he put "a great deal of money" out of his own hands into the King's "upon tallies for Tangier," as interest at 10% was tempting.[3] He also had a "great sum of money" without interest in the hands of Lord Rutherford;[4] but it is not clear in all cases whether these moneys belonged to Pepys himself or were invested by him as Treasurer for Tangier. On September 4, 1667, Sir Samuel Morland, his old College Tutor, wanted a loan on orders upon the Exchequer, offering 12%, but "I would not meddle with them," writes Pepys, "though they are very good; and would, had I not so much money out already on public credit." Perhaps he was encouraged in this resolution by a forced loan to which he had been subjected a few days before. On August

[1] Pepys had already said on September 12, 1664, that he was "doubtful of trusting any of these great dealers because of their mortality," adding, however, "but then the convenience of having one's money at an houre's call is very great."

[2] The record of a loan of £1,900 from Pepys to Warren, dated April 3, 1666, is in the Rawlinson Collection at the Bodleian (A. 174. f. 436).

[3] January 31, 1666-7.

[4] July 29, 1667.

24 "comes a letter from the Duke of York to the Board to invite us, which is as much as to fright us, into the lending the King money." The Clerk of the Acts offered £300, although he found "no delight in lending money now, to be paid by the King two years hence,"[1] even at 10%. On November 3, 1667, he refused a bargain of land in Norfolk, "but it is out of the way so of my life that I shall never enjoy it, nor it may be see it, and so I shall have nothing to do with it"; but a year later[2] he arranged a snug little investment of £1,000 upon mortgage with his cousin Roger Pepys of Impington, "trusting to his honesty and ability, and . . . that I may not have all I have lie in the King's hands." In spite of his distrust of Lord Sandwich as a man of business, Pepys's loyalty to the family held firm to the end of the *Diary*. On May 10, 1668, he could not "deny my Lady" £100, "whatever comes of it, though it be lost, but shall be glad that it is no bigger sum"; and although on August 26, 1666, he had declined to lend Lord Sandwich £500, "being not willing to embarke myself in money there, where I see things going to ruine," on September 28, 1668, he found it "his duty to my Lord" to furnish that sum, "wishing only that I had my money in my purse that I have lent him."[3]

[1] August 30, 1667. [2] November 11, 1668.
[3] November 23, 1668.

The fact that on a salary of £350 a year the Clerk of the Acts succeeded in putting by nearly £7,000 in seven years, raises the question of the means by which this fortune was acquired. It is true that from March 1665 he was also Treasurer for Tangier, and from November 1665 until July 1667 he was receiving an extra salary of £300 a year as Surveyor-General of Victualling; but these additions are not sufficient to explain the discrepancy between his income and his accumulations.

Some of the methods adopted were legitimate enough according to the ideas of the time. On March 5, 1660-1, Pepys's head is beginning to be "full of thoughts how to get a little present money"; and on April 15 he discusses the possibility of venturing something by ships sailing for Portugal. There were pickings to be had out of the purchase of £300 worth of cloth for Lord Sandwich "to give in Barbary as presents among the Turks."[1] On February 21, 1662-3, he was thinking of speculating in freights, and on March 25, 1663, he was seeking "some lawfull profit" from hiring ships for Tangier;[2] but Sir

[1] June 12, 1661. In this connexion should be noted an artless confession of a desire (successfully resisted) to swindle Lord Sandwich over his accounts. "I had some hopes to have made a profit to myself in this account, and above what was due to me (which God forgive me in), but I could not, but carried them to my Lord" (July 8, 1662).

[2] *Cf.* also June 10 and December 9, 1664.

William Warren advised him not "to meddle either in ships or merchandise," but to keep his money at interest, "which is a good, quiett, and easy profit."[1] At the end of October a lavish expenditure on clothes and periwigs led him to the conclusion, "I must look about me to get something more than just my salary."[2] This led him to contemplate himself in the part of an informer, exposing abuses in connexion with the arrears of stores at the Victualling Office at Portsmouth, and securing a grant from the King of a percentage of all that he could discover.[3] On November 23, 1663, he was dabbling in shipping insurance; and it may have been in reference to this that he wrote on December 23, "Did much business at the 'Change, and so home to dinner and then to my office, and there late doing business also to my great content to see God bless me in my place, and opening honest ways, I hope, to get a little money to lay up and yet to live handsomely." On November 16, 1664, he "had much discourse" with Sir William Batten "how to get ourselves into the Prize Office" with a view to profit, but Coventry advised them not to proceed with their application.[4]

In September 1665 Pepys began to embark in

[1] May 5, 1663. This counsel was repeated on January 25, 1665-6.

[2] October 31, 1663.

[3] November 4, 1663.

[4] December 12, 1664.

an important speculation in the purchase of prize goods, which got him into trouble later on.[1] The enterprise was, however, very profitable, and the promise of £500 as his share occasioned him "extraordinary inward joy."[2] In June 1666 he bought four lighters to send down to the fleet, "and I hope to get £100 by this jobb."[3] On September 26 Pepys and Penn talked about buying timber in Scotland, "for timber will be a good commodity this time of building the City." They were both in partnership with Sir William Batten and Sir Richard Ford in the hire of a privateer, the *Flying Greyhound*, which brought in several valuable prizes, but it was found necessary to offer a bribe to the Swedish Resident in connexion with the proceedings for the condemnation of one of them "wherein he puts in his concernment as for his countrymen."[4] An offer of £350 seems to have been insufficient, for when the case came into court the "Swedes' Agent" appeared on the other side; but the partners promised their counsel a coach if they succeeded, and they secured a judgment which was on the whole satisfactory to them. "It is pretty to see what money will do."[5] There was also trouble about other prizes,

[1] The story has been carefully worked out by Mr. Philip Norman; but it must be reserved for the larger *Life*.

[2] November 13, 1665.

[3] June 8, 9, and 11, 1666.

[4] January 21, 1666-7.

[5] March 21, 1666-7.

but the partners effected a composition by paying £1,400.[1] In July 1667 the privateer brought "a rich Canary prize" into Hull,[2] and Pepys declined an offer from Batten of £1,000 for his share in the profits; but these seemed likely to be less than had been expected, and he eventually parted with it for £666 13*s.* 4*d.*[3] When Batten died on October 5, Pepys was left to such satisfaction as he could obtain from his estate.

In October 1667[4] the Clerk of the Acts petitioned the King for the grant of a ship in consideration of his services in the Navy Office, and obtained the *Maybolt* galliot, which proved rather a white elephant. He was advised to send her to Newcastle for coals, which "will be a gainful trade, but yet make me great trouble";[5] and eventually he decided to sell her.

These ways of gaining money, though they appear to modern eyes unseemly for a Principal Officer of the Navy, were not illegitimate according to the ideas then prevailing; but Pepys's doubtful dealings[6] yielded a much larger profit. About these the diarist is perfectly candid; he employs no disguises, and tells himself the worst about himself with the most engaging sincerity. The age was corrupt, and the receiving

[1] April 16, 1667. [2] July 17, 1667. [3] August 14, 1667.
[4] See October 6 and 13. [5] December 31, 1667.
[6] On the reformed Pepys of a later time, see p. 226 below.

of presents for services rendered was condemned only officially and not by public opinion. Pepys's patron, Lord Sandwich, was said to have had £1,500 from the contractors for the Mole at Tangier, which Pepys thought "a very odd thing for my Lord to be a profiter by the getting of the contract made for them."[1] Offices and appointments were regularly bought and sold. In 1668 Sir John Trevor paid £8,000 for the office of Secretary of State, and Prince Rupert £3,500 for the Constableship of Windsor Castle;[2] and the austere reformer Coventry accepted money for the sale of places, although he told Pepys that he had not received more than "what his predecessors time out of mind have taken."[3] Even John Milton when Latin Secretary had accepted £3 from the Hanseatic League.[4] Pepys's clerks had their little perquisites,[5] and Pepys himself, having as an Officer of the Navy saleable commodities to dispose of, thought no shame of taking money for them as long as the King was "not wronged" thereby.

But although these extenuating circumstances

[1] December 27, 1667.

[2] S.P. to the Earl of Sandwich, September 29, 1668 (Braybrooke, iv. 197-8).

[3] June 2, 1663; *cf.* October 28, 1667.

[4] This case is quoted by Mr. Philip Norman from the MS. accounts of the League in London in 1656 in the Chancery Masters' Papers (Horne, 412). See also the same author's "Later History of the Steelyard" in *Archaeologia*, lxi. 389-426.

[5] November 11, 1664.

may be pleaded, the number and scale of the dubious transactions recorded in the *Diary* are such as to scandalise the most lenient modern critic. Pepys began in a small way with acknowledgments from masters and chirurgeons of ships whose warrants passed through his hands.[1] On April 3, 1663, he received a thank-offering from Captain Grove, for whom he had obtained a small appointment,—"a letter directed to myself from himself: I discerned money to be in it, . . . but I did not open it till I came home to my office, and there I broke it open, not looking into it till all the money was out, that I might say I saw no money in the paper if ever I should be questioned about it. There was a piece in gold and £4 in silver."

These gains were paltry, but it was not long before larger sums from more important people began to come in. On December 15, 1663, Mr. Dering promised £50 "if I can sell his deals for him to the King," and on December 19 Pepys records the result with his usual candour. "I laboured hard at Deering's business of his deals, more than I would if I did not think to get something, though I do really believe that I did what is to the King's advantage in it, and yet, God knows, the expectation of profit will have its force and make a man the more earnest." Another

[1] March 12 and 14, 1662-3.

comment on a later transaction with the same merchant brings out still more clearly the nature of the argument by which Pepys justified himself to his own conscience. He draws a sharp distinction between a bribe accepted beforehand and an unsolicited expression of gratitude offered after the service had been rendered, and refuses twenty pieces of gold "to have the contract perfected," "resolving not to be bribed to dispatch business," adding, however, "but will have it done . . . out of hand forthwith."[1] On September 30, when the money was again pressed upon him, he took it, "yet really and sincerely against my will and content." On December 16, 1663, Captain John Taylor the shipbuilder brought him £40, "the greater part of which I shall gain to myself after much care and pains out of his bill of freight;" and later on he received other sums from the same source, possibly for services in connexion with the sale of masts. On January 20, 1663-4, Pepys proposed to himself to "have a good fleece out of Creed's coat," but he only managed to get 20 pieces of gold out of him, "which I did not refuse, but wish and expected should have been more."[2]

[1] August 7, 1665. It was at the end of this month that Pepys wrote, "My late gettings have been very great, to my great content, and am likely to have yet a few more profitable jobbs in a little while."

[2] July 18, 1664.

An entry of January 25, 1663-4, contains an artless confession of corruptibility, although it is only fair to Pepys to say that he never actually did anything quite as corrupt. At a conference between the Navy Board and representatives of the East India Company he "did the King good service against the Company, . . . and yet, God forgive me! I found that I could be willing to receive a bribe if it were offered me to conceal my arguments that I found against them, in consideration that none of my fellow-Officers, whose duty it is more than mine, had ever studied the case, or at this hour do understand it, and myself alone must do it." The East India Company did not expose him to the test, but a week later[1] Sir William Warren, with whom the Navy Office had transactions in timber, "did give me a payre of gloves for my wife wrapt up in paper, which I would not open, feeling it hard." The gloves contained "forty pieces in good gold, which did so cheer my heart that I could eat no victuals almost for dinner, for joy to think how God do bless us every day more and more, and more yet I hope He will upon the increase of my duty and endeavours." On May 3, 1664, Pepys was suitably shocked at the "many rogueries" of Batten, who would do nothing without a bribe; but the day before he had himself received "twenty pieces of

[1] February 2, 1663-4.

new gold, a pleasant sight," from Mr. Bland the merchant, apparently for his services in prevailing on the Navy Office to hire one of Bland's ships. But here again the distinction in Pepys's mind between the bribe before and the present after the event enabled him to place his colleague's alleged proceedings in a different category to his own. On June 22 Lord Peterborough promised him £50 for procuring "present dispatch in his business of freight."

Up to this point Pepys's highest figure had been £50, but now he begins to reckon in hundreds and to share the prey of the larger carnivora. On July 14, 1664, the prospective victuallers of the Tangier garrison promised him £150 a year if he obtained the contract for them at 3*s.* 1½*d.* per week per man, and £300 if at 3*s.* 2*d.* He was successful in carrying the contract at the higher figure, and made sure thereby of the £300 a year, "which do overjoy me."[1] He justified the transaction to his own conscience by saying, "I have therein saved the King £5,000 per annum,"[2] although how this happened does not appear. In spite of his protestations of devotion to the King's service, the usual result followed. When the contractors were accused before the Tangier Commissioners of cheating

[1] July 16, 1664. [2] September 10, 1664.

the King, Pepys writes, "I doubt it true, . . . but will serve them what I can."[1]

Another lucrative source of profit was Mr. Gauden, the Victualler of the Navy. On October 4, 1665, he gave Pepys £60, "which is great mercy to me," but this was only a foretaste of pleasures to come. When the Clerk of the Acts on November 8 became also Surveyor-General of Victualling, his value to Gauden rose at once to a high figure, and on December 8 he received a present of £500, which put him "into great joy." He was also promised 2% of all payments made to Gauden by him in his capacity of Treasurer for Tangier.[2] On February 4, 1666-7, Pepys received another £500 from Gauden "for the service I do him in my victualling business, and £100 for my particular share of the profits of my Tangier imployment as Treasurer." The £500 appears to have been an annual payment,[3] and it led Pepys to write of his benefactor on another occasion, "He is a most noble-minded man as ever I met with, and seems to own himself much obliged to me, which I will labour to make him."[4]

Another "most usefull and thankfull man" to Pepys was Sir William Warren the timber merchant. With him on February 6, 1664-5, he "concluded a firm league," and on January 25,

[1] July 16, 1668. [2] January 9, 1665-6.
[3] June 4, 1667. [4] August 2, 1667.

1665-6, the high contracting parties were "mighty merry" in Pepys's garden in "the discourse of our owne trickes." Warren had already given him £100 on September 16, 1664, for his "pains in his two great contracts for masts," and on January 26, 1665-6, he received another £100 from him, to his "very extraordinary joy." At the same time Warren paid him £220 more, "got clearly by a late business of insurance of the Gottenburg ships," and there are also obscure references to another £200 arising out of "the business of the Tangier boates";[1] but these two last may have been legitimate transactions. On March 19, 1665-6, Pepys hopes "to get something considerably" by Warren "before the year be over," and on April 3, 1666, he "got of him £300 gift" "for my service about some ships that he hath bought, prizes." This was in connexion with the loan of £1,900 referred to above.[2] At the beginning of 1667 their friendship was at its height, and Pepys speaks of Warren as "a very wise man, and full of good counsel, and his own practices for wisdom much to be observed," "whose discourse I love";[3] but soon after Warren offended him by attaching himself to Lord Brouncker, "and so I dare not trust him as I used to do, for I will not be inward with him

[1] November 2 and December 27, 1665.

[2] P. 156. [3] January 11, 1666-7.

that is open to another."[1] The result of this estrangement was that Pepys "did manifestly plead" against Warren at the Navy Board,[2] although there was as yet no declared enmity.[3] On May 4, 1667, however, there was an open quarrel at the Navy Office, "he bringing a letter to the Board . . . part of which I said was not true and the other undecent. . . . So I writ in the margin of the letter, 'Returned as untrue,' and by consent of the Board did give it him again, and so parted." When Warren's accounts came up before the Board for examination on May 15, Pepys appeared "mighty fierce" against him, and "in every thing as much as I can his enemy."[4] For some time they were "pretty strange" to each other,[5] but both had too much to lose by a permanent alienation, and on February 17, 1667-8, a kind of reconciliation was effected.

Among the possible sources of profit to Pepys may be reckoned Thomas Povey, his predecessor in the office of Treasurer for Tangier. Pepys writes of him very contemptuously, criticising his method of keeping accounts[6] and commenting severely on his fatuous behaviour when examined on them at the Committee, where "by his many

[1] March 11, 1666-7. [2] March 16, 1666-7. [3] April 30, 1667.

[4] May 24. [5] October 14 and November 1, 1667.

[6] "Such accounts I never did see, or hope again to see in my days" (January 18, 1664-5).

words and no understanding" he did "confound himself and his business, to his disgrace, and rendering every body doubtfull of his being either a foole or knave."[1] The transaction as described in the *Diary* is not very clear, but apparently Pepys obtained from Povey a note for £117 5*s*. in respect of the "pretended freight" of a Tangier ship.[2] A "pretended" freight did not at this time necessarily mean a false freight but only a freight claimed; the doubtful nature of the proceeding is, however, indicated by the extreme fear of exposure displayed by the recipient of the money. After a prolonged period of panic, he entered the sum in his private accounts as a debt due to Povey, for "a quiet mind and to be sure of my owne is worth all."[3]

A dispenser of substantial gifts was Sir Hugh Cholmley, the engineer engaged in the construction of the Mole at Tangier. When he visited London in November 1665 to try and obtain ready money for carrying on the work, instead of depreciated Exchequer tallies, he called on the Treasurer for Tangier "and we settled all matters about his money, and he is a most satisfied man in me and do declare his resolution to give me £200 per annum."[4] He is afterwards described

[1] January 17, 1664-5. [2] December 9, 1664.
[3] January 31, 1664-5. [4] November 23, 1665.

as "a fine, worthy, well-disposed gentleman."[1] On the other hand, Lord Belasyse the Governor of Tangier, who promised Pepys "the same profits Povy was to have had,"[2] appears in the *Diary*, on Cholmley's authority, to be "as very a false villain as ever was born."[3] It may perhaps be inferred that one paid and the other did not.

Other considerable sums also came in Pepys's way. On April 10, 1665, a certain Mr. Warren, presumably a merchant, offered him £100 "to get him a protection for a ship to go out," although the scheme appears to have miscarried;[4] and soon after he was promised £50 from the same quarter for a press warrant.[5] On August 5, 1665, he discussed with Sir William Warren a scheme in connexion with the provision of a mast dock at Woolwich, "which I hope to compass and get 2 or £300 by." Lord Rutherford gave him £100 "upon clearing his business,"[6] but an unfortunate promise to Creed deprived him of half,—or, as the victim preferred to put it, "of which to my grief the rogue Creed has trepanned me out of £50."[7] He received from the Houblons £200 "for helping them out with two or three ships"[8] soon after he had been

[1] March 6, 1666-7.
[2] May 23, 1666.
[3] March 24, 1666-7.
[4] April 19, 1665.
[5] May 12, 1665.
[6] September 26, 1665.
[7] October 3, 1665.
[8] March 2, 1665-6.

engaged, with the other members of the Navy Board, in "examining abuses of our clerkes in taking money for examining of tickets";[1] and two months later he was displaying a virtuous indignation with Lord Ashley for taking bribes.[2]

Pepys was not quite as omnivorous as some of his contemporaries, and his attitude towards the offers made to him shew a certain discrimination. In 1666, Captain Cocke offered Pepys and Brouncker £500 each if his bargain for hemp went through. Pepys was "no great friend to the proposition," perhaps because he was afraid of Coventry and distrusted Brouncker;[3] and the proposal was "disliked by the King, and so is quite off."[4] On February 5, 1666-7, two flag-makers, "with mighty earnestness," pressed him to accept a box "wherein I could not guess there was less than £100 in gold," but "not thinking them safe men to receive such a gratuity from, nor knowing any considerable courtesy that ever I did do them," he refused it. Another refusal of money is more creditable, and indicates the limits which Pepys placed upon his own corruption. An anchorsmith had given him 50 pieces of gold "to speake for him to Sir W. Coventry for his being smith at Deptford." "After I had got it

[1] January 24, 1665-6. [2] May 20, 1666.

[3] See May 25, June 27, and November 8, 1666.

[4] July 27, 1666.

granted to him, he finds himself not fit to go on with it, so lets it fall" and "has no benefit of my motion. I therefore in honour and conscience took him home the money," though "much to my grief."[1] It is true that the next day he went down to Deptford to try and get it back, but apparently without success. On February 21, 1667-8, Thomas Beckford the slopseller offered "a little purse with gold in it," and after several refusals, "telling him that it was not an age to take presents in," Pepys accepted it, although he confesses to some fear of the Commissioners of Public Accounts. On looking over his memorandum books, however, "which are now of great use to me, and do fully reward me for all my care in keeping them,"[2] he was convinced that he could put up some sort of defence for the gifts which he had received. His justification would probably have been that indicated in his exposition of the ethics of bribery to William Hewer, when he was summoned before the Commissioners for receiving a present of £30 from Mr. Mason the timber merchant,—that there was no harm in it, "he having done them several lawful kindnesses and never demanded anything."[3] Sir William Warren also was a tower of strength, for he denied to the House of Commons that he had ever made

[1] May 8, 1666. [2] February 25, 1667-8.
[3] August 19, 1668.

any presents to the Officers of the Navy, "though he knows that he is forsworn as to what relates to me."[1] Warren probably agreed with Drake's sailors, who "had rather venture their souls into the hands of a merciful God by perjury, than their fortunes . . . in the hands of unmerciful men."

The General Instructions to the Navy forbade any officer to trade in any commodities used in the navy, but this prohibition was widely ignored. On December 4, 1669, the Commissioners of Public Accounts reported that "great sums, amounting to £79,064. 12*s.* 2¼*d.*," have been paid by the Treasurer of the Navy "to several officers of the navy for commodities so used and served in," and among these Pepys appears as the recipient of £757. 17*s.* 5¾*d.* for flags and cork.[2] In the *Diary* there are several references to the trade in flags, from which the diarist expected "considerable profit."[3] On January 28, 1664-5, he thanks God that he has obtained a clear £50 by it, "and earned it with dear pains and care and issuing of my owne money, and saved the King near £100 in it." He was at some trouble to disguise his transactions, for finding his name in a list of payments for flags intended for presentation to Parliament, it vexed him "mightily."

[1] February 25, 1667-8.

[2] Historical MSS. Commission, *Eighth Report*, Part i. p. 133.

[3] November 27, 1664.

"At last I concluded of scraping out my name and putting in Mr. Tooker's, which eased me; though the price was such as I should have had glory by."[1]

In addition to presents of money, Pepys received many gifts in kind, and especially plate. The first present of value came from Sir William Warren the timber merchant on February 10, 1662-3,—"a fair state dish of silver and cup, with my arms ready cut upon them, worth I believe about £18; which is a very noble present and the best I ever had yet." On November 7, 1663, Captain Taylor brought him "a little small state dish, he expecting that I should get him some allowance for demorage of his ship *William* kept long at Tangier, which I shall and may justly do" On February 11, 1663-4, Mr. Falconer, the clerk of the ropeyard at Woolwich, gave Mrs. Pepys "a silver state-cup and cover" valued at £5. 16*s*., which her husband afterwards exchanged for "a fair tankard." On July 21, 1664, Mr. Gauden the victualler sent him "a pair of the noblest flaggons that ever I saw all the days of my life," "to oblige me to him in the business of the Tangier victualling." The recipient at first regarded this as a temptation, but Gauden assured him that it was a recognition of past kindnesses and not a bribe for the future,

[1] September 24, 1666.

"which I was glad to hear, and, with my heart in good rest and great joy, parted."[1] On November 8, 1664, Mr. Lever the purser-general sent Mrs. Pepys "a pair of silver candlesticks, very pretty ones"; and on March 16, 1664-5, Mr. Harris the sailmaker offered Pepys "a noble present of two large silver candlesticks, and snuffers, and a slice to keep them upon, which indeed is very handsome." This was followed on March 21 by "a couple of state cups, very large," from John Burrowes the slopseller, and on April 17 by a "neat silver watch" from "one Briggs, a scrivener and sollicitor." On February 2, 1665-6, Mr. Waith the paymaster tried to give Pepys silver chafing-dishes, "but I would not accept of that, . . . not knowing any courtesy I have yet done him to deserve it." In December 1666 Captain Cocke, who dealt in hemp, invited Pepys to order plate to the value of £100,[2] and Mr. Foundes presented "a fair pair of candlesticks and half a dozen of plates, . . . which cost him full £50, and is a very good present."[3] On January 1, 1668-9, Beckford the slopseller produced "a noble silver warming-pan" as a New Year's gift; and on January 28, Mr. Sheres, in the full flood of gratitude for a payment of £100 for his service at Tangier, had a silver candlestick

[1] September 16, 1664. [2] December 13, 1666.

[3] December 14, 1666.

made "after a form he remembers to have seen in Spain, for keeping the light from one's eyes," "but I do intend to force him to make me pay for it."

Among other proffered gifts were: a barrel of sturgeon; "a very noble parti-coloured Indian gowne for my wife,"[1] which Pepys returned to the donor with a note to say that he expected at least £50; "an excellent mastiff, his name Towser"; "a case of very pretty knives with agate shafts"; "a very fine African mat to lay upon the ground under a bed of state"; "a Japan cane with a silver head"; and "a ring with a Woolwich stone, now much in request." On December 9, 1663, Mrs. Russell the tallow-seller gave Mrs. Pepys "a very fine St. George in alabaster, which will set out my wife's closett mightily." This produced a characteristic reflection in the *Diary* for the following day:—

"Up, pretty well, the weather being become pretty warm again, and to the office, where we sat all the morning, and I confess having received so lately a token from Mrs. Russell, I did find myself concerned for our not buying some tallow of her, (which she bought on purpose yesterday most unadvisedly to her great losse upon confidence of putting it off to us). So hard it is for a man not to be warped against his duty and master's interest that receives any bribe, or present though not as a bribe, from any body else. But she must be contented and I, to do her a good turn when I can without wrong to the King's service."

[1] November 21, 1663.

On May 3, 1664, Pepys listened eagerly to a whole series of complaints against Sir William Batten which included his taking of " bribes . . . of cabinetts and other things." On May 18 this austere critic of his colleague's alleged frailties cheerfully accepted " a pretty cabinet sent me by Mr. Shales, which I give my wife, the first of that sort of goods I ever had yet, and very conveniently it comes for her closett."

CHAPTER XVI

Some Personal Characteristics

By his early training Pepys was a Puritan. When the Civil War broke out he was a boy of nine at school in the Puritan eastern counties; while it was being fought he was being educated in Parliamentarian London; and when the King was executed he was only just sixteen,—so his later youth and early manhood belonged to the Commonwealth and the Protectorate. On November 1, 1660, his old school-fellow Mr. Christmas, now "a deadly drinker" and "grown exceeding fat," dined with him and indulged in most inconvenient reminiscences. "He did remember that I was a great Roundhead when I was a boy, and I was much afraid that he would have remembered the words that I said the day the King was beheaded, that were I to preach upon him my text should be—'The memory of the wicked shall rot.'" Thus there are to be found in the man of the *Diary* traces of the Roundhead boy. His reflections on the exhumation of Cromwell's remains went as far as any Restoration writer could be expected to go,—" which (methinks) do trouble me that a man of so great courage as he was should have that dishonour, though otherwise he might deserve it enough," [1]—but, taken by itself, admiration of the Protector would not prove Pepys's Puritanism, for it was shared by many of his contemporaries who were not Puritans. On February 8, 1666-7, Pepys and three of his colleagues on the Navy Board, over " an exceedingly good dinner," talked much of Cromwell, " all saying he was a brave fellow, and did owe his crowne he got to himself as much as any man that ever got one." On July 12, 1667, Pepys writes, " It is strange how . . . every body do now-a-days reflect upon Oliver and commend him, what brave things he did, and made all the neighbour princes fear him " ; and on January 31, 1667-8, he speaks highly of the old Cromwellians who, with general approval, had found their way into the Commission of Public Accounts. But his fundamental Puritanism emerges in other entries in the *Diary* which distinguish him sharply from the ordinary Cavalier. His devout appeals to God Almighty, his passionate outpourings of grief over and repentance for his sins, are real and not hypocritical, for they were intended

[1] December 4, 1660.

for his eye alone. Repentance for sin was not a monopoly of Puritanism, but we discern in these an inheritance from the days when religious emotion would naturally express itself in Puritan forms and phrases. His Puritan instincts also appear in unexpected places. In 1661 a half-hearted attempt to keep Lent soon broke down, for when at the dinner of March 26, 1661, to celebrate the anniversary of his operation for the stone, some of his guests ate no flesh, Pepys "had a great deal of good flesh, which made their mouths water." And the next year, when Batten and Penn were "unwilling to eat flesh," Pepys and Captain Cocke "had a breast of veal roasted."[1] It was some time before he ceased to be a Sabbatarian, and after "composing some ayres" on a Sunday, he writes, "God forgive me!"[2] Like Evelyn at a later time,[3] he was shocked to see the Court playing cards on Sunday, "having not believed it."[4] It vexes him to hear his rector advocating confession,[5] and he finds the surplice somewhat ridiculous;[6] while the Roman service in the Duke of York's Chapel is "but silly devotion, God knows."[7] He disliked his wife's

[1] February 17, 1661-2. [2] February 9, 1661-2.

[3] Evelyn's *Diary*, February 9, 1684-5.

[4] February 17, 1666-7. [5] August 24, 1662.

[6] October 26, 1662.

[7] April 15, 1668; *cf.* December 24, 1667.

false hair although it was fashionable,[1] and he loathed Mrs. Pearse because she painted.[2] On November 11, 1661, he combines two Puritan prejudices in a single entry reflecting upon the folly of gaming and the impropriety of allowing young girls to dance before an audience.

Concerning the weak points in his own character Pepys displays a most engaging candour. He recognises the fact that he was of a timid and nervous disposition. In the presence of the imposing Mrs. Clerke "and the number of fine ladies that were with her" he was "much out of countenance," and could hardly carry himself "like a man among them";[3] and meeting the Duke of York he was fearful that he might not go far enough with his hat off.[4] He observes that he is in his nature "mighty unready to answer no to anything,"[5] thus falling under Coventry's censure, who held "that a man that cannot sit still in his chamber . . . and he that cannot say no . . . is not fit for business."[6] He knows how difficult it is for him to resist any kind of pleasure. "But, Lord!" he writes, on May 18, 1665, "to see how fraile a man I am, subject to my vanities, that can hardly forbear, though pressed with

[1] March 24, 1661-2; March 13, 1664-5.

[2] September 16, 1667; *cf.* September 28 and October 26.

[3] May 2, 1662.

[4] July 27, 1663.

[5] January 5, 1667-8.

[6] August 8, 1662.

never so much business, my pursuing of pleasure"; although later on he attempts a justification :—

> "The truth is, I do indulge myself a little the more in pleasure, knowing that this is the proper age of my life to do it; and out of my observation that most men that do thrive in the world do forget to take pleasure during the time that they are getting their estate, but reserve that till they have got one, and then it is too late for them to enjoy it with any pleasure."[1]

He observes "something of ill-nature" in himself,[2] although good humour, "when all is done," is "the greatest felicity of all."[3] He finds his spirit "very poor and mean as to the bearing with trouble."[4] On September 9, 1668, there were "high words" at the Treasury, "and I all that night so vexed that I did not sleep almost all night, which shews how unfit I am for trouble: so, after a little supper, vexed, and spending a little time melancholy in making a base to the Lark's Song, I to bed."

The *Diary* makes no secret of the fact that physically Pepys was a coward. On October 23, 1660, one of Mr. Shepley's pistols "flew off, and it pleased God that, the mouth of the gun being downwards, it did us no hurt, but I think I never was in more danger in my life, which put me into a great fright." When he was hiding from bailiffs sent to arrest him in connexion with the

[1] March 10, 1665-6. [2] December 20, 1666.
[3] June 21, 1668. [4] February 3, 1667-8.

troublesome case of Field, "a little dirty boy" standing before the Merchants' Gate "under which we pass to go into our garden" "did make me quake and sweat to think he might be a Trepan."[1] "It is hard to believe with what fear I did walk," he writes, in connexion with another writ issued against him over the same affair, "and how I did doubt at every man I saw, and do start at the hearing of one man cough behind my neck."[2] When walking from Woolwich to Greenwich on May 11, 1663, Pepys was "set upon by a great dogg, who got hold of my garters, and might have done me hurt; but, Lord! to see in what a maze I was, that having a sword about me I never thought of it or had the heart to use it, but might for want of that courage have been worried."

Although Pepys found in himself "little desire of fighting,"[3] an insult to his wife roused him to administer "a good cuff or two on the chops" to the offender, but the entry continues characteristically, "seeing him not oppose me, I did give him another; at last found him drunk, of which I was glad, and so left him."[4] On July 11, 1664, a noise at night caused him to fall "into a most mighty sweat" for fear of burglars, knowing he had much money in the house; but he was

[1] February 23, 1662-3. [2] December 11, 1663.
[3] May 28, 1667. [4] October 20, 1663.

relieved to discover that "it was only the dogg wants a lodging." On November 29, 1667, a similar alarm turned out to be the sweep. A chimney on fire put him "into much fear and trouble"[1] and news of a mutiny of seamen "into a great fright."[2] Ghost stories after supper made him "almost afeard to lie alone," but, he adds, "for shame I could not help it."[3]

With this physical cowardice there was associated a very high degree of moral courage. When his friend and patron Lord Sandwich fell into evil courses and began to imperil his reputation in the world, Pepys risked the loss of his friendship and support, and wrote him a dignified letter of remonstrance[4] which accomplished its purpose, although it occasioned a coolness between them which lasted for some time. On July 27, 1665, owing to the increase of the Plague in London, the Navy Board resolved to sit at Deptford, but Pepys thought the decision premature. He made his will, "so that I shall be in much better state of soul, I hope, if it should please the Lord to call me away this sickly time,"[5] and remained in London until orders came from the King for the removal of the Navy Office to Greenwich. On September 4 he wrote to Lady Carteret from

[1] January 24, 1666-7. [2] January 23, 1666-7.
[3] March 23, 1668-9. [4] See November 18, 1663.
[5] August 13, 1665.

Woolwich giving an account of his experiences which incidentally reveals a remarkable courage and tenacity :—

"The absence of the Court and emptiness of the City takes away all occasion of news, save only such melancholy stories as would rather sadden than find your Ladyship any divertisement in the hearing ; I having stayed in the City till above 7400 died in one week, and of them above 6000 of the Plague, and little noise heard day or night but tolling of bells ; till I could walk Lumber-street [1] and not meet twenty persons from one end to the other, and not 50 upon the Exchange ; till whole families, 10 and 12 together, have been swept away ; till my very physician, Dr. Burnet, who undertook to secure me against any infection, having survived the month of his own house being shut up, died himself of the Plague ; till the nights, though much lengthened, are grown too short to conceal the burials of those that died the day before, people being thereby constrained to borrow daylight for that service ; lastly, till I could find neither meat nor drink safe, the butcheries being every where visited, my brewer's house shut up, and my baker, with his whole family, dead of the Plague." [2]

With this should be compared another letter written by Pepys about this time, addressed to Coventry, which contains a passage of extraordinary dignity and resolution,—" The sickness in general thickens round us, and particularly upon our neighbourhood. You, Sir, took your turn of the sword ; I must not therefore grudge to take mine of the pestilence." [3]

Pepys could also be courageous where his

[1] Lombard Street. [2] Braybrooke, iv. 192.

[3] Quoted in Wheatley's edition, vol. i. p. xxviii.

personal loyalties were involved. On January 29, 1665-6, he was appearing before the Council at a time when his patron was under a cloud, and "my Lord Sandwich come in in the middle of the business, and, poor man, very melancholy, methought, . . . and sat at the lower end, just as he come, no roome being made for him, only I did give him my stoole and another was reached me." Pepys did not like his colleague Lord Brouncker, but he walked with him in Westminster Hall when he was under the displeasure of Parliament, thinking him unjustly accused.[1] When his friend Sir William Coventry was committed to the Tower, he hastened thither "to give him comfort,"[2] and he visited him nine times during the sixteen days of his imprisonment. Finally, on April 5, 1669, when the Officers of the Navy were dreading dismissal, Pepys writes, "I have not a mind indeed at this time to be put out of my office if I can make any shift that is honourable to keep it; but I will not do it by deserting the Duke of York."

To those about him, and especially to old friends, Pepys shewed steady kindness. His relations with his "gang of clerks" were friendly and familiar. They often came to dine with him, and he was "mightily pleased" with their society "and very good discourse and company they give

[1] February 18, 1667-8. [2] March 4, 1668-9.

me";[1] nor did he disdain upon occasion to treat to wine the clerks of the Exchequer among whom he had formerly served.[2] When his cousin Anthony Joyce drowned himself, Samuel took an immense amount of trouble to save the estate for his widow, and sat with her awhile comforting her, "though I can find she can, as all other women, cry, and yet talk of other things all in a breath."[3] He pitied Christopher Pett's widow and pleaded her cause with the Duke of York. His sympathies also covered a wider field. It "grieved" him "to the heart" to hear the wailings of the wives of the pressed men sent off from the Tower on July 1, 1666, and their "natural expression of passion" as they "wept over every vessel that went off, . . . looking after the ship as far as ever they could by moone-light." There is other evidence of his sympathy with seamen and their wives, and on one occasion he went so far as to bestow half-a-crown on a starving mariner who "lay in our yard a-dying."[4]

There is no doubt that the diarist was very fond of children and young people. On April 11, 1661, on his way from Dartford to London, he "met two little schoolboys going with pitchers of ale to their schoolmaster"; he appropriated some

[1] December 5, 1667.

[2] See May 19, 1665, and February 20, 1666-7.

[3] January 22, 1667-8. [4] March 12, 1666-7.

of the ale and gave the bearer twopence. Soon after, he came upon "two little girls keeping cows" and a similar transaction took place, after he had induced the prettier of the two to kneel down and ask his blessing. On a Sunday expedition to Islington, on May 3, 1668, he gave "two pretty fat boys each of them a cake." On May 3, 1662, he took Sir Thomas Crew's children to the Tower and shewed them the lions; and on June 16 he organised a children's party to Greenwich to see the King's yacht, the House, and the Park. On June 10, 1661, when "some persons of condition" came in to dine with Lady Sandwich, "the children and I rose and dined with ourselves, all the children and I, and were very merry and they mighty fond of me"; and when on August 19, 1661, they were not allowed to come and see him, he confessed that it a little troubled him to lose their company. As he admitted to himself later on, he loved other people's children;[1] and when Bab and Betty Pepys, Roger Pepys's daughters, came on February 18, 1668-9, to stay for a fortnight, although he recognised that he was "not company light enough to be always merry with them," and that his papers were likely to continue "in mighty disorder" while their visit lasted, he gave them a royal time. Bedlam was selected as an appropriate first objective, but

[1] May 12, 1669.

they were taken to four plays, accompanied Mrs. Pepys on her shopping expeditions, saw Westminster Abbey (including the tombs), and were shewn how glass was made. There was a supper at Hercules' Pillars after the play, a little dance at Mrs. Batelier's, and "a pretty little treat" at William Hewer's, and the visit ended with "a noble dinner," followed in the evening by a dance in the office which lasted until 2 in the morning.

Pepys did not like animals out of their place,[1] but it made him "mad" to see a dog ill-treated,[2] and the death of "poor Fancy" at Brampton "troubles me, as being one of my oldest acquaintances and servants."[3] He also mourned over the death of his canary.[4]

The instinct for neatness which made the Clerk of the Acts so methodical in the office comes out quite as strongly in his private life. "Now my delight is in the neatness of everything," he writes on August 10, 1663, "and so cannot be pleased with anything unless it be very neat, which is a strange folly." The disorder occasioned by the presence of workmen in the house makes him "a little pettish."[5] He takes "much pains in sorting and folding of papers,"[6]—a business "which though I can hardly bring myself to do,

[1] November 6, 1660. [2] May 18, 1668.
[3] September 16, 1668. [4] January 11, 1664-5.
[5] July 23, 1662. [6] March 12, 1661-2.

yet do please me much when it is done."[1] "This Christmas," he writes in 1664, "I judged it fit to look over all my papers and books, and to tear all that I found either boyish or not to be worth keeping or fit to be seen, if it should please God to take me away suddenly"; but he entered up in the *Diary* some interesting notes which escaped destruction.[2]

As Mr. George Whale, the President of the Pepys Club, has pointed out, Pepys was what psychologists call a "visualiser": he enjoyed spectacles of all kinds, and he was extraordinarily observant of details. For instance, on May 22, 1663, some one gave him "a fine blackbird," for which 20*s.* had been offered, "he do so whistle." The bird whistled to such effect that it woke Pepys between 4 and 5 in the morning, and he at once observed that it rendered "the beginning of many tunes very well, but there leaves them and goes no further." Again, on July 27, 1665, when he kissed the Duchess of York's hand for the first time, he noticed at once that "it was a most fine white and fat hand." This power of observation is brought into play in wicked little thumb-nail sketches of persons, of which the *Diary* contains a good many. We are introduced to Mrs. Blackborne, "a very high dame and a costly

[1] October 1, 1661. [2] See December 31, 1664.

one" ;[1] to Major Waters, "a deaf and most amorous melancholy gentleman who is under a despayr in love, . . . which makes him bad company though a most good-natured man" ;[2] to Mrs. Goldsborough, with her "devilish tongue" ;[3] to the wife of the King's Falconer, who was "an ugly pusse, but brought him money" ;[4] and to old Delkes the waterman, "that carries pins always in his mouth."[5] The gallery also includes "my aunt James, a poor, religious, well-meaning, good soul, talking of nothing but God Almighty";[6] Mr. Case the minister, "a dull fellow in his talk and all in the Presbyterian manner,—a great deal of noise and a kind of religious tone, but very dull" ;[7] and Lady Paulina Mountagu, who made "a very good end," being "mighty religious in her life-time, and hath left many good notes of sermons and religion wrote with her own hand which nobody ever knew of, . . . but she was always a peevish lady."[8]

There are not a few shrewd sayings embedded in the *Diary*, the fruit of observation and experience. "By how much greater the Council and the number of councillors is, the more confused the issue is of their counsels,"[9] reminds us

[1] October 18, 1660.
[2] January 12, 1660-1.
[3] October 18, 1661.
[4] August 6, 1663.
[5] August 11, 1665.
[6] May 30, 1663.
[7] May 8, 1668.
[8] April 14, 1669.
[9] January 2, 1667-8.

of Bacon on a kindred subject.[1] With the remark in the *Diary* upon the debauchery of princes as "the effect of idleness, and having nothing else to employ their great spirits upon,"[2] may be compared a sentence from a private letter of his about feminine influence at Court, "that ladies lie longest in bed, and govern all when they are up."[3] The Russian Ambassador's comely attendants, "in their habits and fur caps very handsome," made a fine show in the City, "but, Lord! to see the absurd nature of Englishmen, that cannot forbear laughing and jeering at every thing that looks strange."[4] On revisiting the scenes of his youth, Pepys exclaims, "Lord! how in every point I find myself to overvalue things when a child";[5] and he reflects wisely and well upon death.[6] We also find him recording the noteworthy sayings of others:—the remark of Mr. Gray, "a very worthy and studious gentleman in the business of trade," "how it is not the greatest wits but the steady man that is a good merchant";[7] Sir William Warren's variation of *in nocte consilium*, "not to do anything suddenly, but consult my pillow";[8] and the witty saying of the priest

[1] Essay, *Of Counsel.*
[2] November 3, 1662.
[3] S.P. to Lady Sandwich, February 8, 1666-7 (printed in Smith, i. 115-117).
[4] November 27, 1662.
[5] April 25, 1664.
[6] October 19, 1663.
[7] October 18, 1664.
[8] May 19, 1665.

to the discontented Spanish generals, "that the three great trades of the world are, the lawyers who govern the world, the churchmen who enjoy the world, and a sort of fools whom they call souldiers, who make it their work to defend the world."[1]

With all his seriousness and shrewdness, Pepys had a boyish capacity for happiness. When some one gave him a watch, he wrote on May 13, 1665, "But, Lord! to see how much of my old folly and childishnesse hangs upon me still, that I cannot forbear carrying my watch in my hand in the coach all this afternoon, and seeing what o'clock it is one hundred times." And his enjoyment of life persisted, even under the sinister shadow of the Plague. "By and by to dinner about 3 o'clock," he writes on September 24, 1665, "and then I in the cabbin to writing down my journall for these last seven days to my great content, it having pleased God that in this sad time of the Plague every thing else has conspired to my happiness and pleasure more for these last three months than in all my life before in so little time. God long preserve it and make me thankfull for it!" On May 15, 1668, he even contrived to be "very merry" at Sir Thomas Teddiman's funeral.

[1] December 20, 1668.

CHAPTER XVII

Miscellanea

PEPYS has been called a "gossip," but a gossip talks to an audience and he had no audience but himself. He has also been called "credulous," but he writes down everything he hears, not because he believes it but because it would be interesting to see whether any of it afterwards turned out to be true. Thus the *Diary* contains a vast number of references to current events, and, when checked from other sources, is an important authority for the history of the Plague, the Fire, and the Dutch attack on the Medway. It also re-creates for us the social and political atmosphere of the reign of Charles II, thus achieving something at which its author never aimed. This is not the place to discuss Pepys as an historical authority, or to quote his gloomy forecasts or his biting criticisms of the King and Court, but he makes a number of interesting observations upon miscellaneous topics which are not inappropriate to the present volume.

On the political side, we find Pepys on May 4, 1663, making an inspired guess in advance of the rumour of ten days later, that Monmouth was to be made heir to the crown. On June 24, in discourse with Coventry, he also refers to a point the importance of which it has been reserved for modern historians to accentuate,—the depreciation inflicted on the Cavaliers by exile or exclusion from politics. He compares them to the Papists who, "though otherwise fine persons, yet being by law kept for these fourscore years out of employment," are now "wholly uncapable of business." He philosophises upon the nature of assemblies, calling the House of Commons "a beast not to be understood, it being impossible to know beforehand the success almost of any small plain thing, there being so many to think and speak to any business, and they of so uncertain minds and interests and passions."[1] The final entry for the year 1666, with its characteristic anti-climax, may also be quoted here:

> "A sad, vicious, negligent Court, and all sober men there fearful of the ruin of the whole kingdom this next year; from which good God deliver us! One thing I reckon remarkable in my owne condition is, that I am come to abound in good plate, so as at all entertainments to be served wholly with silver plates, having two dozen and a half."

[1] December 19, 1666.

There are a good many references in the *Diary* to the manners and customs of the time :—for instance, to the ceremony of beating the parish bounds on Holy Thursday, followed by a dinner at the Three Tuns Tavern with the rector in the chair ;[1] to the milkmaids' procession on May Day " with their garlands upon their pails, dancing with a fiddler before them " ;[2] to the celebrations proper to Twelfth Night and Valentine's Day and to the practice of exhibiting the effigy of a Welshman on St. David's Day. On December 28, 1668, a day which, owing to the intervention of a Saturday and Sunday, seems to have done duty as Boxing Day, Pepys was " called up by drums and trumpets, these things and boxes having cost me much money this Christmas already, and will do more." On May 10, 1669, Mrs. Pepys and her maid rose at 3 and went abroad in the coach to gather May-dew ; and on May 29 there were fireworks for the King's birthday. In this connexion it is possible to appreciate the sly humour of the diarist's remark when the King was caught in the wet upon the River,—" Methought it lessened my esteem of a king, that he should not be able to command the rain."[3] On June 12, 1663, he notes that masks were again becoming the fashion for ladies, as in Queen Elizabeth's time ; and on December 12, 1667, the appearance

[1] May 16, 1667. [2] May 1, 1667. [3] July 19, 1662.

of a French lady in the pit of the theatre " with a tunique just like one of ours, only a handkercher about her neck," struck him as not at all decent. On December 1, 1662, he saw for the first time " people sliding with their skeates " in the Park, and thought it " a very pretty art."

On November 25, 1662, Pepys hears great talk of the end of the world, " and that next Tuesday is to be the day; against which, whenever it shall be, good God fit us all ! " On August 22, 1663, he had his fortune told by a gipsy, who bade him " beware of a John and a Thomas, for they did seek to do me hurt, and that somebody should be with me this day se'nnight to borrow money of me, but I should lend him none." On the day named he was " mightily displeased " with his brother Tom for trying to borrow £20 of him, and he acted as the gipsy had foretold.[1]

We also learn from the *Diary* that the use of pumice stone is a " very easy, speedy, and cleanly " method of shaving;[2] that Lord Rutherford, " being a Scott," is " resolved to scrape every penny that he can get by any way ";[3] that Mr. Newburne " is dead of eating cowcumbers ";[4] that Aunt Wight thinks a copper kettle unwholesome;[5]

[1] August 29, 1663; and *cf.* September 3.

[2] May 25, 1662; *cf.* also May 31.

[3] April 13, 1663. [4] August 22, 1663.

[5] February 14, 1663-4.

and that Mrs. Turner wears false teeth "set in with wire."[1] On June 5, 1667, Pepys tells a story of a justice of the peace in Lincolnshire who was "laid by the heels" by the Council "for saying that a man and his wife are but one person, and so ought to pay but 12*d.* for both to the Poll Bill, by which others were led to do the like."[2] On January 1, 1667-8, he visits a gaming-house, and enters in the *Diary* a remarkable description of the "prophane, mad entertainment they give themselves" there.

On January 30, 1663-4, Pepys and his legal adviser "made perfect and signed and sealed" one of his numerous last Wills and Testaments, "which is so to my mind, and I hope to the liking of God Almighty, that I take great joy in myself that it is done."

[1] October 10, 1664.

[2] *Cf.* Fuller's account of the position of the recusants under the Act of 1581. They were liable to a fine of £20 a month, "paid severally by every recusant for himself and as much for his wife, which though one flesh in divinity are two persons in law" (*Church History*, iii. 20).

CHAPTER XVIII

The End of the Diary

FROM the careful record of all his symptoms which Pepys kept in the *Diary*, we know that his eyes first troubled him as early as February 1662-3,[1] and by the beginning of the following year [2] they were giving him actual pain, "which I impute to sitting up late writing and reading by candle-light." The writing of shorthand, in particular, made them "ake ready to drop out." [3] On October 5, 1664, he consulted Cocker the arithmetician about "some glasse or other to helpe my eyes by candle-light," and perhaps this accounts for the fact that the complaints do not become frequent until the winter of 1666, when there was snow on the ground all day to dazzle him and long hours of working by candle-light at night. On December 24, on the advice of Lord Brouncker, he bought a pair of green spectacles, but from

[1] February 19, 1662-3. [2] January 19, 1663-4.

[3] June 8, 1664.

these he can have obtained but little benefit, for on January 18 following he speaks of "writing till my eyes were almost blind therewith."

From this time onward the complaints are constant. In August 1667 Pepys writes that his eyes "every day grow worse and worse by over-using them," and will not suffer him to do anything by candle-light.[1] On September 1 he has to get his wife to read to him, and on the 22nd he is "fain to get the boy to come and write" for him. On October 18 he buys "two new pair of spectacles" with "very young sights,"—*i.e.*, with lenses of low power, the green ones having been presumably plain,—but the experiment was a failure. The last entry for the month of April 1668 refers to "some trouble for my friends . . . and more for my eyes, which are daily worse and worse, that I dare not write or read almost any thing." By June they were "now constantly so bad that I must take present advice or be blind";[2] and he therefore consulted Dr. Turberville the oculist, who prescribed pills, bleeding, and some drops for his eyes. This rather drastic treatment does not appear to have done the patient much good, for on July 29 he writes that his eyes have been for these four days his trouble, and his heart "mighty sad." Two days later he is "mighty hot upon trying the late printed experiment of

[1] August 19 and 20, 1667. [2] June 20, 1668.

paper tubes," and on August 21 he buys a reading-glass. On April 25, 1669, he obtained from Lead the vizard-maker a "vizard with a tube fastened within both eyes; which, with the help which he prompts me to of a glass in the tube, do content me mightily." From this alarming apparatus he expected relief, but there was no real improvement. On May 8 Pepys changed his place at the office "after above eight years" because he was not now able to bear the light of the windows in his eyes; and on May 12 at the play "the trouble of my eyes with the light of the candles did almost kill me."

Sir D'Arcy Power, who has investigated the problem of Pepys's eyesight,[1] has come to the conclusion that he was suffering from "hypermetropia with some degree of astigmatism," causing "eyestrain and undue sensitiveness of his retinae." The glasses supplied by Cocker and Lead were probably sufficient to correct the hypermetropia, but, since astigmatism was not recognised until the beginning of the 19th century, his own age could do little for Pepys, and although there was no danger of the blindness which he dreaded so much, the eyestrain continued.

It is to this trouble with his eyes that we owe the irreparable loss involved in the discontinuance

[1] In a paper entitled "Why Samuel Pepys discontinued his Diary" (Pepys Club *Occasional Papers*, 1903-14, p. 64).

of Pepys's *Diary*. On May 16, 1669, he drew up a petition to the Duke of York asking for leave of absence from the Navy Office on account of the state of his eyesight, with a view to travelling abroad. This was presented in person three days later to the Duke, who "discoursed about my eyes and pitied me," and on May 24 his leave to depart was confirmed by the King.

The final entry for May 31, 1669, "Thence to the World's End, a drinking-house by the Park; and there merry, and so home late," is followed by a memorandum of the same date but conceived in a different spirit:—

> "And thus ends all that I doubt I shall ever be able to do with my own eyes in the keeping of my Journal, I being not able to do it any longer, having done now so long as to undo my eyes almost every time that I take a pen in my hand, and therefore, whatever comes of it, I must forbear: and therefore resolve from this time forward to have it kept by my people in longhand, and must therefore be contented to set down no more than is fit for them and all the world to know; or, if there be any thing, which cannot be much now my amours to Deb are past and my eyes hindering me in almost all other pleasures, I must endeavour to keep a margin in my book open, to add here and there a note in shorthand with my own hand.
>
> And so I betake myself to that course, which is almost as much as to see myself go into my grave; for which, and all the discomforts that will accompany my being blind, the good God prepare me!" S. P.

Thus on a note of the purest pathos the immortal *Diary* ends.

CHAPTER XIX

The Diary as Literature

"It is generally supposed," writes Robert Louis Stevenson, "that as a writer Pepys must rank at the bottom of the scale of merit";[1] and although he argues that this is to place the *Diary* too low, he convicts the author of it by implication of writing in a style that is ungrammatical, inelegant, and full of mistakes. A later writer[2] arrives at a sounder conclusion when he assigns distinction to the *Diary*, due partly to "the absolute sincerity and transparent truth of the narrative"[3] and partly to "the vitality of the man and his intense interest in the pageant of life"; and then points out that the supreme merit of his style lies in the fact that it is suitable to the character of what the

[1] *Familiar Studies of Men and Books*, p. 313.

[2] In the *Cambridge History of English Literature*, viii. 258.

[3] Mr. Russell Lowell at the unveiling on March 18, 1884, of the monument erected in St. Olave's Church to the memory of Pepys, remarked that the sincerity of the author of the *Diary* with himself "argued a certain greatness of character" (Wheatley's edition, vol. i. p. 58).

diarist had to relate. As the author is his only reader, he never writes for effect. He does not emit correct sentiments with one eye on the public, but delivers himself of his real mind. The result is that he writes simply and without effort, in words that exactly express his thoughts about people and things. Any attempt at elegance would have destroyed the characteristic charm of the *Diary*, because it would have disfigured with insincerity a literary work which is absolutely sincere. It is scarcely too much to say that we have here the perfection of style, because it is so entirely appropriate to the purpose for which it is used.

How profoundly the character of style can be modified by the introduction of a public can be seen in the other writings of Pepys himself. The narrative of his voyage to Tangier in 1683, his journal in Spain, and his account of the voyage home,[1] are dull and pedestrian records of daily happenings, only rarely illuminated by the penetrating observations and criticisms which the *Diary* so freely dispenses.

"1683. August 12. Sunday.—Morning, prayers and sermon by Dr. Ken; prayers in the afternoon. Evening, came the Cleveland yacht with the money for Tangier. Sir J. Berry sailed, and we came to anchor again. Mr. Bankes went to Windsor."

[1] Printed in the *Life, Journals, and Correspondence* edited by the Reverend John Smith (1841).

How insipid is this entry in the Tangier Journal after the lively descriptions of earlier Sundays which are to be found in the *Diary*; and the rest is all of a piece with it, for Pepys is playing up to his reputation as a serious naval administrator. The author is very observant and makes interesting remarks about discipline and navigation. He finds "Spanish onions mighty good"; he is "uneasy with the chinchees or musquittoes"; he suffers from "a mighty cold" that made him dumb; he hears "a silly sermon"; and he writes "a merry, roguish, but yet mysterious" letter,—but the life and sparkle have gone, and the greater part of the Tangier Journal might have been written by any dull official.

If the style of this Journal has little in common with that of the *Diary*, still less has Pepys's official correspondence preserved in the *Admiralty Letters*.[1] This is always perfectly clear and business-like, but ponderous and processional. The sentences are long and labyrinthine, in which "the thread of thought winds deviously through an infinity of dependent clauses, but the thread is never lost, and the reader always arrives in the end at the destined goal."[2] One letter[3] contains a single

[1] *Catalogue of Pepysian MSS.* vols. ii. and iii.

[2] *Samuel Pepys and the Royal Navy*, p. 14.

[3] S. P. to the Navy Board, June 2, 1677, printed from the Pepysian MSS. *Admiralty Letters*, vi. 43 in *ib.* p. 15.

colossal sentence of 333 words, yet the grammatical construction is faultless and the sense is absolutely clear. Pepys's only acknowledged work, the *Memoires of the Royal Navy*, 1679-88, published in 1690,[1] is written in much the same style, and one of the sentences runs to 247 words. The official speaks in quite a different tone to the diarist, but in both cases the style is admirably adapted for its purpose.

When he corresponds as a "virtuoso" with other collectors and men of taste, Pepys adopts yet another literary style, as far removed from that of the *Diary* as it is possible for a style to be. He models himself on his friend Evelyn, and writes letters which are strained, artificial, and full of cryptic allusions and "coagulated compliment." In a letter of September 1693 to Dr. Charlett, Master of University College, Oxford,[2] the earlier Pepys flashes out for a moment through the obscurity of the later style. After apologising for the "clamminess" of his memory, he refers to "Mr. Wood's no-mortification, and the further kicks he means to expose his teeth to from the heels of truth." A later letter to the same correspondent, written on November 9, 1698,

[1] Reprinted in 1906 by the Clarendon Press in the "Tudor and Stuart Library."

[2] Printed from the Ballard Letters in *Academy*, xxxviii. (1890), 109.

concerning Mr. Isted's election as a Fellow of the Royal Society,[1] is however a more typical specimen of the "virtuoso" at his simplest; his more contorted productions are all too long for quotation.

"I did with great pleasure join in the unanimous election of him . . . into our Society at Gresham College; and that therefore, besides your commands and his own apparent merits, I am now by colleagueship become his humble servant and honourer, and by your leading me to it will as an elder brother take upon me to read to him (as he favours me with opportunities for it) upon the great subject of this world out of a register I carry about me of my own mistakes in it."

Simple and almost homely as the style of the *Diary* is, it sometimes attains a high level of literary distinction, and there are to be found in it not a few gems of English prose. Pepys's account of his first sight of the Fire, on Sunday September 2, 1666, is as a whole extraordinarily impressive. He and his friends took refuge upon the water and found themselves under "a shower of fire-drops."

"When we could endure no more upon the water, we to a little alehouse on the Bankside, over against the Three Cranes, and there staid till it was dark almost, and saw the fire grow; and, as it grew darker, appeared more and more, and in corners and upon steeples, and between churches and houses, as far as we could see up the hill of the City, in a most horrid malicious bloody flame, not like the fine flame of an ordinary fire. . . . We staid till, it being darkish, we saw the fire as only one entire arch of fire from this to the other side the bridge, and in a bow up the hill for

[1] Printed from the Ballard Letters in *Academy*, xxxviii. (1890), p. 174.

an arch of above a mile long: it made me weep to see it. The churches, houses, and all, on fire and flaming at once; and a horrid noise the flames made, and the cracking of houses at their ruine. So home with a sad heart." . . .

In contrast with this is a charming pastoral scene on Epsom Downs on July 14, 1667. Pepys sprained his right foot when leaping down a little bank, but the pain passed off,

"And so the women and W. Hewer and I walked upon the Downes where a flock of sheep was; and the most pleasant and innocent sight that ever I saw in my life—we find a shepherd, and his little boy reading, far from any houses or sight of people, the Bible to him; so I made the boy read to me, which he did, with the forced tone that children do usually read, that was mighty pretty, and then I did give him something and went to the father and talked with him. . . . He did content himself mightily in my liking his boy's reading, and did bless God for him, the most like one of the old patriarchs that ever I saw in my life, and it brought those thoughts of the old age of the world in my mind for two or three days after."

In his account of the funeral of Sir Christopher Myngs,[1] who had been mortally wounded in action on the last day of the great battle with the Dutch off the North Foreland, June 1-4, 1666, Pepys reaches his highest plane. He was present at the funeral in a coach with Sir William Coventry, at which, he tells us,

"there happened this extraordinary case—one of the most romantique that ever I heard of in my life, and could

[1] *Diary*, June 13, 1666. The comments on the episode are taken from the present writer's short work entitled *Samuel Pepys and the Royal Navy*, pp. 13-14.

not have believed but that I did see it; which was this:—About a dozen able, lusty, proper men come to the coach-side with tears in their eyes, and one of them that spoke for the rest begun and says to Sir W. Coventry, 'We are here a dozen of us that have long known and loved and served our dead commander Sir Christopher Mings, and have now done the last office of laying him in the ground. We would be glad we had any other to offer after him, and in revenge of him. All we have is our lives; if you will please to get his Royal Highness to give us a fireship among us all, here is a dozen of us, out of all which choose you one to be commander, and the rest of us, whoever he is, will serve him; and, if possible, do that that shall shew our memory of our dead commander and our revenge.' Sir W. Coventry was herewith much moved (as well as I, who could hardly abstain from weeping), and took their names, and so parted; telling me that he would move his Royal Highness as in a thing very extraordinary, which was done."

No more touching tribute than this has ever been paid to the memory of a great seaman, nor better evidence given of the simple loyalty of sea-faring men which in their descendants has served us so well of late. "The truth is," continues Pepys,

"Sir Christopher Mings was a very stout man, and a man of great parts and most excellent tongue among ordinary men. . . . He had brought his family into a way of being great; but dying at this time, his memory and name . . . will be quite forgot in a few months as if he had never been, nor any of his name be the better by it; he having not had time to will any estate, but is dead poor rather than rich."

A writer who was alive to the pathos of this scene and could describe it in a style which comes so near distinction, reflecting with dignity upon the swift passing of human greatness, is something more than the "delightful old diarist" and "garrulous gossip" which he has been called by undiscerning readers; but it is characteristic of Pepys that he should conclude his entry for the day with an anti-climax: "In my way home I called on a fisherman and bought three eeles, which cost me three shillings."

CHAPTER XX

The Later Life of Pepys[1]

When the *Diary* came to an end on May 31, 1669, three months after its author's 36th birthday, it had covered less than 9½ years of his life, and he still had 34 years before him, 20 of which were to

[1] For the private life of Pepys after the close of the *Diary* the biographer is largely dependent upon his correspondence, and it is unfortunate that this has not yet been collected in one authentic edition. Many of the letters printed by the Reverend John Smith in his *Life, Journals, and Correspondence of Samuel Pepys*, 2 vols. 1841, are incorrectly copied; and although Lord Braybrooke appended to his editions of the *Diary* a number of letters from the Pepys Cockerell Collection and other sources (afterwards reprinted in the Mynors Bright edition), the editing of them, although it passed muster in his own time, is from the point of view of to-day positively unscrupulous. In those taken from the Pepys Cockerell Collection, at any rate, sentences, paragraphs, and even whole pages are omitted without any indication, and in some cases the omissions have been disguised by tampering with the grammatical structure of the sentences. Letters printed elsewhere, as for instance the correspondence of Dr. Charlett, in the *Academy* for 1890, are carefully edited, but these are not numerous. The Rawlinson MSS. and the Pepys Cockerell Collection have still to be thoroughly explored.

A list of the printed sources which have been utilised for the biographical part of the book is given on p. 299. References to manuscript authorities are supplied in the footnotes.

be spent, if not all in high office, at any rate in close association with naval affairs. Thus there is some justification for the view that the importance of the *Diary* in relation to the whole life of Pepys has been exaggerated, and that it was, after all, only a by-product of his genius. In order to provide the right perspective, it is therefore necessary to add to this volume a sketch of his later life. This falls naturally into five periods: (1) The Clerkship of the Acts after the *Diary* (1669-73); (2) the first Secretaryship of the Admiralty (1673-79); (3) his first retirement (1679-84); (4) the second Secretaryship of the Admiralty (1684-89); and (5) his final retirement (1689-1703).

LAST YEARS OF THE CLERKSHIP OF THE ACTS
(May 31, 1669, to June 18, 1673)

In June 1668 Pepys had taken his wife and a small party of friends on a fortnight's tour in England, and of this he gives a charming account in the *Diary*. They visited Oxford ("a very sweet place"), Salisbury (where they found Old Sarum and Stonehenge "prodigious" and the Cathedral "most admirable"), and Bath, where they bathed in the waters. It is a matter for regret that no similar account survives of the tour in Holland and France, but the state of his eyes which was the occasion of the journey prevented Pepys from exercising his descriptive powers.

In his correspondence, however, he refers to it at the time as a voyage "full of health and content," and writing to Evelyn on December 24, 1701, in praise of foreign travel, he recalls it as despatched "to a degree of satisfaction and solid usefulness that has stuck by me through the whole course of my life and business since." He returned to England on or about October 22, 1669, but on the day of her arrival in London Mrs. Pepys fell ill of "a fever so severe as . . . to render her recovery desperate,"[1] and on November 10 she died, aged 29. She was buried in her parish church of St. Olave's, Hart Street, where her husband erected to her memory a monument with a Latin inscription.

It is possible that the date of his return to England may have been determined by Pepys's parliamentary ambitions. On December 5, 1668, he wrote in the *Diary*, "my great design, if I continue in the Navy, is to get myself to be a Parliament-man," and his opportunity came when the death of Sir Robert Brooke in 1669 created a vacancy in the representation of the town of Aldborough (now Aldeburgh) in Suffolk. In a letter to one of the Bailiffs dated July 1, 1669, Pepys offered himself as a candidate, and he was supported by James, Duke of York, and by the

[1] Sir D'Arcy Power thinks that Mrs. Pepys may have died of typhoid fever.

influence of the Howards, exercised at the Duke's request. The issue of the writ on October 19 almost coincides with his return from the continent, but "the sorrow and distraction" caused by the death of his wife forced him to a long neglect of his "private concernments," and he took no part in the election, at which John Bruce the Opposition candidate was returned.

For nearly four years more Pepys continued to discharge the duties of the office of Clerk of the Acts. His first business after his return was to draft an elaborate and methodical defence of the Navy in reply to certain "observations" addressed to the Principal Officers, upon "some proceedings of theirs in reference to the late war and the management thereof," by the Commissioners of Public Accounts. This was presented to the Commissioners on November 27, 1669, and was afterwards supplemented by a "particular defence" relating to Pepys's "own single conduct," dated January 6, 1669-70. The "observations" of the Commissioners and Pepys's written defence of himself and his colleagues were discussed during January and February at meetings of the Council Board, when all the honours of the debate fell to the Clerk of the Acts.[1]

[1] A fuller account of these proceedings is given in *A Descriptive Catalogue of the Naval Manuscripts in the Pepysian Library*, ed. J. R. Tanner (Navy Records Society's Publications), i. 33-6.

For the rest of the four years we possess but scanty knowledge of Pepys's activities. In 1670 he fell out with Sir John Barckman Leyenbergh, the Swedish Resident, and there was some talk of a duel; but from this he was saved by the welcome intervention of the King, who, "to prevent any further inconvenience that may happen," signified his pleasure on November 9 that he should be required "neither to send any challenge to the said Resident of Sweden nor to accept of any from him." We know also that Pepys was at this time active in the affairs of the Trinity House. On November 29, 1671, he "laid open" before the Duke of York and Lord Arlington (the Master and several Brothers attending), the right of the Corporation to choose consuls at Leghorn. Perhaps it was in recognition of this service that he was promoted to be an Elder Brother on January 24, 1671-2,—a capacity in which he often sat at the Courts. On June 24, 1672, he was one of the six "Bannerolles" in the procession at Lord Sandwich's funeral in Westminster Abbey.

On January 29, 1672-3, a fire broke out at the Navy Office in Seething Lane; and a reference in the *Admiralty Journal* to the ground "whereon the Navy Office stood" suggests that it must have been very destructive.[1] The Officers of the Navy

[1] The destructive character of the fire seems to have escaped the late Mr. Wheatley, for opposite p. 192 of the first volume

residing there were burnt out of their houses; and it was found necessary to transfer the business of the Navy Board to the Prize Office in Mark Lane and a private house adjoining it, and to deposit many of the books and papers at the Trinity House.[1] It is not certain where Pepys went to live when his house at the Navy Office became uninhabitable, but in a letter from Mrs. Houblon of a later date (December 3, 1683) there is a reference to "your old fusty residence" in Winchester Street, and on November 2, 1674, he writes from that address. This affords some ground for the conjecture that early in 1673 he went to live in Winchester Street, and that he was there until the autumn of 1674. Like the other Officers of the Navy affected by the fire, he received an allowance for rent, "not exceeding £80 per annum," until "other provision of housing" could be made for him.

FIRST SECRETARYSHIP OF THE ADMIRALTY

(June 18, 1673, to May 21, 1679)

The passing of the Test Act on March 29, 1673, led, as it was intended to do, to the resigna-

of his edition of the *Diary* he inserts a "Prospect of the Navy Office" dated 1714 as if it represented the building as in 1660. But this was the Office as rebuilt in 1682 under an Act of Parliament (25 Car. II. c. 10) on an enlarged and "more commodious" site (*Catalogue*, iv. 109).

[1] Historical MSS. Commission, *Fifteenth Report*, Appendix, Pt. ii. p. 172.

tion of the office of Lord High Admiral by James, Duke of York. This took place on June 15, and on July 9 the Admiralty was placed in commission, the King reserving to himself all Admiralty profits and patronage for England, and his brother retaining the Admiralty of Scotland, Ireland, and the plantations abroad.[1] The King presided in person at the meetings of the new Admiralty Commission, but the Duke remained an important influence behind the throne. It was said of the former by the Duke of Buckingham that "the great, almost the only pleasure of his mind to which he seemed addicted, was shipping and sea affairs"; and the latter was a naval expert, who had commanded fleets and had had actual experience of fighting at sea. The new Admiralty Commission needed an efficient secretary, and "his Majesty was pleased" to call Mr. Pepys, "the only survivor of the first . . . set of Officers of the Navy at his Restoration, from his charge of Clerk of the Acts to that of Secretary to himself and the said Commission."[2] This important promotion surprised no one, for by this time the industry and method of the Clerk of the Acts had placed him in the front rank of the naval administrators available.

[1] A fuller account of this reorganisation is given in *Catalogue of Pepysian MSS.*, i. 36 ff.

[2] Pepysian MSS., *Miscellanies*, xi. 221.

As Lord High Admiral, the Duke of York had had a succession of secretaries,—Sir William Coventry (1660-7), Matthew Wren (1667-72), and Sir John Werden (1672-3).[1] Pepys was now to occupy the same relation to the composite Admiralty as these had held to the individual Admiral; and the salary of £500 a year assigned to him was the same as had hitherto been paid to them. But the new appointment had an immediate result of great importance, for it involved the creation of a proper Admiralty Office. The Secretary to the Lord High Admiral had acted very much like a private secretary, and he had only had one or two clerks to help him. Pepys, coming straight from the organised Navy Office, introduced an office tradition and office methods, and in this way succeeded in systematising proceedings which hitherto had been somewhat haphazard. From this time also the Secretary himself, no longer hampered, as the Clerk of the Acts had been, by colleagues of equal standing, could speak with a new note of authority. Constitutionally he was under the control of the King and the Commissioners, but as their expert adviser on navy business he soon succeeded in controlling them. "Laborious drudge," untrue before as a description of Pepys, becomes merely ridiculous now.

[1] Werden was appointed a Commissioner of the Navy to compensate him for his displacement by Pepys.

At the beginning of January 1673-4 the Lords of the Admiralty occupied Derby House in Canon Row,[1] which had been leased from the Duke of Ormonde for their office, and for "the residence of the said Mr. Pepys as Secretary,"[2] and on January 3 Pepys's official correspondence begins to be dated thence; but work had still to be done to the house and garden, and this no doubt explains why Winchester Street continued to be his private address during the greater part of 1674.

In the year of his appointment as Secretary of the Admiralty, Pepys was able to realise his ambition of becoming a "Parliament-man." On August 19, 1673, Sir Robert Paston, who sat for Castle Rising, was created Baron Paston and Viscount Yarmouth, and on October 27 a writ was issued for a new election. Pepys's candidature was supported by the Duke of York and the Duke of Norfolk, and in spite of the untimely death of the Mayor, whom the latter describes as "a perfect creature I could depend upon," the burgesses of Castle Rising elected Pepys. But the defeated candidate, Robert Offley, petitioned against the return, and on February 6, 1673-4, the Committee of Privileges reported that Mr. Pepys was not elected and the election was void.

[1] The site of Derby House is now occupied by New Scotland Yard.

[2] *Mariner's Mirror*, ix. 273.

In the debate which followed on February 10,[1] the question was raised which was to give infinite trouble later on. The House was informed by some members—

> "That they had received an account from a Person of Quality that he saw an altar with a crucifix upon it in the house of Mr. Pepis; And Mr. Pepis, standing up in his place, did heartily and flatly deny that he ever had any altar or crucifix, or the image or picture of any saint whatsoever in his house, from the top to the bottom of it."

There are references in the *Diary* to "a fine crucifix," [2] but a subsequent entry [3] suggests that it was only a varnished print of the Crucifixion; and the portrait of Mrs. Pepys as St. Catharine may very well have been taken for a saint. The original calumny was traced to Shaftesbury, but he withdrew it, and the prorogation of Parliament ended the controversy, leaving Pepys in possession of the seat. It appears that the question had been already raised at the election, for the candidate had found it necessary to put in a certificate, dated November 3, 1672, and signed by three clergy, that "the said Samuel Pepys, Esq., is both otherwise a worthy person, and particularly that he hath constantly manifested himself to be a firm Protestant, according to the rites of the Church of England, and a true son thereof." During the debates in Parliament he had further fortified him-

[1] *Commons' Journals*, ix. 306.

[2] July 20 and August 2, 1666. [3] November 3, 1666.

self by obtaining from his brother-in-law, Balthazar St. Michel, a rather flamboyant letter declaring his readiness to prove ("to the hazard of my life . . . with my sword in my hand") that Robert Offley was "a false liar in his throat" in asserting that there had ever been an altar in his house, or that Mrs. Pepys "had the least thoughts of Popery." Readers of the *Diary* for November 29 and December 6, 1668, will realise that with regard to his sister St. Michel's letter goes far beyond the facts; but Dr. Milles's certificate of May 22, 1681,[1] testifies to her regular attendance at church, and shews that she received the Sacrament upon her death-bed.

The atmosphere of suspicion which surrounded Pepys was not dispelled when, either at the end of 1674 or early in 1675, the Italian musician Cesare Morelli took up his residence in his house. This young man, "born in Flanders but bred at Rome," had been recommended to Pepys by Mr. Hill the merchant, one of his early musical friends,[2] as one

[1] Printed in Wheatley's edition of the *Diary*, vol. i. p. xli.

[2] Mr. Hill was also an enthusiastic admirer. On July 1, 1675, he acknowledges, with many expressions of gratitude, the gift of his friend's portrait. "The picture is beyond praise, but causes admiration in all that see it,—its posture so stately and magnificent, and it hits so naturally your proportion and the noble air of your face that I remain immovable before it hours together." Mr. Lionel Cust thinks that this may be the portrait by Hales now in the possession of the Clothworkers' Company (Pepys Club, *Occasional Papers*, 1903-14, p. 30).

"who has a most admirable voice, and sings rarely to his theorbo, and that with great skill." He could also speak Latin, Italian, French, and Spanish. The ultimate result was an offer, on November 22, 1674, of £30 a year, "with his lodging and entertainment." "He shall not only on his part be welcome," writes his new patron, "and possibly find me not the most uneasy to be lived with; but myself, or mine also, shall (I am apt to believe) find in him a servant not of less real use by his languages, in reading, writing, translating, or other offices depending thereon, than satisfaction to myself in his excellent qualifications in music,[1] in which my utmost luxury still lies, and is likely to remain so." But Morelli was a Roman Catholic.

For the history of Pepys's first Secretaryship of the Admiralty we are fortunate in having abundant materials in the minute-book of the Commission[2] and the Secretary's office letter-book.[3] From these sources we learn that the chief business of the new administration established in 1673 was to carry through the third Dutch war to its close, and

[1] A large collection of music, copied, arranged, or composed by Morelli, is in the Pepysian Library (see P. Lubbock, *Samuel Pepys*, p. 218).

[2] Calendared in vol. iv. of the *Catalogue of Pepysian MSS.* (Admiralty Journal).

[3] Calendared as far as May 7, 1677, in *ib.* vols. ii. and iii. (Admiralty Letters).

then to repair, by an energetic shipbuilding policy, that depreciation of the navy which was one of the results of the war. In this work it was on the whole successful. The Admiralty Commissioners were sensible and vigilant, and they were well served by their Secretary; while the Navy Board was strong on the technical side of its work, and in 1675 it was fortunate in acquiring as one of its members an official so thoroughly capable in his own department as was Sir Anthony Deane. Moreover, although the financial difficulty was not solved, and still continued to hamper and cripple the navy, Parliament was beginning to give better support to naval expansion. The idea of the importance of sea power had already acquired a considerable hold upon the political classes of England, and the wars with the Dutch had served to strengthen it. Charles II read rightly the feelings of his subjects when he allowed his Chancellor to say, in his speech to the Pension Parliament at the beginning of its eleventh session, "There is not so lawful or commendable a jealousy in the world as an Englishman's of the growing greatness of any prince at sea." [1]

The most important event in the history of the Admiralty Commission of 1673-9 is the Act of 1677 assigning £600,000 for the building of 30 new ships. Pepys modestly ascribed the passing

[1] *Parliamentary History*, iv. 587.

of the Act through the House of Commons to his own great speech in Parliament on February 23 of that year;[1] and in the spending of the money he initiated a far-sighted policy of preparation which did much to account for the ease and rapidity with which the new ships were built. His genius for organisation, already shewn as Clerk of the Acts, is now applied in a wider field, and as an administrator he attains to real greatness. The new establishment of May 4, 1676, for "midshipmen extraordinary and volunteers"; the establishment of November 3, 1677, for men and guns; the establishment of December 15, 1677, for naval chaplains; and the regulations of December 18, 1677, setting up an examination for the office of lieutenant, were all of his drafting and probably of his suggestion. He also appears as a strict naval disciplinarian. It may further be said of him that, unlike many officials, he was accessible to new ideas. On May 3, 1677, we find Mr. James Houblon the merchant unfolding to him a scheme for establishing "intelligencers" in foreign ports, charged with the duty of collecting not only political information but also particulars of the

[1] The substance of this speech is given in *Catalogue of Pepysian MSS.* i. 48-53. Pepys's speeches were packed with facts and figures,—the oratory of the expert; but on May 11, 1678, a member complained of his haughtiness. He "speaks rather like an admiral than a secretary, 'I' and 'We'" (*Parliamentary History*, iv. 976).

delinquencies of English naval officers abroad, "that the management of the King's fleet in all particulars may be executed by sober, discreet, and diligent persons and men of business, and that all drinking, swearing, gaming, and expensive and sumptuous eating, may be banished the fleets." [1]

During his first tenure of the office of Secretary of the Admiralty there is no trace of the corruption which Pepys had practised as Clerk of the Acts. A reference in the *Diary* suggests that he had already reached the point of satiety,[2] and the activities of the Commission of Public Accounts had made corruption dangerous. Moreover, he was now exceedingly well off. In addition to his regular salary of £500 a year, he received the same "allowance of travelling charges" as was made to members of the Navy Board, and he was also entitled to fees on the renewal of the commissions of the vice-admirals of the maritime counties. But a far more lucrative source of income was his claim to a fee of 25*s.* each for the passes granted to ships under the treaties with the Mediterranean powers. This "he claimed as his due, as being

[1] This scheme, entitled "Considerations touching the importance of some provision to be made for publique marine intelligence," is printed from the Rawlinson MS. by Lady Alice Archer Houblon in *The Houblon Family* (1907), i. 221.

[2] On March 11, 1666-7, Pepys refers to his "indifference now more than heretofore to get money"; *cf.* April 20, 1669: "I thank God my condition is such that I can retire, and be able to live with comfort, though not with abundance."

lower than was anciently and as low as was at any time ever taken by his predecessors." Some of his critics hinted that the number of these passes had run up to 8000 in a year, and " it was generally taken for granted " in the House of Commons that there were 4000 ; but even if Pepys's own figure of 1000 is accepted as correct, £1250 a year was a comfortable addition to his official salary. A more creditable reason may however be assigned for his reformation. His office correspondence certainly gives the impression that the Secretary of the Admiralty had become too proud of the navy, and of his own share in making it what it was, to lend himself any longer to corruption of the cruder kind. He had developed that eagerness for the efficiency of his own department which high responsibility always arouses in those for whom the salt of life has not yet lost its savour, and therefore he was able to resist those meaner temptations to which the young man beginning life without resources had fallen an easy prey. Such an impression would of course be valueless against direct evidence of corruption, but such evidence as we have is all the other way. Nothing could be better than the dignified rebuke which he administered on May 5, 1675, to a naval commander who in applying for a commission had hinted at a reward :

" But that which I have reason to take amiss from you is your thinking that any consideration of benefit to myself or expectation of reward from you should be of any inducement with me. Therefore pray reserve that sort of argument for such as will be guided by it, and know that your meriting well of the King is the only present that shall ever operate with me."[1]

In September 1675 another captain offered him £100 to procure the command of a ship, but the bribe was refused and the offender wrote a second letter "confessing his fault in so doing." And on May 3, 1677, his friend Mr. James Houblon offered Pepys an unsolicited testimonial, referring to "those petty advantages and sneaking perquisites your predecessors did stoop to and which you have to your hurt rejected."

During the period under consideration the activities of Pepys were by no means limited to the official business of his Secretaryship. On February 1, 1675-6, he was appointed a Governor of Christ's Hospital,[2] but his interest in the School was of an earlier date. On August 19, 1673, Charles II had established by letters patent a Foundation of forty poor boys "who having attained a competent skill in the grammar and common arithmetic to the rule of three in other schools in the said Hospital, may be fit to be further educated in a Mathematical School, and

[1] *Catalogue of Pepysian MSS.* (Admiralty Letters), iii. 46.

[2] Pepysian MS. No. 2612, *A Collection of Matters relating to Christ's Hospital*, p. 175. From this manuscript a whole chapter might be written on the work of Pepys in connexion with the Foundation.

there taught and instructed in the art of navigation and the whole science of arithmetic," with a view to their being apprenticed to the sea. While he was still Clerk of the Acts Pepys had taken a great interest in the project, and when in 1675 the time came for working out the details of a system of apprenticeship, he was ready with a complete scheme, which was confirmed by Order in Council on November 12, 1675. Under this boys who were reported by the authorities of the School to be qualified to go to sea, were to be examined and certified by the Trinity House. In 1677, the year after he became a Governor of the Hospital, Pepys was elected a member of the Schools Committee, and he at once threw himself with energy into his new duties. On October 22 he set forth to the Governors what he conceived to be the defects of the Mathematical School, and on November 3 he received a letter of thanks from Sir John Frederick the President of the Hospital. It was probably at his suggestion that on January 3, 1677-8, it was "proposed by his Majesty that some method might be digested . . . for the settling a breed of pilots out of the King's mathematical boys, to be constantly borne upon his yachts." On May 22 (Trinity Monday), 1676, Pepys was elected Master of the Trinity House, and in that capacity he opposed in Committee, on March 22, 1676-7, the Seamen's and

Watermen's Bill then before Parliament, urging that it would be wholly ineffectual for the purpose for which it was designed.[1] The opposition was successful, and the Bill was eventually dropped. On August 8, 1677, he was elected Master of the Clothworkers' Company, to which he presented the famous silver cup and the rose-water dish and ewer still used at banquets; and on July 4, 1678, his arms were ordered by the Company to be placed in one of the windows of their Hall. On September 10, 1677, he was one of the stewards at a Feast of the Honourable Artillery Company at Merchant Taylors' Hall, his colleagues being Viscount Newport the Treasurer of the Household, and Sir Joseph Williamson one of the Secretaries of State. During his Secretaryship Pepys continued to hold the office of treasurer for Tangier to which he had been appointed in 1665. He resigned, or was ejected, in 1679, when the Popish Plot for a time ruined his career, but his accounts run to April 30, 1680.

When the Pension Parliament was dissolved on January 24, 1678-9, and a new one summoned for March 6, "the gentlemen of Castle Rising" exhibited "forgetfulness" towards their former member, but "three several corporations of somewhat greater names,"—Portsmouth, Harwich, and

[1] Historical MSS. Commission, *Ninth Report*, Pt. ii. and Appendix, p. 87.

one of the Isle of Wight boroughs, competed for his services. He was eventually chosen for Harwich, his colleague being Sir Anthony Deane the famous shipbuilder, and he sat in that capacity in the short Parliament of 1679. But the suspicion of his Popish sympathies which had ruined his chances of re-election at Castle Rising, pursued him into his new constituency, and on March 6 he writes to Captain Langley "touching the discourses . . . about the election Harwich has made in their choice of Sir Anthony Deane and me, as if he were an Atheist and myself a Papist." He adds that Deane "hath too much wit to be an Atheist," and he indignantly repudiates the other charge against himself.

Of the private life of Pepys during the period 1673-9 we know little. His eyes continued to give him trouble, and he therefore "fell to employing clerks" for all purposes "save on the occasions of utmost importance," and from this practice of delegation he obtained great benefit.[1] But if the *Admiralty Journal* is in Pepys's own hand,[2] the large and straggling writing which

[1] A memorandum of November 7, 1677, on "The present ill state of my health" (Rawlinson MSS., A. 185, f. 206) gives a minute and exhaustive account of all his various symptoms. Incidentally he confesses that on his "occasions of crossing the sea between this and France" he is sea-sick "to the utmost extremity."

[2] These minutes were taken down by Pepys in shorthand, and were afterwards written out in a hand that closely resembles the

occurs between November 1674 and January 1675-6 suggests that at that time his eyesight was giving him more than ordinary trouble.

In 1674 his loyalty to the Sandwich family led Pepys to interest himself in the election of " the hopeful young gentleman " John Mountagu, his patron's fourth son, to a Fellowship at Trinity College, Cambridge. In 1683 Mountagu was appointed Master of Trinity by the Crown and in 1699 he became Dean of Durham. In 1674 Pepys carried out a long-standing promise to set up a Table of Commandments in the chancel of Chatham church, and he repaired the windows there. He also responded generously, both by subscription and by loan, to an appeal made to him in 1677 to contribute to the new buildings at Magdalene. On August 27, 1675, we find Mr. Gibbon corresponding with him about an apparition of " a human feminine shape " which appeared to Pepys while he was " one night playing late upon some musical instrument " ; and on December 4, 1676, Captain Prowd was furnishing him with information concerning a loadstone by letter, as " at present a swelling in my face hinders me from the payment of my respective duty " of calling in person.

longhand version of the King's escape from Worcester, which has always been supposed to be his. On the other hand it is difficult, on this supposition, to account for some ill-spelt Latin in the *Journal*.

The adoption by Charles II of Sir William Temple's scheme for a new Privy Council, to represent at once landed wealth and "the conflicting interests of office and opposition," necessitated the dissolution of the old Privy Council, and the Admiralty Commission went with it. This was dissolved on April 21, 1679, and was succeeded by a new Commission of quite a different composition. The alteration of persons did not, as has been commonly supposed, of itself involve a change of Secretary. Pepys at first remained in office under the new Commission, and on April 25 the Duke of York wrote to him from the Hague, "Be assured you shall find me as kind to you as ever." The King also informed him that he relied upon his experience of the navy to supply, as their Secretary, the notable ignorance of the new Commissioners;[1] but the state of his health and the fact that some of the Commissioners were his declared enemies, who had not "spared publicly to let fly," in opposition to his continuance in office, "that so long as Mr. Pepys should be there his Royal Highness remains in effect Admiral," led him to renew a petition which he had already made, that he might be withdrawn

[1] "I could wish," writes Pepys on May 6, "his [Majesty's] naval arrangements to be such as for a time might allow these worthy gentlemen opportunity of being informed in the work of their great office before they be urged to much execution in it."

from "this odious Secretaryship," and might either himself be appointed a member of the Commission or at least have some other provision made for him "as one superannuated" in the King's service. On May 22, 1679, the Duke of York wrote warmly to his brother in support of the former alternative, as the new Commissioners, "though in other affairs they are very able men, yet must needs be very raw" in the service of the navy, "and will want one amongst them that understands it"; but on May 21, the day before this letter was written, Pepys had of his own accord resigned the Secretaryship. He was succeeded by his old clerk Thomas Hayter, the Clerk of the Acts.

FIRST RETIREMENT

(May 21, 1679, to June 10, 1684)

The storm which was to overwhelm Pepys, depriving him of his liberty and even threatening his life, had long been brewing. On November 1, 1678, his clerk, Samuel Atkins, had been arrested and charged with being an accessory to the murder of Sir Edmund Berry Godfrey, the London magistrate, who had disappeared on Saturday October 12, and whose body had been found in a ditch on Thursday October 17. The testimony of Bedloe the informer was to the effect that on the night of Monday October 14 Atkins had assisted in the removal of the body. According to Roger North, he was arrested in the expectation that he would accuse Pepys, and that then Pepys in his turn, under the pressure of threats and promises, "for he was an elderly gentleman, who had known softness and the pleasures of life,"[1] would accuse the Duke of York. At his trial on February 11, 1678-9, Atkins proved an *alibi*, and was acquitted by the jury without leaving the box; but the *alibi* had been obtained by the exertions of Pepys himself, and by his use of his official position to bring the necessary witnesses from sea. Atkins was saved by the testimony of the commander and the boatswain of the *Katherine* yacht, which was to the effect that on Monday October 14, the critical day, the prisoner was entertaining some friends on board the yacht from half-past four in the afternoon until half-past ten at night, when he departed, "very much fuddled." The sailors, rowing against the tide, did not actually land him until half-past eleven.[2]

Though routed in the Courts of Law, the enemy returned to the charge in Parliament, and succeeded in involving Pepys in the discredit of the Popish Plot. On April 28, 1679, a Committee was appointed by the House of Commons to

[1] *Examen*, p. 243. The "elderly gentleman" was 45!

[2] See J. R. Tanner, "Pepys and the Popish Plot" (*English Historical Review*, 1892).

enquire into the miscarriages of the navy, the chairman being Mr. William Harbord, a personal enemy of Pepys who was scheming to supplant him in the office of Secretary of the Admiralty.[1] On May 20 this Committee reported to the House, making formidable charges against Pepys and Deane :—That they did, "in conspiracy together cause divers maps and sea journals to be made," with draughts and models of the King's ships, and "divers other treasonable matters," which Deane had carried over to the French Government when he visited France in 1675. It was also stated, "That the said Mr. Pepys is either a Papist himself or a great favourer of that party." The House ordered that Deane and Pepys should be taken into custody, that the Attorney-General should forthwith undertake their prosecution, and that the evidence collected by the Committee should be placed at his disposal for that purpose. On May 22 they were accordingly committed to the Tower on the Speaker's warrant, and on June 2, when the prisoners came before the Court of King's Bench, bail was refused.

Against Deane there seems to have been no

[1] This is frequently referred to in the correspondence of the time, *e.g.* Southwell's letter to the Duke of Ormonde on May 3, 1679, which suggests that "Mr. Pepys is to be pulled to pieces" by the Parliamentary Committee expressly in order that Harbord might succeed him (Mr. Wheatley's MS. : *cf.* Historical MSS. Commission, *Seventh Report*, p. 472).

evidence, but the case against Pepys depended mainly upon the testimony of two witnesses, John James his discharged butler, and John Scott (who called himself Colonel Scott), an enemy of long standing. The evidence of James principally related to remarks which he overheard when he was in Pepys's service, but he also made a good deal of the frequent visits of the Italian musician Morelli to his house. Morelli was no longer living there, for it had been recognised that he was a dangerous inmate. In 1678 Mr. James Houblon had made an attempt to induce him to change his creed, but on November 2 he wrote to Pepys, "I find Morelli so resolved in his religion that it will be in vain to hope his conversion." It was therefore arranged that he should go into lodgings at Brentwood, "at the house of a most obliging family." Titus Oates stated that he was a Jesuit who had "with great importunity procured himself to have the care of the English business."[1] This was quite untrue, for Morelli was not even a priest, but the association with him prejudiced Pepys's cause. When Oates's statement was communicated to the House of Commons a member exclaimed, "This is one of the branches of the Plot; we have a land-plot, this is a sea-plot."[2] In March 1680 James, on his death-bed, signed two confessions to the effect that he had been

[1] Grey's *Debates*, vii. 305. [2] *Ib.*

suborned by Harbord and Colonel Mansell to give false evidence against his former master. The perjured testimony of Scott was due not to subornation but to malice. He had engineered fraudulent sales of land in Long Island, and in 1669 his victim had petitioned the Crown for redress. Pepys was instructed by the Duke of York to investigate Scott's career, and he succeeded in bringing together a number of depositions with regard to his dishonest proceedings in New England and elsewhere.[1] Returning to London full of wrath against the man who had exposed him, Scott made common cause with Titus Oates and the informers, and was used by Shaftesbury and Harbord as a weapon against Pepys; but their witness's character was too bad to stand cross-examination, and he kept out of the way. The prosecution failed to obtain other evidence, so on July 9, 1679, the prisoners were released, on their obtaining bail for £30,000 each.[2] Mr. James Houblon and three of his friends furnished the necessary security. The public trial was four

[1] An account of Scott's career of fraud is given in G. D. Scull, *Dorothea Scott* (1883).

[2] In some quarters their liberation was not popular. Charles Hatton wrote on July 10, "Mr. Pepys and Sir Anthony Deane was bailed yesterday, and if my Lord Chief Justice hang 500 Jesuits he will not regain the opinion he hath thereby lost with the populace, to court whom he will not act against his conscience" (*Hatton Correspondence*, Camden Society, i. 187). The judge referred to was the notorious Scroggs.

times postponed on the ground that further evidence for the prosecution was expected, but when Scott failed to stand by his original deposition, Pepys and Deane were relieved of their bail on February 12, 1679-80, and on June 30, 1680, the last day of the following term, they were finally discharged.

With the proceedings against Pepys in Parliament and in the Courts was associated a scurrilous attack on him in the press. In 1679, probably in October,[1] two pamphlets were issued, accusing Pepys and his clerk William Hewer of corruption of the grossest kind. The first is entitled *A Hue & Cry after P. and H.*, the second, *Plain Truth, or a Private Discourse betwixt P. and H.*; and both proceed from a witty and practised pen. In the *Hue and Cry* Pepys and Hewer are charged with taking money unjustly from the owners of ships for permissions and protections; with receiving excessive fees from commanders for their commissions and warrant-officers for their warrants, and taking "great lumps" from Sir Dennis Gauden the Victualler of the Navy; with making false certificates of Turkish passes "to those that

[1] It is clear from internal evidence that the pamphlets were issued after the fall of Pepys, and it is possible that one of them was the subject of James Houblon's reference in a letter of October 14, 1679. "I see the malice of the enemy increases; God forgive them for that vilanous paper published yesterday. If they call the master Beelseebub, they will not spare them of the household" (Rawlinson MSS., A. 173, f. 18).

had never been at sea, nor did deserve any" ; and with favouring Roman Catholics for promotion.

P. and *H.*, you must also refund those before-hand Guinies or Broad-peeces ; and also the Jars of *Oyl*, and Boxes of *Chockolet*, and Chests of *Greek Wines*, and Chests of *Saracusa Wines*, and Pots of *Anchovis*, and Quarter-Casks of *Old Mallago*, and Butts of *Sherry*, and *Westphalihams*, and *Bolonia Sauceges*, and Barrels of Pickel'd *Oysters*, and Jars of *Ollives*, and Jars of *Tent*, and *Parmosant* Cheeses, and Chests of *Florence* Wine, and Boxes of *Orange* Flower Water ; And all those dryed *Cods* and *Lings ;* and Hogsheds of *Claret*, *White-Wines*, and *Champaynes*, and Dozens of *Syder* ; And also all those *Mocos*, Parrots and Parakeets, *Virginia* Nightingales, and Turtle-Doves, and those Fat Turkeys and Pigs, and all those *Turkish* Sheep, *Barberry* Horses, and Lyons, and Tygers, and Bears ; and all those fine *Spanish* Matts.

All which were received from Sea-Captains, *Consuls*, Lieutenants, Masters, Boatswains, Gunners, Carpenters, and Pursers ; or from their Wives, or Sons, or Daughters ; Or from some of the Officers in the *Dock-Yards* ; as Master Ship-Wrights, Master[s] of Attendance, or Clark of the Cheques, and Storekeepers, etc. . . .

As the fallen Pepys was now fair prey, the pamphleteer did not scruple to launch a venomous attack upon his private life :—

There is one thing more you must be mightily sorry for with all speed : Your Presumption in your Coach, in which you dayly Ride as if you had been Son and Heir to the great Emperor *Neptune* ; or as if you had been Infallibly to have succeeded him in his Government of the Ocean. All which was Presumption in the highest Degree.

First, You had upon the Fore-part of your Chariot Tempestuous Waves and Wracks of Ships : on your Left-hand, Forts and great Guns and Ships a-fighting : on your Right-hand was a fair Harbor and Town, with Ships and

Galleys riding with their Flags and Penants sp[r]ed, kindly saluting each other,—just like *P.* and *H.* Behind it were high Curl'd Waves and Ships a-sincking; and here and there an Appearance of some Bits of Land.

And now really Consider with your self that you are but the Son of a Taylor, and wipe out all this presumptious Painting, And new Paint it with those things agreeable to your quality: In the first place, paint upon the fore-part as handsome a Taylor's shop-board as you please, with the Old Gentleman your Father upon it at work and his Journey-men sitting about him, each Man with his Pint of Ale and half penny Loaf before him; and the good Old Matron your Mother and your self and the rest of your Brothers and Sisters standing by: this will be agreeable to your Qualities. Then behind your Coach Paint all the evil deeds of *P.* and *H.* in particulars: Also on your Right Hand Paint your Jesuite *M.* Playing upon his Lute and Singing a Holy Song: On your Left Hand Paint two or three poor Cripples which *P.* Reformed, and giving them his Charity, which he never was wont to do. All this will shew *P.'s* great Humility and Reformation, and Reducement to his Right Station. You must also, *P.*, Correct your Barge and take out all those Damask Curtains and Cushions and put in good Shaloon ones, and some of your Shop-Board Cushions: And wipe out those little Seas that are Painted, and Paint it a *New* with an honest Green; and here and there a pair of great Shears with open Mouths,—the Ignorant sort of People may take them for some Strange and Monstrous Fishes: all this will do very well.

The pamphlet ends with a mock hue and cry offering "a great Reward" to any who "can Apprehend *P.* and *H.*, or either of them."

While Pepys was in the Tower his friends did not desert him. James Houblon visited him frequently, and Evelyn dined with him twice and also sent him venison ; while Mr. D'Oyly deemed the occasion appropriate for an attempt to borrow £50 of him. On June 9, 1679, Pepys indited from the Tower a loyal letter to the Duke of York. "Hardships . . . I do and shall suffer contentedly," he wrote, "and the more in that I had the honour of having my duty to your Royal Highness assigned for the real cause of what my adversaries are pleased artificially to pretend of Popery and other like chimeras." He also referred to "the payment of that gratitude which even that Protestancy of mine the world would be thought so doubtful of exacts from me towards your Highness, and shall have it to the last point of my fortune and my life." The Duke sent him a valuable witness to the frauds of Scott, "our infamous adversary," as Pepys calls him, and for this, on January 6, 1679-80, he despatched a grateful letter. Pepys was denied the opportunity of establishing his innocence at a public trial, but he had taken characteristic pains to place it beyond doubt should a public trial be allowed him. He conducted from the Tower a voluminous correspondence with his friends, gathered witnesses from all quarters, sent messengers to the Continent for materials for his defence, and even despatched his brother-in-law, Balthazar St. Michel, to America to obtain additional information about Scott's career. St. Michel was engaged for more than nine months in looking up witnesses and collecting evidence,[1] and the expense was a severe strain upon Pepys's private resources;[2] but the result was that he was prepared with a complete answer to all the charges made against him. It must have been a bitter disappointment to him that he was never allowed to present his vindication in court, but the fruits of his labours remain for the defence of his reputation to posterity. The original documents are among the Rawlinson MSS. in the Bodleian at Oxford,[3] and the fair copies are in the Pepysian Library at Cambridge.[4]

On his liberation from the Tower, Pepys, now ejected from the official residence at Derby House, went to live with his friend Hewer in York Buildings, Buckingham Street, Strand. On July 14, 1679, he writes from there, "I am now with Will Hewer at his house, and have received from him all the care, kindness, and faithfulness of a son on this occasion, for which God reward him if I

[1] Pepys warned him "to be most slow to believe what we most wish should be true."

[2] Pepys banked at Hoare's, and his account there did not always shew a large balance. He had a great regard for his banker, and Sir Richard Hoare, "Goldsmith," was among those who received mourning rings at his funeral.

[3] A. 175.

[4] In the "two volumes or Mornamont." Colonel Scott styled himself as "of Mornamont," a place which has no existence, even among castles in Spain, and the name caught Pepys's fancy.

cannot."[1] This house stood at the south-west corner of the roadway, close to the River, and opposite to the house where Peter the Great lived in 1697. Dr. Thomas Gale called it "the Paradise which looks into the Thames, near the Water-gate in York Buildings," and this proximity to the Water-gate was very convenient at a time when the Thames was constantly used as a means of communication. The Gate is a fine example of Inigo Jones's architecture, but the steps leading up to it are now destroyed, or buried in the Embankment garden, and the symmetry of the design is much impaired thereby.[2] Here Pepys arranged his books; and there are in the Pepysian Library two drawings of the library in York Buildings shewing the identical bookcases now at Magdalene. In one of these views there is a glimpse of the River through the windows at the end. The rate-books of the parish of St. Martin's in the Fields shew that Buckingham Street was begun in 1675 and that Hewer first occupied the house in 1677. He continued to pay the rates on it until 1684, and letters are addressed to Pepys "at Mr. Hewer's house," but in 1685 he is replaced in the rate-books by "Esquire Pepys," who continued to be the tenant for the rest of his

[1] Quoted in Mr. Wheatley's MS.

[2] Mr. Philip Norman's MS., from which the particulars which follow of Hewer's and Pepys's tenure of this house and the house at Clapham are also taken.

life. It is probable that Hewer lived with Pepys in York Buildings, notwithstanding the change of tenancy, until he became a Commissioner of the Navy in 1686, and had a house assigned to him in the Navy Office, now rebuilt. The two friends appear to have lived in some style. There were two coachmen and a footman, and on June 3, 1680, there is a reference to the sale of Pepys's black boy,[1] possibly the one offered to him by Lieutenant John How in 1675.[2]

The house at Clapham where Pepys and Hewer ended their days was also acquired during this period. It had been built by Sir Dennis Gauden, the Victualler of the Navy, on an estate which he had probably bought as early as 1655, although when Pepys visited it on July 25, 1663, the house itself was not quite finished. It had been intended for his brother Dr. John Gauden, Bishop of Exeter and then of Worcester, the author of *Eikon Basilike*, but he died in 1662. Gauden became involved in financial difficulties, and as early as 1678 Hewer acquired an interest in the Clapham estate, perhaps by the way of mortgage. It appears from the Clapham rate-book, 1664-87, that Gauden continued to pay assessments on the property there until 1683, when his name was replaced by that of William "Ewers." Hewer already had a domicile at Clapham and Pepys visited him there.

[1] Rawlinson MSS., A. 181, f. 317. [2] *Ib.* A. 185, ff. 66, 70.

On October 30, 1680, in a letter to Pepys at Brampton, he tells him that his chests and hampers have been sent to Clapham, " where they will be safe from danger, as yourself may be, whenever you shall think fit to return." [1] In all probability this was not the " excellent, useful, and capacious house on the Common " referred to by Evelyn in his *Diary*.[2] Hewer's first occupation of Gauden's house may perhaps be assigned to 1688, as in a letter to Pepys dated March 12, 1687-8, James Houblon writes, " You have full employ about the elegancy of furnishing your new house," a reference which is intelligible if we suppose that Hewer had just departed to Clapham taking his furniture with him and leaving Pepys in sole possession of the house.

On October 2, 1680, Pepys was with the King at Newmarket, in the hope of " getting something settled towards my satisfaction upon the arrear due to me for my almost twenty years' service," [3]

[1] Rawlinson MSS., A. 183, f. 150.

[2] *Diary*, July 25, 1692 ; *cf.* September 23, 1700.

[3] In his last Will he included in his estate a debt of £28,007 2*s.* 1¼*d.* due from the Crown "upon the Ballance of two Accompts, One as Clerke of the Acts of the Navy and Secretary of the Admiralty of England, The other as Treasurer for Tangier, to their said late Majesties King Charles and King James the Second." The claim had been acknowledged by Charles II on March 2, 1678-9, and in a letter of November 17, 1688, James II recommended it to the Lords Commissioners of the Treasury, but it was ignored by the government of William and Mary and was never satisfied.

with the intention of staying a day at Brampton on his return, but it is probable that the death of his father, who was buried there on October 4, converted what was to have been a flying visit into a long stay. In September his sister Paulina had lost her husband, and as Samuel was his father's executor and principal heir there was family business to be transacted, and he did not return to London until November 19. During his stay at Brampton, Hewer conducted with Pepys an important correspondence, partly in cipher,[1] furnishing him with political information and sending him the Parliamentary votes. One or two of the political references are of special interest. Hewer reports that on Lord Mayor's Day, October 29, the Duke of Monmouth was present at the dinner "and was, both coming and going, very much cried up by the rabble, and the general discourse now is, 'York must be taken off without more ado.'" We learn that on November 17, which Hewer calls "Queen Elizabeth's birthday," there were to be "great doings of burning the Pope." Elizabeth was born on September 7, 1533, so the day of her accession, November 17, 1558, must be intended. It is clear that she was still regarded by the London populace as in a special sense the representative of the Reformation.

[1] Rawlinson MSS., A. 183, ff. 124-155. The correspondence is copied in Mr. Philip Norman's MS.

The correspondence shews that Pepys was employing his leisure at Brampton in preparing an exposure of the villainies of Scott, who haunted the two friends like a spectre, and still appeared a potential danger.[1] In the midst of these greater matters, Pepys refers to "my Lord of Rochester's Poems, written before his penitence in a style I thought unfit to mix with my other books,"[2] and directs that it should remain in the drawer where it is. In the letter of November 11 Hewer has an encouraging piece of information to communicate. Mr. Harbord had greeted him in the lobby of the House of Commons "with an unusual way of civility," and "with his hat off" had asked how he did.

The new Admiralty Commission of 1679 was intended to be a commission of retrenchment, but its members were entirely without naval experience and they did not find in Pepys a lenient critic. "No king," he wrote, "ever did so unaccountable a thing to oblige his people by, as to dissolve a Commission of the Admiralty then in his own hand, who best understands the business of the sea of any prince the world ever had, and things

[1] Although the prosecution had been withdrawn, Pepys did not yet feel that he was out of the wood. On November 9, 1680, Hewer reports to him that new witnesses had appeared "to make further discoveries of the late Hellish Plot."

[2] This book is now in the Pepysian Library, but its owner was so ashamed of its contents that he had it lettered on the back, "Rochester's Life."

never better done, and put it into hands which he knew were wholly ignorant thereof, sporting himself with their ignorance."[1] In a letter to Hewer of May 19, 1682, he also refers to "the shameful and ridiculous proceedings" of the Commissioners. Nor was Pepys their only critic. "The King's service goes to rack," wrote Hewer on May 6, "and is at this day in such a pickle as it never was since I can remember." And if Hewer is regarded as suspect by reason of his close association with Pepys, it should be noted that their conclusions were confirmed by Bonrepaux, an expert from the French Admiralty.

After his fall the discarded Secretary was still in favour with the King and the Duke of York. In April 1680, three months before the proceedings against him were finally withdrawn, Pepys was commanded to the Court at Newmarket. In October he was there again, taking down in shorthand from the King's own lips the story of his escape after the battle of Worcester.[2] His

[1] Pepysian MSS. No. 2866 (*Naval Minutes*), p. 76. The last phrase brings before us vividly Charles II's characteristic way.

[2] This manuscript, with a transcript in longhand, is now in the Pepysian Library. The latter has been published, in the same volume with Grammont's *Memoirs*, in the Bohn Standard Library. By the irony of fate, while John Smith was labouring for three years to decipher the shorthand of the *Diary*, this convenient key to it lay all the while, undiscovered by him, ready to his hand.

contemporaries still drew upon his naval experience, and on November 6, when Mr. Finch "moved in Council relating to salutes, the King was pleased to respite the doing anything therein till they had discoursed" with the late Secretary of the Admiralty.[1] Although out of office, he was regarded as an influence to be reckoned with, and applications were still made to him for employment. On July 7, 1680, he was approached on behalf of a candidate for the office of Clerk to the Trinity House, and he interested himself in ecclesiastical and academical preferments.

On the death of Sir Thomas Page, the Provost of King's College, Cambridge, on August 8, 1681, it was suggested that a Royal mandate should be obtained appointing Pepys to the vacant post. At first he thought the proposal "most agreeable," although he doubted his academic qualifications. He was also uncertain whether the Provostship would give him the kind of retirement he coveted, "a total seclusion from pomp and envy, as well as noise and care." It was pointed out to him that he might "live in the pomp, without either envy, noise, or care," and on August 16, in a letter to Colonel George Legge, he gave a qualified assent, declining to allow his name to be put forward against that of Legge's old Tutor, Dr. John Copleston, who was already

[1] Rawlinson MSS., A. 183, f. 140; *cf.* also f. 130.

in the field, but undertaking, if " it shall fall out that those his pretensions shall come under any danger of being overborne by a foreigner," to allow his own claims to be considered. In that case, he proposed to hand over to the College the whole of the Provost's stipend of £700 for the first year and not less than half in succeeding years; and to occupy himself during his tenure of the office " in putting together (for the public use) " his " collections so many years in the Navy and Admiralty," which " nothing but an entire leisure " would ever enable him to do. This singularly public-spirited conception of his duty, far in advance of anything ordinarily expected from Heads of Colleges in those days, was never realised, for Dr. Copleston was not " overborne by a foreigner," and became in due course Provost of King's.

On March 14, 1681-2, Pepys was again at Newmarket, where he found the Duke of York " plumper, fatter, and all over in better liking " than he had ever known him; and on May 4, 1682, he was on board ship in Margate Roads, ready to accompany the Duke on his visit to Edinburgh. In this unfortunate voyage, the Duke's ship, the *Gloucester*, through the carelessness of the pilot, was wrecked upon the Lemon and Oar Sand, about 16 leagues from the mouth of the Humber, and many lives were lost. Pepys had received "abundant invitation" to sail on board the *Gloucester*, but he had preferred to remain in the *Katherine* yacht, "for room's sake and accommodation." This was not known to his friends in London, and he was "numbered among the dead by all the City almost"; but a letter of May 8 from Edinburgh relieved their anxiety. Pepys stayed some days in Edinburgh, and was invited by the Duke to be present at two Councils, which impressed him with the "order, gravity, and unanimity of their debates." From Edinburgh, in company with Colonel Legge, he visited Stirling, Linlithgow, Hamilton, and Glasgow. The last he thought "a very extraordinary town indeed for beauty and trade, much superior to any in Scotland," but "the truth is, there is so universal a rooted nastiness hangs about the person of every Scot (man and woman), that renders the finest show they can make nauseous, even among those of the first quality." On May 19 Pepys was at Berwick and on May 26 at Newcastle, whence he "made a step to Durham, where the Bishop seems to live more like a prince of this than a preacher of the other world." At Newcastle the "personal freedom" of the city was conferred upon Colonel George Legge who had at the beginning of the year been appointed Master-General of the Ordnance, Sir Christopher Musgrave his Lieutenant-General, Sir George Fletcher, and Samuel Pepys.[1] This was not Pepys's first association with Newcastle, for on March 27, 1677, he had received a letter of thanks from the Mayor and Burgesses for opposing in Parliament a scheme to which they objected. From Newcastle he went to Scarborough and thence to Hull, the last port touched at before returning to London. He must have reached home about June 5, some days after the Duke, who had made the journey direct by sea.

In 1683 Pepys went again upon his travels. In that year George Legge, now Lord Dartmouth, was despatched with a fleet to superintend the evacuation of Tangier and the destruction of the Mole, and Pepys sailed with him as his Secretary, although at the time of his appointment he was ignorant of the purpose of the expedition, which he strongly disapproved. This was the occasion of his second *Diary*[2]—the narrative of his voyage to Tangier and of his subsequent travels in Spain. Pepys set out from London on July 30, 1683, perhaps accompanied by Hewer, who was attached to the expedition, and reached Portsmouth on August 1, but he did not go on board the *Grafton* until August 9, arriving on September 14 in

[1] This information from the town records of Newcastle was supplied to the author by Mr. H. M. Wood of Alnmouth.

[2] Deciphered from the shorthand MSS. in the Bodleian, and printed by Smith in the *Life, Journals, and Correspondence.*

Tangier Bay. The work of demolishing the Mole by mines began on October 1, but at first it made slow progress as the structure was solidly built,—" such a piece of masonry as our engineers say was never yet put together in the world," [1]—and it was not completed until the end of the year. Pepys's own share of the business was finished earlier, and on December 1 he and Hewer left Tangier by sea for Cadiz, where they were detained by floods until after the New Year. On January 5, 1683-4, he was at St. Lucar, and on February 3 at Seville, where he finished his sight-seeing in six days, but was " kept out of any capacity of quitting it " by the height to which the waters had risen. By February 12 he was back at Cadiz trying to get a ship for Tangier, but he found that the commanders " wholly prefer their own profit to the King's service." This led him to note how " this business of money, which runs through and debauches the whole service of the navy, is now come to the highest degree of infamy, and nobody considers it." The remedy was afterwards applied by Pepys himself, by the regulations of July 15, 1686, " about plate-carriage and allowance for captains' tables," which aimed at so improving the position of naval commanders as to place them beyond the reach of the temptation to neglect their public duty for private

[1] The sum of £340,000 had been spent upon it.

gain. The fleet sailed from Tangier on March 5, 1683-4, and returned home on March 30, having carried out the work entrusted to it "very exactly and effectively." Pepys received for his service £992, reckoned at the rate of £4 a day for 248 days. Among the Rawlinson MSS. is a bill from a Spanish tailor at Cadiz for making him a "sea-gown," and another for some Spanish books which he bought at Seville.

Christ's Hospital was still an important interest with Pepys, and on March 9, 1680-1, he proposed, "after a two years' troublesome interruption," to return to the affairs of the King's Mathematical Foundation.[1] On February 17, 1681-2, he borrowed Alderman Sir Thomas Beckford's scarlet gown "for Signior Verrio, the King's painter, to make use of in the picture he is preparing for Christ's Hospital." This important work shews James II on his throne, surrounded by official personages, and it includes a portrait of Pepys. In his opinion, however, all was not going well at the Hospital, and in a letter of May 2, 1682, to Sir John Frederick the President, he refers to the "present unsettlement and disorder" of the Mathematical School, and complains that it is "in itself most absurd that a foundation expressly instituted for the improvement of navigation should be under the conduct of one wholly uncon-

[1] Pepysian MSS., No. 2612, p. 380.

versant with ship or sea." On June 23 he retired from the Schools Committee,[1] although he continued to attend the public Courts; [2] and an entry of 1684 at the end of the MS. in the Pepysian Library [3] explains his attitude:—

"MEMORANDUM.—That from my despairs long since conceived and frequently in this Collection mentioned of any satisfactory success to this Foundation from the methods of its then management, and being therein daily confirmed by my observation of the still greater inproficiencies of its children at their examinations at the Trinity House, I persisted in my first withdrawing myself from the care thereof, to the time of the general dissolution of the government both of the Hospitals and City. Nor, though re-chosen thereunto by the succeeding Commission of his Majesty's, bearing date the 26th of October, 1683 (which God prosper), can I yet find any encouragement to the re-engaging myself in any new charge therein."

During his retirement, when office was no longer open to him, Pepys was vigorously pursuing his intellectual interests in correspondence with his friends. He received from John Evelyn, his brother diarist, learned communications upon a variety of subjects:—the affairs of the Royal Society; English navigation; the history of the Dutch War; "our pretence to Dominion on the Seas"; and "the martial performances of dogs." On June 17, 1682, Dr. Robert Wood, the mathematical master at Christ's Hospital, sent him "some papers containing Sir William Petty's

[1] Pepysian MSS., No. 2612, p. 613. [2] *Ib.* p. 719.
[3] *Ib.* p. 722.

scheme of Naval Philosophy,"[1] and on July 3, 1683, Petty himself wrote to him from Dublin, "Notwithstanding many troubles, I every day do something on the design of shipping and sailing, and, I thank God, succeed pretty well." A correspondence of 1680 with Dr. John Turner, a former Fellow of Magdalene, shews that Pepys was interested in Sixtus V's edition of the Vulgate; and on December 3, 1681, he receives from the learned Dr. Thomas Gale, the Headmaster of St. Paul's School, an answer to his enquiry "touching the true construction of the word *versoria*, etc., and the antiquity of the title and office of steerman, both in England and Norway." He also appears as a borrower and lender of books. Between December 11, 1682, and April 26, 1683, Pepys was corresponding with Dr. Nathaniel Vincent of Clare Hall, Cambridge, about the latter's invention of a method of secret writing, to which he had given the uninviting name of *Cryptocovianicon*.

"It bears reading but a very few minutes, and then its characters vanish. Directions may be given to read it which shall not discover its way of writing, so that no letter written by it can ever be a witness against its author, nor shall the writer be engaged to the faithfulness of his messenger; whilst another may carry the instructions for reading, by which means the writer is secured as well against falseness and interception as against curiosity, sauciness, or accidental discoveries. Neither is it more useful than surprising, pleasant, and diverting."

[1] This is copied into Pepys's *Miscellanies*, ii. 477.

The enthusiastic inventor found in his correspondent a courteous but faithful critic.

The correspondence for this period illustrates the close friendship between Pepys and the Houblon family. In 1679 he sent to James Houblon, who knew the language, a Dutch account of English shipbuilding, and Houblon's abstract, dated October 18, 1679, is among the Rawlinson MSS. On November 14, 1680, he wrote to James Houblon a charming letter accompanying the gift of his own portrait, which was duly delivered at Winchester Street by William Hewer, "carefully done up in a coarse cloth."[1] He also sent a present to each member of the family,—"a small bribe" to get them to call attention to the portrait every time they passed it:—

"As thus, 'Was Mr. Pepys in these clothes, father, when you used to go to the Tower to him?' Or thus, 'Lord, cousin, how hath this business of Scott altered my poor Cousin Pepys since this was done!' Or thus, 'What would I give for a Plot, Jemmy, to get you laid by the heels, that I might see what this Mr. Pepys would do for you!'"[2]

A portrait supposed to be this one is preserved by the Houblon family at Hallingbury Place in Essex,[3] but Mr. Lionel Cust is disposed "to dis-

[1] Rawlinson MSS., A. 183, f. 13.

[2] This letter suggests how profound was the impression made upon Pepys's mind by his sufferings when under suspicion of being concerned in the Popish Plot.

[3] Reproduced in *The Houblon Family*, vol. i. facing p. 201.

credit the attribution, and to look for the portrait of Pepys elsewhere among the portraits at Hallingbury, disregarding the inscription on the canvas, which probably dates only from the close of the eighteenth century."[1] The portrait is certainly very unlike Pepys. When old Mr. Houblon, the father of his friend James, died on June 20, 1682, at nearly ninety years of age, Pepys wrote an epitaph in Latin which was placed on a memorial tablet in the church of St. Mary Woolnoth, where he was buried. It also appears on copies of a miniature of him made after his death, one of which hangs in the Bank of England.

During this period Pepys was also corresponding with Cesare Morelli about music. When Morelli went to Brentwood in 1678, his patron had treated him with great consideration, paying for his board and continuing the allowance of £30 a year. On September 25, 1679, Pepys promises to spend a day with him in order to consult him about the guitar, "for the little knowledge in music which I have, never was of more use to me than it is now, under the molestations of mind which I have at this time, more than ordinary, to contend with." He adds disconsolately, that he has nothing left to practise upon but the Lamentations of Jeremiah. On April 11, 1681, hearing of his master's "painfull feaver," the

[1] Pepys Club *Occasional Papers*, 1903-14, p. 33.

grateful Morelli produced an infallible remedy. "There is here a man," he writes, "that can cure it with simpathetical power, if you please to send me down the parings of the nails of both your hands and your foots, and three locks of hair of the top of your crown." On March 8, 1681-2, he wrote to Pepys to inform him of the death of the landlady at his Brentwood lodgings, and it is probable that soon after this he went abroad. On November 13, 1686, in a letter written in French, he asks Pepys to procure him a musical appointment in James II's chapel, where his religion would be a recommendation; and on February 16, 1686-7, he excuses the concealment of his marriage.

SECOND SECRETARYSHIP OF THE ADMIRALTY

(June 10, 1684, to February 20, 1688-9)

The Admiralty Commission of 1679 was revoked by letters patent on May 19, 1684, and from this date until his death the office of Lord High Admiral was executed by the King, with the advice and assistance of "his royal brother the Duke of York." On June 10 the office of "Secretary for the Affairs of the Admiralty of England" was created by letters patent under the Great Seal, and thus it conferred on its holder a higher position and greater powers than had been enjoyed by the secretaries to the Lord High

Admiral before 1673, or by the secretary of the collective Admiralty between 1673 and 1679. To this new office Pepys was appointed, with a salary of £500 a year and an allowance of £700 a year for clerks and house-rent. The important episode of this administration was the establishment, at Pepys's suggestion, of the Special Commission of 1686 "for the Recovery of the Navy." This experiment in organisation was based upon the result of an enquiry made by him, soon after he took office, into the state of the navy and "the disorders and distresses it had been suffered to fall into" under the Commission of 1679-84. This the author presented to Charles II, "in a book fairly written and sealed up," on January 1, 1684-5, "opening to him at the same time the general contents of it . . . by discourse," but this was "all the knowledge" the King "ever had of it," as owing to his illness the book remained unopened until the day of his death on February 6. The scheme was, however, vigorously pursued by James II, who now became his own Lord High Admiral, and the Special Commission began to act in March, 1686, although the patents were not signed until April 17. It was intended to last for three years, the time estimated to be necessary for putting the navy into a state of thorough repair; but the work was so energetically carried through that on October 12, 1688, it was found possible to dissolve it and to restore the old method of administration by the Principal Officers.[1]

Pepys's second Secretaryship of the Admiralty is associated with the re-appearance, in private correspondence,[2] of a curious echo from the *Hue and Cry* of 1679. In a letter of April 6, 1686, it is stated that "Eure" and Pepys "neglect all where money chinks not"; and in another of April 10 the writer says, "I know the griping temper of both him and Eure, and what rates every poor bo'sun pays for what he has purchased with his blood and many years' hardship." There is no reason to suppose that Pepys the Secretary of the Admiralty and Hewer who had just become a Special Commissioner of the Navy were engaged in a conspiracy to defraud the boatswains, but some of the mud thrown in 1679 was sticking still. It is true that Pepys still received presents from his friends, but "three brace of partridges and a barrel of small carps" from one quarter, and "fifteen fine little birds in a small cage" and "a very grave walking-cane" from another, would not lead to any serious declension from the way of righteousness.

[1] A fuller account of the history of the Special Commission of 1686, from a manuscript in the Pepysian Library (No. 1490), is given in *Catalogue of Pepysian MSS.*, pp. 66-91.

[2] Ellis, *Original Letters*, 2nd Series, iv. 92.

On December 1, 1684, by 29 votes out of 39, Pepys was chosen President of the Royal Society, and on December 10 he was sworn in, and took the chair at a meeting of the Society, Evelyn being then one of the Council. During the two years of his tenure his occupations at the Admiralty prevented the President's frequent attendance; and he was only present at eleven Councils and at six meetings of the Society. He paid for sixty plates of Francis Willoughby's *Historia Piscium* and the book was dedicated to him; and on June 30, 1686, the Society ordered "that a Book of Fishes of the best paper, curiously bound in Turkey leather, with an inscription of dedication therein, likewise five others bound also, be presented to the President." Newton's *Principia*, accepted and published by the Society and licensed by Pepys as President, bears on the title-page the words *Imprimatur, S. Pepys, Reg. Soc. Praeses, Julii 5*, 1686.

When James II called a Parliament in 1685, Pepys, who was regarded as having the King's ear, was elected member for both Harwich and Sandwich. He chose to serve for the former, but at the Coronation he walked in the procession immediately after the Royal canopy as one of the Barons of the Cinque Ports. On July 12, 1687, on the rumour that a second Parliament was about to be summoned, he was approached privately on behalf of Sandwich, but this Parliament never met; and he was not elected to serve again for Harwich in the Convention Parliament of 1689. A contemporary account of the election, dated January 16, 1688-9,[1] shews that although it was carried against Pepys by the thirty-one persons entitled to vote, the unenfranchised were in his favour, "most of the freemen, and particularly the seamen, . . . declaring that, had they been concerned in it, they would have chosen Mr. Pepys." The cry that was raised against him, *No Tower men, no men out of the Tower*, was "echoed by nobody."

On May 30, 1685, Pepys was appointed a Deputy-Lieutenant for Huntingdonshire; and in the same year he was for a second time chosen Master of the Trinity House, being named as Master in the new Charter. This document, which had been drafted by Pepys himself, was so voluminous that it could not be got ready by Trinity Monday, and the election was accordingly postponed until July 20. "We went to church according to custom," wrote Evelyn, "and then took barge [from Deptford] to the Trinity House in London, where we had a great dinner, above eighty at one table."

During his second Secretaryship Pepys continued to live in York Buildings, and there he

[1] Printed in Braybrooke, iv. 245.

entertained on Saturday evenings some of the most distinguished members of the Royal Society. It is to these meetings that Evelyn referred when he wrote on January 20, 1702-3, after Pepys had returned to Clapham, "In the mean time I feed on the past conversation I once had in York Buildings, and starve since my friend has forsaken it." The house was sometimes spoken of as the Admiralty, and regarded as if it were an office, and on April 27, 1689, Pepys, who had then ceased to be Secretary, forwarded to the Navy Board a bill dated November 2, 1688, from Matthias Fletcher, Carver to the Navy at Deptford and Woolwich, for "carved work done for the Office of the Admiralty in York Buildings," together with a Royal warrant of James II's for its payment, dated December 3, 1688. The charge was "for a shield for the front of the Office towards the Thames, containing the anchor of the Lord High Admiral of England, with the imperial crown and ciphers . . . £30," and "for the King's arms at large, with ornaments, for the pediment . . . £73 15*s.* 0*d.*" In his covering letter Pepys writes, "The shield . . . has been erected a year or two. The King's arms designed for the pediment, being not finished till a little before the late great Revolution, has been prevented being set up, and remains in Mr. Fletcher's hands, ready, he tells me, to be placed wherever you direct."

Although he was immersed in official business, the Secretary of the Admiralty still found time to correspond with the "virtuosoes," and especially with his friend John Evelyn. On September 23, 1685, Evelyn wrote to him at length upon the use of colours in war; and on October 2 the friends were dining together and discussing the conversion of Charles II to Rome. On December 13, 1685, Evelyn saw "a very noble experiment" at Pepys's house; and on April 19, 1687, he heard the famous singer Cifaccio, "esteemed the best in Europe." "This was before a select number of particular persons whom Mr. Pepys invited to his house; and this was obtained by particular favour and much difficulty, the Signor much disdaining to shew his talent to any but princes." Evelyn's son, John Evelyn the younger, also makes a brief and inglorious appearance. In 1684 he sent Pepys a feeble poem of fifty-four verses in praise of the Duke of York, with a request that the Secretary of the Admiralty should offer them to the Duke's consideration if he himself should "think them worthy of being laid at his Royall Highnesses feet." [1] James Houblon again figures among the correspondents, and there is an interesting reference to Sir William Petty. The copy of his

[1] Historical MSS. Commission, *Fifteenth Report*, Appendix, Pt. ii. p. 177, where the letter is wrongly assigned to 1680.

Dialogue between A. and B. on Liberty of Conscience, 1687, in the Rawlinson Collection has been endorsed by Pepys, " Sir William Petty's paper, written at my desire, and given me by himself a little before his death."

At the Revolution of 1688 Pepys was destined to suffer a final political eclipse, for his relations with James II were too intimate[1] for the new government to leave him in office undisturbed. As the drama of the Revolution drew to its end, he made a brief appearance on the stage at the Trial of the Seven Bishops in June 1688. The prosecution was trying to prove that the Bishops had owned their signatures and their petition at the Council Board, and Pepys was called to give evidence as to what had happened at the Council, where he had chanced to be present; but neither the Lord Chief Justice nor the Attorney-General succeeded in getting anything out of him that was of use to the prosecution.

James II's first withdrawal from London took place on December 11, 1688, and on the same day the Secretary of the Admiralty was summoned to attend the Lords Spiritual and Temporal who were taking over the control of public affairs, and from them he received his orders. It was from

[1] James was sitting to Kneller for a portrait commissioned by Pepys when the news arrived of the landing of the Prince of Orange in Torbay.

this first withdrawal that the end of the reign came to be dated, and on December 12, Evelyn wrote to Pepys:

"I left you indisposed, and send on purpose to learn how it is with you, and to know if in any sort I may serve you in this prodigious Revolution. You have many friends, but no man living who is more sincerely your servant or that has a greater value for you."

With this should be compared another letter, written on December 19, two days after James's second and final withdrawal, and signed "Your ever faithful and obedient servant, WM. HEWER:"

"You may rest assured that I am wholly yours, and that you shall never want the utmost of my constant, faithful, and personal service; the utmost I can do being inconsiderable to what your kindness and favour to me has and does oblige me to. And therefore as all I have proceeded from you, so all I have and am is and shall be at your service."[1]

This was endorsed by Pepys, "A letter of great tenderness at a time of difficulty."

The Secretary of the Admiralty remained at his post for more than two months after the abdication of James, working under William of Orange until he became king. The Crown was formally accepted by William and Mary on February 13, 1688-9, and on February 20 Pepys ceased to act. On March 9 he was directed to hand over his books and papers to Phineas Bowles, who had been appointed to succeed him.

[1] Rawlinson MSS., A. 179, f. 59; also printed in Braybrooke, iv. 244.

FINAL RETIREMENT

(February 20, 1688-9, to May 26, 1703)

On August 26, 1689,[1] six months after his surrender of his post, Pepys wrote to the Trinity House "desiring his being discharged from his relation thereto," assigning as the reason his inability to attend. His friend and colleague Sir Anthony Deane, who had shared both his tribulations and his triumphs, wrote to him on October 29 in terms which suggest a complete withdrawal from public life:

"These are only to let you know that I am alive. I have nothing to do but read, walk, and prepare for all chances attending this obliging world. I have the old soldier's request,[2] a little space between business and the grave, which is very pleasant on many considerations...."

In an undated letter Pepys replies:

"I am alive too, I thank God! and as serious I fancy as you can be, and not less alone.... The worse the world uses me, the better, I think, I am bound to use myself..."

But he was not yet able to realise that the world had ended for him. On February 8, 1689-80, two days after the dissolution of the Convention Parliament, he began to make interest with his friends to find him a "berth" in the new Parliament which had been summoned for March 20. He had no hopes of Harwich, "being fallen

[1] Rawlinson MSS., A. 170, f. 146.

[2] To the Emperor Charles V.

wholly into new hands," but he flattered himself that his "being in this Parliament might not be wholly unuseful." This last bid for a career failed, and the Government of the Revolution, with singular ingratitude to the man who had in 1686 regenerated the navy, committed him to the Gatehouse on June 25, 1690, "on suspicion of being affected to King James." His second imprisonment was of short duration, for on June 30 Evelyn writes, "I dined with Mr. Pepys, now suffered to return to his house on account of indisposition"; and in October the proceedings were dropped. On October 15, "being this day become once again a free man," he writes to his bailors, Sir Peter Palavicini, Mr. James Houblon, Mr. Blackborne, and Mr. Martin, inviting them to share "a piece of mutton" with him on the following day. But to the end of his life Pepys was an object of suspicion to the Government. When in 1698 he sent his nephew John Jackson to travel abroad, the enterprise was at first supposed to have a sinister significance. "I hope you will have an eye upon Mr. Pepys's nephew that he doth not go astray," wrote James Vernon to Matthew Prior at Paris on August 16, 1698;[1] "I believe the old gentleman means fairly, and hath sent no underhand compliments to his old master, having professed the contrary; but young

[1] *Calendar of the Bath Papers*, iii. 256, 261.

men and ladies may sometimes be libertines and forget good advice." These fears proved to be groundless, for Prior replied on September 3, "By what I have yet seen of the conduct of Mr. Pepys's nephew, it is likely to prove innocent enough."

On September 29, 1693, John Jackson had shared with his uncle an exciting adventure, for when travelling in the latter's coach to Chelsea with some ladies, they had been robbed by masked highwaymen, who, "holding a pistol to the coachman's breast and another against Mr. Pepys's, ... demanded what they had, which Mr. Pepys readily gave them." The spoil included five mathematical instruments and a magnifying glass. On December 6-9 two men were tried for the crime at the Old Bailey, and in spite of alibis of the usual type were convicted and sentenced to death.

Although Pepys was now out of office, his knowledge, experience, and influence were still appealed to in connexion with naval affairs. A letter of December 9, 1689, written from Chatham by his cousin Charles Pepys, suggests that he was popular in the navy. "Blessed be God, I scarce speak to any officer of the King's ships but ask me how your Honour doth, and say they are in hope your Honour will shortly come into power again." On August 6, 1697, he was furnishing Davenant with information concerning the strength of the Royal Navy in 1666 and 1688,[1] probably for use in one of his Essays; and even as late as May 20, 1700, the Bishop of Ely was seeking to obtain through his good offices a clerkship in the Navy Office for the "poor orphan son of an honest clergyman."

When Pepys withdrew from the Admiralty in 1689, an attempt was made to turn him out of his house in York Buildings and to assign it to office purposes, but the occupant displayed the greatest reluctance to go, and eventually the new Commissioners of the Admiralty gave up their project in despair. On April 12, 1689, Sir John Lowther wrote, "The Committee, finding their affairs could not bear the want of a house for so long time as you required to remove, have agreed for a house elsewhere."[2]

In York Buildings Pepys continued to keep up a certain state. The rent of the house was £150 a year, and a paper of 1697[3] gives particulars of a staff of eight servants,—a porter at £12, a footman at £10, a housekeeper and a coachman at £8, and a junior footman, a cook, a laundrymaid, and a housemaid, all at £6. Pepys also rented a "little house" in York Buildings at £25 a year for his servant Jones, who may have been a

[1] Copies of letters found among Mr. H. B. Wheatley's papers.

[2] Rawlinson MSS., A. 170, f. 66.

[3] Among some uncalendared papers in the Pepysian Library.

personal attendant. If he was involved in domestic difficulties, it was not for want of good advice, for on October 3, 1685, Evelyn had sent him at his request a memorandum on housekeeping[1] which his wife had drawn up in 1675 for the use of a friend who was about to be married. It furnishes estimates for a family of eight persons, "as many as were in the Ark," and contains a priceless maxim,—"Use but seldom chare women and out-helpers as you can, they but make gossips." On November 29, 1685, Mrs. Evelyn followed up this general counsel by a particular recommendation. She had picked out as a housekeeper for Pepys "a very neat, an excellent housewife, not ungentile, sightly and well-behaved, yet of years to allow the necessary experience and prudence to direct in a family and preserve respect," and it may fairly be conjectured that this was Mrs. Fane, with whom he parted in anger in 1689. On July 10 he wrote to James Houblon, who had known Mrs. Fane "from her bib upwards" and was trying to mediate between them,

"I do not believe a more knowing, faithful, or vigilant person, or a stricter keeper at home, or (which is to me a great addition) a person more useful in sickness as well as health than Mrs. Fane is can anywhere be found.... At the same time, I must also tell you that with all these excellences she hath a height of spirit, captiousness of humour, and bitterness and noise of tongue that, of all

[1] Mr. S. J. Davey's Collection (now dispersed).

womankind I have hitherto had to do withal, do render her conversation and comportment as a servant most insupportable. This I say to you after three years and a half's grievous experience. . . ."

A housekeeper is included in the staff of 1697 referred to above, but the comfort of the household came to depend mainly upon Mrs. Skynner, who kept house for Pepys in York Buildings, probably after the departure of Mrs. Fane, and remained with him until the close of his life. In a codicil to his Will he left an annuity of £200 in acknowledgment of his "esteem, respect, and gratitude to the Excellent Lady, Mrs. Mary Skynner, for the many important Effects of her Steddy friendship and Assistances during the whole course of my life within the last thirty-three years"; and he also left her £5000 out of the debt due from the Crown, if it should ever be paid.

In January 1689-90 Pepys's friend Dr. Gale sent him a description of Walcote House, about two miles out of Stamford, which was then in the market, but he remained faithful to York Buildings. In 1696 he was assessed there for capitation tax, paying double for not taking the oaths; [1] and a receipt for watch money, paid on May 3, 1703, "by the order of Squire Peepes," proves that he retained the house until his death.

From York Buildings Pepys maintained an unabated interest in the Royal Society; and he

[1] Uncalendared Pepysian papers.

was still consulted from time to time about the affairs of Christ's Hospital. In 1692 it was proposed to establish a Drawing School at the Hospital, and Pepys was asked for his advice. He replied that he could only send "the opinion of one whom age and idleness have now spoiled for a counsellor in anything," but he supported the view already taken by Wren, that foreign artisans, and especially the French, are ahead of the English in the mechanic arts because they are taught drawing as the foundation of them.[1] After 1693 Pepys reappeared as a reformer, putting forward plans which aimed at securing better teaching and stricter examination; and on April 27, 1699, the Court of Aldermen, "in acknowledgment of the great zeal and concern for the interest of Christ's Hospital which Samuel Pepys Esquire hath manifested upon all occasions, and in hopes of his continuing the same regard and inclinations for its preservation and advancement for the future, doth present him with the Freedom of the City. . . ."[2] This may have been a sop to Cerberus, for Thomas Tanner writes in a letter to Dr. Charlett dated the following day,

"I hear [Mr. Pepys] has printed some letters lately about the abuses of Christ's Hospital; they are only privately

[1] Letter of November 17, 1692, quoted in E. H. Pearce, *Annals of Christ's Hospital*, 1st edn. 1901, p. 159.

[2] *Antiquary* (December 1883), viii. 233.

handed about. A gentleman that has a very great respect for Mr. P. saw one of them in one of the Aldermen's hands, but wishes there had been some angry expressions left out, which he fears the Papists and other enemies of the Church of England will make ill use of."[1]

In June of the same year, when Alderman Sir John Moore, the President of Christ's Hospital, asked to be relieved of some of his duties by the appointment of a Vice-President, Pepys was chosen for that office.[2]

At the date of his final retirement Pepys was only 56, and such records as exist for the remaining 14 years of his life shew an amazing intellectual activity exercising itself over a vast and varied field. Very soon after his surrender of office he began collecting "heads," and on August 26, 1689, Evelyn wrote, with ponderous learning and at prodigious length, a letter "upon occasion of Mr. Pepys's design of adorning his library with some of the most learned and otherwise eminent living heads of our own nation,"[3] remarking modestly, "I did not in the least suspect your intention of placing my shallow head amongst those heroes"; and Pepys was still adding to his collection of prints as late as 1702. He also gave much time to the sorting and weeding

[1] Printed in Braybrooke, iv. 263.

[2] Minutes of the Court of Aldermen, June 20 and 28, 1699; *Antiquary*, viii. 238.

[3] Rawlinson MSS., A. 171, f. 316.

out of his library, and to the acquisition of new treasures.

> "Were the *Diary* non-existent [writes Mr. F. Sidgwick], and were no other source of knowledge available, a judgement of Pepys's character formed upon a consideration of the contents of his Library would reveal him to have been a man of great breadth of interest and catholicity of taste, an inquisitive scholar conversant with more languages than his own, and a person in whom a love of order and neatness in detail was paramount."[1]

He commissioned friends travelling abroad to buy books for him, and in a letter to Evelyn of December 4, 1701, he refers to "my two or three months' by-work of sorting and binding together my nephew's Roman marketings." He also acquired books by gift, and sometimes by simple appropriation. In 1700, with the consent of the Dean and Chapter, he cut out and carried off for his "Calligraphical Collection" two slips from the MS. Gospels in the Cathedral Library at Durham; and in a letter to Evelyn of March 28, 1692, he refers to "that vast treasure of papers which I have had of yours so many years in my hands,"—an acquisition which was never restored to its rightful owner. We learn from an important letter of August 4, 1694,[2] written to Dr. Charlett, that Pepys himself contributed an account of his own manuscripts to *Catalogi librorum manu-*

[1] In *Bibliotheca Pepysiana*, Pt. ii. p. i.

[2] Printed from the Ballard Letters (i. 140) in *Academy*, xxxviii (1890), 110.

scriptorum Angliae et Hiberniae in unum collecti, published in 1697,—"the noble work you virtuosi of Oxford are upon, of enriching our English world with the knowledge of a wealth it is itself mistress of and does not yet know it." The place of Pepys in the literary world of his day was also recognised by the fact that books were dedicated to him.[1]

Pepys was a friend and patron of authors, but apart from the *Diary* he produced little himself. In the *Bibliotheca Britannica* Robert Watt, who calls him "a liberal benefactor to the literature of his country," assigns to him the authorship of *Portugal History: or a Relation of the Troubles in the Court of Portugal in 1667 and 1668*, by S.P. Esqre, London, 1677, probably translated from, or at any rate closely related to, a work in French with a similar title published in Amsterdam in 1674. Although there is a copy of the book in the Pepysian Library, the ascription must be regarded as doubtful. The style is not in any way characteristic of Pepys, and it is unlikely that in 1677, when he was in the full tide of business at the Admiralty, he would have turned aside to write on a subject so remotely connected with the sea. Attempts have also been made to father various pamphlets upon him, and Macray doubtfully ascribes to him *A Friend to Caesar*, because one of the copies in the Bodleian is bound up with his letter of 1665 to

[1] A list of these is given in Wheatley, *Pepysiana*, pp. 55-60.

Coventry about the victualling, and the volume is labelled on the back, probably by a later hand, "Pepys on the Treasury and Navy." The tract is almost entirely concerned with the Treasury, of which Pepys knew little, and it is more likely that the author was Coventry, who had been a Treasury Commissioner. James II's *Memoirs of the English Affairs, chiefly Naval, from 1660 to 1673*, was probably edited by Pepys, but the *Memoires of the Royal Navy*, 1679-1688, published in 1690, remains his only acknowledged work. In this criticism of the blunders of the Admiralty Commission of 1679 he appears "as a naval administrator pure and simple, defending an official position in official language, with the help of statistics and official documents."

Quite early in his career, Pepys had conceived a grandiose scheme for a History of the Navy, and for this he was collecting materials throughout his life, although he did not proceed very far in the arrangement of them. On June 13, 1664, he talked with Coventry "of a History of the Navy of England, how fit it were to be writ; and he did say that it hath been in his mind to propose to me the writing of the history of the late Dutch War, which I am glad to hear, it being a thing I much desire, and sorts mightily with my genius, and, if well done, may recommend me much." Entries in the *Diary* of March 15 and 16, 1668-9, shew that he had by that time accumulated materials for the period 1618-42, " in order to my great business now of stating the history of the Navy." His correspondence with Evelyn and Sir William Dugdale suggests that the project was conceived on the broadest lines, and would have included in its scope the antiquities of the navy, and possibly the history of navigation ; and this impression is confirmed by the miscellaneous memoranda,—many of them notes for the History,—entered in a manuscript volume in the Pepysian Library entitled *Naval Minutes*. The numerous papers copied in the twelve volumes of *Miscellanies* also cover a good deal of ground. Writing on August 4, 1694, to Dr. Charlett,[1] Pepys describes his collection as a " mass of papers, for the most part unconnected, and those out of any of the trodden roads of common reading," relating mainly to " the History Laws, and Oeconomy " of the Navy ; but in this sphere he claims that it was complete. " And a just reproach I should think it of to me to have one hole found unsearched by me, or knowingly to have failed of rendering myself master of any one written sheet that either pains or price could help me to on that subject." A year before this was written, on July 5, 1693, in an epistle " to Mr. Southwell, newly a Clerk of

[1] Printed from the Ballard Letters (i. 140) in the *Academy*, xxxviii. (1890), 109.

the Council, part compliment, part business,"[1] Pepys asks him to look up a point of naval history for him in the Council-books, and as late as January 2, 1699-1700, he was enquiring after Monson's *Naval Tracts*; but the great undertaking was never finished. On May 26, 1703, when the news of his friend's death reached him, Evelyn wrote in his *Diary*, "Besides what he published of an account of the navy as he found and left it, he had for divers years under his hand the History of the Navy, or *Navalia* as he called it; but how far advanced and what will follow of his is left, I suppose, to his sister's son."

During his retirement Pepys corresponded upon a variety of subjects with some of the most learned and distinguished men of the day,—Sir Isaac Newton, Sir Hans Sloane, John Dryden the poet, John Evelyn the diarist, Sir Godfrey Kneller the painter, John Wallis the mathematician, and Humfrey Wanley the palaeographer. He also exchanged numerous letters with Dr. Arthur Charlett, Master of University College, Oxford, and kept in close touch with the great merchant family of Houblon.

[1] Printed in the *Athenaeum*, 1890 (i.), p. 705. This letter includes a characteristic reflection: "But Time has some lessons which it keeps for its own teaching only, unless you can and will borrow them of a friend that has paid for them. I say *will*, for 'twas not Solomon's fault that I learnt too late, nor shall be mine if you do so too. To shun being too righteous as much as being too wise, There's one of them."

The correspondence with Evelyn was the most voluminous, for the relations between the two friends had grown closer with advancing years. On July 8, 1689, Kneller was painting Evelyn's portrait on a commission from Pepys, and on August 29, 1692, Evelyn writes to Pepys from his country-house at Wotton,

"I have been philosophising and world-despising in the solitudes of this place, whither I am retired to pass [the time] and mourn the absence of my worthiest friend. Here is wood and water, meadows and mountains, the Dryads and Hamadryads; but here's no Mr. Pepys, no Dr. Gale. Nothing of all the cheer in the parlour that I taste; all's insipid, and all will be so to me till I see and enjoy you again."

Among the subjects discussed between them are, the buying of pictures; collections of coins and medals; the dearth of libraries in England; the nature of dreams; and the praise of music. On August 15, 1690, the Bishop of St. Asaph "expounds his prophecies" to them;[1] and on January 9, 1691-2, Evelyn is asked to meet Newton and Dr. Gale at Pepys's house. On May 30, 1698, he dined there to hear "the rare voice of Mr. Pule" singing some of Purcell's compositions; and on August 6, at another dinner at Pepys's house, he met Captain Dampier, "who

[1] Evelyn's *Diary*. William Lloyd, one of the Seven Bishops, was an eager student of the book of Daniel and the Apocalypse, and claimed to be able "to read the prophecies as he read history" (*D.N.B.* xxxiii. 437).

had been a famous buccaneer," and found him "a more modest man than one would imagine by the relation of the crew he had assorted with." The correspondence with Newton relates to "the doctrine of determining between the true proportion of the hazards incident to this or that given chance or lot," and includes a series of letters[1] giving a full exposition of Newton's views. One of Kneller's letters to Pepys[2] contains the *obiter dictum*, "All Frenchmen require to be made [civil], being born under a slavish government." On May 2, 1699, Dr. Wallis was writing to Pepys about secret ciphers, and on October 24 concerning "the eclipse lately seen at Oxford," describing his experience of the difficulty of steering a boat on the Thames in a thick mist and the bearing of this upon "ancient circumnavigations." Wanley's letters are of value to the biographer because they shew that as late as 1702 Pepys was able to interest himself in the appointment to the Keepership of the Cottonian Library; and also for the character which Wanley gives of Pepys. In a letter to Dr. Charlett of March 8, 1700-1, he refers to his "obliging kindness" as a host, "which engages all that he converses with into a love and respect for his person," and to "his

[1] In the Pepys Cockerell Collection; only two of them have been printed by Lord Braybrooke.

[2] January 16, 1689-90.

judgment in men and things, in placing his friendships and shewing his countenance on those only whose merit gave them some pretensions thereto."

An exchange of letters of peculiar interest is that between Pepys and Dryden. In 1698 Dryden had dined with Pepys, who had suggested to him the character of Chaucer's Good Parson as a subject for his pen, and the ultimate result was a folio volume, published in 1700, entitled *Fables Ancient and Modern: translated into verse from Homer, Ovid, Boccace, and Chaucer; with Original Poems*: By Mr. Dryden. In a letter of July 14, 1699, beginning *Padron Mio*, Dryden offers to bring to Pepys a copy of the "Character," and Pepys replies on the same day, inviting the poet "to a cold chicken and a salad any noon after Sunday, as being just stepping into the air for two days." Dryden's letter, endorsed "Mr. Dryden to S.P. upon his translating at his request Chaucer's Prologue to his Parson's Tale," together with a copy of the reply to it, is inserted in Pepys's own volume of Dryden's *Fables*.

With so much leisure now at his command, Pepys could eagerly investigate such problems as provoked his characteristic curiosity. On September 10, 1698, he wrote out an account of some tests applied to the "singular memory" of Mr. Meheux, who could repeat 60 words given him in a numerical order "in the same order backwards and forwards " eight minutes after they had been dictated to him.[1] From October 1699 to May 1701 Pepys was corresponding with Lord Reay and others about second-sight; and on March 8, 1702-3, little more than two months before his own death, he was receiving from Roger Gale, the son of the Dean of York, the story of the apparition of his absent father in his stall in York Minster, and its very mundane explanation. On October 10, 1702, he was describing to Dr. John Hudson, Bodley's Librarian at Oxford, the remarkable performance of Mr. Dundas, who for five guineas wrote out a document which included the Creed and other matter, and ended with a Latin dedication to Pepys himself, in a hand so minute that the whole could be covered "with the common hammered penny of King Charles the First."

In the latter part of his life Pepys came into close relations with the University of Oxford, which he calls "my dear Aunt." His affection for Oxford even undermined his loyalty to Cambridge, for in a letter from Wanley to Charlett,

[1] This was not his first experiment, for Evelyn in his *Diary* for January 27, 1688-9, describes the examination by Pepys and himself of an infant prodigy of twelve years of age, the son of Andrew Clench the physician. After an overwhelming display of "the most prodigious maturity of knowledge" in chronology, history, geography, astronomy, Latin and French, "the tenets of the Gnostics, Sabellians, Arians, Nestorians," "the difference between St. Cyprian and Stephen about re-baptization," and "both natural and moral philosophy" including metaphysics, the two examiners "left questioning further."

dated May 13, 1698,[1] referring to the possibility of the Cottonian Library being acquired by Oxford, the following statement occurs: "Mr. Pepys says he looks upon that Library as one of the jewels of the Crown of England; and declared to me that, though he is a Cambridge man, yet he had much rather the Library was carried to Oxford." In a letter to Dr. Charlett of May 5, 1695,[2] he acknowledges a List of Benefactors, "which God increase!" and asks for a copy of the Oxford Service for their Commemoration, having already obtained the corresponding Cambridge Service through the good offices of Dr. Quadring, the Master of Magdalene. In another letter to Charlett, dated April 27, 1699,[3] we find the earliest mention of his plan for presenting to the University a portrait of the venerable Dr. Wallis, the Savilian Professor of Geometry, "which I should with great pleasure see done by the best hand, whether Sir Godfrey Kneller, Cloysterman,[4] or any other that Mr. Dean [of Christ Church] and you shall propose; to be there lodged *in perpetuam Wallesii memoriam.*" Kneller was eventually selected, and the portrait was painted in Oxford. On March 24, 1701-2,

[1] Ellis, *Original Letters* (Camden Society), p. 260.

[2] Printed from the Ballard Letters (i. 151) in the *Academy*, xxxviii. (1890) 152.

[3] *Ib.* p. 175 (Ballard Letters, i. 160).

[4] John Closterman, the portrait painter from Hanover.

the artist wrote to Pepys, "I never did a better picture, nor so good a one, in my life, which is the opinion of all as has seen it." The work must have been rapidly executed, for on September 3, 1702, Charlett tells Pepys that "the painter's fancy was warm, and his imaginations not to be controlled . . . with delays." The finishing touches were applied in London, and the picture was duly delivered to Pepys, who had undertaken responsibility for the frame. "A very proper place" was provided for it in the Gallery of the Schools, "next to Sir Harry Savile, the Founder of the Mathematic Lectures," and on September 12[1] the donor wrote from Clapham to Charlett to say that it would be in Oxford by Tuesday. On September 26 Dr. Wallis returned thanks to Pepys for "that noble present," and on October 30 a letter of thanks was sent to Pepys by Charlett, then acting in place of the Vice-Chancellor, on behalf of Convocation, "for his noble testimony of respect and affection to learning and this University," accompanied by a Latin Diploma drawn by the Public Orator.[2] On November 14 Pepys wrote in acknowledgment to Charlett, adding, "I would not be thought, neither, unmindful of the superlative performance of your Orator therein,

[1] Letter printed in the *Academy* from the Ballard Letters, i. 173.

[2] This is printed in Wheatley's edition of the *Diary*, vol. i. p. xlviii.

whose every period seems to raise a new world of glory to me out of nothing, even to the putting me out of countenance to own it." This was followed, on December 5, by a more formal letter of thanks from the Vice-Chancellor, Dr. Delaune.

Writing to Evelyn on August 14, 1694, Pepys had confessed to being "a good deal out of order," and in 1697 he had a serious illness. On May 15 Dr. Thomas Smith wrote to Mr. Wanley,

> "My very worthy and excellent friend Mr. Pepys has been very ill of late, and was brought so low that we were afraid we should have lost him; but now, God be praised, the danger is over, and he by advice of physicians and friends is gone into the country, but not far from London, for full and perfect recovery of his health, which I dare say you, and indeed all others who know what a brave, publick-spirited gentleman he is, wish as well as I." [1]

It is probable that the reference is to Clapham, whither Pepys went from time to time as Hewer's guest. It was not until the end of 1699, or the beginning of 1700, that the return of his old enemy the stone began to render him a permanent invalid.[2] On May 6, 1700, Thomas Tanner wrote to Dr. Charlett, "Mr. Pepys has been in a very ill state of health this winter, and is now

[1] Ellis, *Original Letters*, 2nd series, i. 241.

[2] In a letter from Clapham to Sir Godfrey Kneller, dated March 26, 1702, he writes, "so it has fallen out that by an unexpected return of an old evil the stone, I have been ever since under a continued incapacity for these two years and more of stirring out of doors, and at length was forced for life ... to be brought hither, where I still am, and am likely to be."

gone to Clapham for the air." The change was beneficial, for on May 10 Evelyn congratulates him on the improvement in his health, and on May 14 Roger Gale, writing from Cambridge, refers to his "happy recovery." His doctor would not yet allow him books, but a letter of September 19 shews that he had been making country excursions to Windsor, Hampton Court, Epsom, Richmond, and Streatham Wells, "with other places in our neighbourhood," and by October 29 he was looking forward to returning to town within ten days "at farthest." On December 3 he was once more writing from York Buildings. The improvement was, however, only temporary. On June 7, 1701, Pepys informs Evelyn that under medical advice he is now hastening his return to Clapham, "with some prospect of setting up my future rest there." On October 10 he refers to his "long and forlorn want of health," but the change again proved beneficial, and on November 19 he writes to Evelyn from Clapham, "As much as I am (I bless God !) in perfect present ease as to my health, 'tis little less however than a very burial to me, as to what of all my worldly goods I put most price upon, I mean the few old and learned friends I had flattered myself with the hopes of closing the little residue of my life in the continued enjoyment of." To one of these friends, Dr. Sloane, he makes a pathetic appeal in a letter of July 31, 1702: "I have not thanked you neither, as I ought long since to have done and now do, for the favour of your last visit; almost wishing myself sick, that I might have a pretence to invite you for an hour or two to another by yourself."

It is probable that when Pepys went to live at Clapham for good, he took with him his whole establishment of men and women servants, for mourning rings are provided for seven of them in his Will; and references in letters make it clear that Mrs. Skynner was keeping house for him there as she had done in York Buildings. Until the final removal to Clapham, most of his books remained on the other side of the River, for on October 12, 1700, Paul Lorrain, his copyist, reports to him from York Buildings, and on October 29 Pepys writes from Clapham to Dr. Charlett, "As impatient as I am to be among my old friends again (as you know who called them) my books, my friends on this side the water are obstinately bent to prevent it, as long as there is one mouthful of serene air to be hoped for this season."[1] On the other hand, a reference in his Will to "my Collections of Books and papers contained in my Library, now remaining at Mr. Hewer's at Clapham or in any other place or places," suggests that part of them

[1] *Academy*, xxxviii. 200 (from the Ballard Letters, i. 165).

had accompanied him thither on his final retirement.

It is strange that there should be so much uncertainty about the site of the house to which Evelyn refers as "your Paradisian Clapham."[1] Sir Dennis Gauden's mansion was famous in its day, but the tradition of it seems to have been lost. It has been suggested that its position was that now occupied by The Elms or Elm House (No. 29, North Side), where Sir Charles Barry, the architect of the Houses of Parliament, formerly lived, but the case cannot be regarded as completely made out and there is no good plan of the site in existence.[2]

Although he shewed remarkable constitutional vitality, which "supported him under the most exquisite pains, weeks beyond all expectations," the painful disease from which Pepys was suffering had made alarming progress, as was proved by examination after death.[3] He died at Clapham on the morning of May 26, 1703, at about a quarter to four, and was buried at nine on the night of June 4 by his friend Dr. George Hickes, the non-juring Bishop of Thetford, in a vault by the communion-table of St. Olave's, Hart Street,

[1] Letter of January 20, 1702-3, printed in Braybrooke, iv. 320.

[2] Mr. Philip Norman's MS.

[3] Historical MSS. Commission, *Ninth Report*, Pt. ii. Appendix, p. 466.

just beneath the monument to the memory of Mrs. Pepys. On the day of his death John Evelyn wrote in his *Diary*,

"This day died Mr. Samuel Pepys, a very worthy industrious and curious person, none in England exceeding him in knowledge of the Navy.... He was universally beloved, hospitable, generous, learned in many things, skilled in music, a very great cherisher of learned men of whom he had the conversation.... Mr. Pepys had been for near forty years... my particular friend."

During the next century the name of Samuel Pepys carried great weight in the navy; and in the first report of the Commission of 1805 on naval administration he is described as "a man of extraordinary knowledge in all that related to the business of" the Admiralty, "of great talents, and the most indefatigable industry." Thus to the 18th century he bequeathed a fine record of public service, and to the 19th the priceless heritage of the *Diary*. The private confession for long obscured the public service: but the 20th century has done something to bring the two traditions into their right relation to each other and so to restore to us the real Pepys.

BIOGRAPHICAL SUMMARY

1633	Feb. 23	Samuel Pepys born in Salisbury Court, Fleet Street.
	Mar. 3	Baptised in St. Bride's Church.
c. 1644		At Huntingdon Grammar School.
c. 1646-50		At St. Paul's School.
1650	June 21	Entered at Trinity Hall, Cambridge.
	Oct. 1	Transferred to Magdalene College.
1651	Mar. 5	Began residence at the University.
	July 4	Matriculated.
1654	March	Proceeded to the B.A. Degree.
1655	Dec. 1	Married Elizabeth St. Michel.
c. 1656		Steward to his kinsman Edward Mountagu, afterwards Earl of Sandwich, and lived in Mountagu's lodgings at Whitehall.
1656 ?		Appointed a Clerk of the Exchequer.
1658	Mar. 26	Operated on for the stone.
1659	June	Accompanied Mountagu to the Sound.
1659		Living in Axe Yard, Westminster.
1660	*Jan.* 1	*Began to write the Diary.*
	Feb. 24-28	Visited Cambridge.
	Mar. 22	Appointed Secretary to the Generals of the Fleet sailing to Holland to bring over the restored King.
	May 25	Witnessed Charles II.'s landing at Dover.
	June 9	Returned to London.
	June 28	Resigned Clerkship of the Exchequer.
	June 29	Appointed Clerk of the Acts.
	July 23	Sworn in as a Clerk of the Privy Seal.
	Sept. 24	Sworn in as a Justice of the Peace.

1660 Proceeded to the Degree of M.A.
1661 Apr. 30-May 6 Visited Portsmouth.
July 6-22 Went to Brampton on the death (July 5) of his uncle, Robert Pepys.
Aug. 3-7 Visited Cambridge, Impington, and Brampton.
1662 Feb. 15 Admitted a Younger Brother of the Trinity House.
Apr. 22-May 2 Visited Portsmouth.
Apr. 30 Made a Burgess of the Town of Portsmouth.
Aug. 17 Resigned his Clerkship of the Privy Seal.
Oct. 9-15 Visited Cambridge and Brampton.
Nov. Nominated on the newly-appointed Commission for the Affairs of Tangier.
1663 Sept. 14-21 Visited Brampton.
1664 Mar. 15 Death of his brother Tom.
Apr. 8 Nominated on the new Corporation for the Royal Fishing.
Sept. 5 Elected a member of the standing Fishery Committee.
Oct. 13-16 Visited Brampton.
1665 Feb. 15 Elected a Fellow of the Royal Society.
Mar. 20 Appointed Treasurer for Tangier.
July 5 Removed family to Woolwich on account of the Plague.
c. Nov. 8 Appointed Surveyor-General of Victualling.
1666 Jan. 7 Returned to London.
Sept. 2 Saw the beginning of the Fire.
1667 Mar. 25 Death of his mother at Brampton.
July 28 Resigned the Surveyorship of Victualling.
Oct. 7-12 Visited Brampton to dig up the gold buried there during the panic caused by the appearance of the Dutch in the Medway.
Oct. 22 Defence of the Navy Office before the House of Commons in Committee.
1668 Feb. 27 Marriage of his sister Paulina to John Jackson.

1668	Mar. 5	Speech at the bar of the House of Commons in defence of the Navy Office.
	May 23-26	Visited Brampton and Cambridge.
	June 5-17	Tour in the West of England.
	Oct. 25	The domestic tragedy.
1669	*May* 31	*The Diary discontinued.*
	June-Oct.	Tour in Holland and France.
	Nov. 10	Death of Mrs. Pepys.
	Nov. ?	Fails to be elected M.P. for Aldborough.
1670	Mar. 30	His brother John appointed Clerk to the Trinity House.
	Nov. 9	Duel with the Swedish Resident forbidden by the King.
1672	Jan. 24	Admitted an Elder Brother of the Trinity House.
	June 24	One of the six "Bannerolles" at Lord Sandwich's funeral in Westminster Abbey.
1673	Jan. 29	Destructive fire at the Navy Office in Seething Lane; Pepys moves soon after to Winchester Street.
	June 15	The Duke of York surrendered the Office of Lord High Admiral of England.
	June 18	Pepys became Secretary of the Admiralty; his brother John appointed Joint Clerk of the Acts with Thomas Hayter.
	July 9	The Admiralty placed in commission.
	Oct. ?	Elected M.P. for Castle Rising.
1674	Jan. 3	Began to date his official correspondence from the new Admiralty Office at Derby House.
	Dec. ?	Moved from Winchester Street to Derby House.
1676	Feb. 1	Appointed a Governor of Christ's Hospital.
	May 22	Elected Master of the Trinity House.
1677	Feb. 23	Speech in the House of Commons in support of the Bill for 30 new ships.
	Mar. ?	Death of his brother John.

1677	Aug. 8	Elected Master of the Clothworkers Company.
	Sept. 10	Steward at a Feast of the Honourable Artillery Company.
	Oct. ?	Elected a member of the Schools Committee of Christ's Hospital.
1679	Feb. 11	His clerk, Samuel Atkins, acquitted for the murder of Sir Edmund Berry Godfrey.
	Mar. 6	Appeared as M.P. for Harwich in the short Parliament of 1679.
	Apr. 21	Dissolution of the Admiralty Commission of 1673-9 and appointment of a new Commission.
	May 14	Wider powers conferred on them by a Commission of their own drafting.
	May 21	Pepys resigned the Secretaryship of the Admiralty and ceased to be Treasurer for Tangier.
	May 22	Pepys and Deane committed to the Tower on a charge of treasonable correspondence with France.
	July 9	Pepys and Deane released on bail; Pepys went to live with William Hewer at his house in York Buildings.
	Oct. 13	Publication of two pamphlets attacking Pepys and Hewer for corruption.
1680	Feb. 12	Pepys and Deane relieved of their bail.
	June 30	Proceedings against them finally abandoned.
	c. Aug. ?	Death of his sister Paulina's husband, John Jackson.
	c. Oct. 2	At Newmarket: took down, at Charles II.'s dictation, the story of his escape after the battle of Worcester.
	Oct. 4	His father buried at Brampton.
	c. Oct. 4-Nov. 19.	Remained at Brampton, settling the affairs of the family and preparing an exposure of the villainies of Scott.
1681	Mar. 9	Returned to the affairs of Christ's Hospital.

1681	Aug.	Proposed appointment by royal mandate as Provost of King's College, Cambridge.
1682	May 4	Accompanied the Duke of York on his unfortunate voyage to Edinburgh.
	May 26 ?	Received the freedom of the City of Newcastle.
	June 23	Retired from the Schools Committee of Christ's Hospital.
1683	July 30	Set out from London to accompany Lord Dartmouth as his Secretary on his voyage to Tangier to superintend the evacuation of the town and the destruction of the Mole.
	Dec. 1	Left Tangier to travel in Spain.
1684	Mar. 5-30	On return voyage from Tangier.
	May 19	Dissolution of the Admiralty Commission of 1679-84.
	June 10	Pepys again appointed Secretary of the Admiralty.
	Dec. 1	Elected President of the Royal Society.
1685	*c.* Apr.	Elected M.P. for both Harwich and Sandwich.
	Apr. 23	Walked in James II.'s coronation procession as a Baron of the Cinque Ports.
	May 19	Sat in Parliament as M.P. for Harwich.
	May 30	Appointed a Deputy Lieutenant for Huntingdonshire.
	July 20	Master of the Trinity House for the second time.
1686	Mar.	Special Commission of 1686 "for the Recovery of the Navy" began to sit.
1688	June 29	Called as a witness at the Trial of the Seven Bishops.
	Oct. 12	Dissolution of the Special Commission of 1686.
	Dec. 11	James II.'s first withdrawal.
1689	Jan. 16	Unsuccessfully contested Harwich at the election for the Convention Parliament.

1689	Feb. 20	Surrendered the Secretaryship of the Admiralty.
	Aug. 26	Resigned the Trinity House.
1690	June 25-30	Imprisoned in the Gatehouse "on suspicion of being affected to King James."
1690		Published his *Memoirs of the Royal Navy*, 1679-88.
1693	Sept. 29	Robbed on the highway when going to Chelsea.
1697	*c.* Apr.	Was for a time dangerously ill.
1699	Apr. 27	Received the freedom of the City for his services to Christ's Hospital.
	June	Appointed Vice-President of Christ's Hospital.
1700	*c.* May	Visited Clapham for reasons of health.
	c. Dec.	Returned to York Buildings.
1701	*c.* June	Final retirement to William Hewer's house at Clapham.
1702	Sept.	Presented to the University of Oxford a portrait by Sir Godfrey Kneller of Dr. Wallis, Savilian Professor of Geometry.
	Oct. 30	Diploma sent him by Convocation.
1703	May 26	Death of Samuel Pepys at Clapham, in the 71st year of his age.
	June 4	Burial in the Church of St. Olave's, Hart Street.

BIBLIOGRAPHICAL NOTE

THE following are the chief printed sources which have been used in preparing the biographical part of this volume. References to manuscript authorities are given in the footnotes.

Wilbur C. Abbott, "The Serious Pepys" (in *Yale Review* for April 1914).

Bibliotheca Pepysiana: Pt. i. "Sea" MSS. (1914); Pt. ii. General Introduction and Early Printed Books (1914); Pt. iii. Mediaeval MSS. (1923).

Thomas Birch, *History of the Royal Society* (1756). 4 vols.

Lord Braybrooke, *Diary and Correspondence of Samuel Pepys, F.R.S.* Fourth edition (1854). Letters in iv. 183–368.

Sir Frederick Bridge, *Samuel Pepys, Lover of Musique* (1903).

Dr. Charlett's letters printed in the *Academy*, xxxviii. (1890).

John Evelyn, *Diary and Correspondence.*

Sir C. H. Firth, "The Early Life of Pepys," in *Macmillan's Magazine*, lxix. (1894), 32.

Sir Archibald Geikie, article on Pepys's connexion with the Royal Society, in *Nature*, lxxi. 415.

F. R. Harris, *Life of the First Earl of Sandwich* (1912). 2 vols.

Lady Alice Archer Houblon, *The Houblon Family* (1907). 2 vols.

Sir Sidney Lee, "Pepys and Shakespeare," in the *Fortnightly Review*, 1906.

J. Lucas-Dubreton, *La petite vie de Samuel Pepys Londonien* (1923).

Percy Lubbock, *Samuel Pepys* (1909).

Miss E. Hallam Moorhouse, *Samuel Pepys* (1909).

E. H. Pearce, *Annals of Christ's Hospital.*

Samuel Pepys, *Memoires of the Royal Navy*, 1679-1688 (1690); reprinted in the Tudor and Stuart Library; ed. J. R. Tanner (1906).

Pepys Club, *Occasional Papers*, 1903-1914.

Miss E. M. G. Routh, *Tangier*, 1661-1684 (1912).

John Smith, *Life, Journals, and Correspondence of Samuel Pepys* (1841). 2 vols.

R. L. Stevenson, *Familiar Studies of Men and Books* (1886).

J. R. Tanner (ed.), *A Descriptive Catalogue of the Naval Manuscripts in the Pepysian Library* (Navy Records Society's Publications): vol. i. General Introduction (1903); vols. ii. and iii. Admiralty Letters (1904 and 1909); vol. iv. Admiralty Journal (1923).

J. R. Tanner, *Samuel Pepys and the Royal Navy* (Lees Knowles Lectures for 1919).

H. B. Wheatley, *Samuel Pepys and the World he lived in* (1895).

H. B. Wheatley, *Pepysiana* (1899).

H. B. Wheatley, *The Diary of Samuel Pepys*: short life prefixed to vol. i.

Dictionary of National Biography; Grey's *Debates*; Historical MSS. Commission, *Seventh*, *Eighth*, *Ninth*, *Eleventh*, and *Fifteenth Reports*; *Commons' Journals*; *Lords' Journals*; *Parliamentary History*; *State Trials*.

INDEX